SUZY GERSHMAN

BORN TO SHOP

NEW YORK

The Ultimate Guide for
Travelers Who Love to Shop

8th Edition

IDG Books Worldwide, Inc.
An International Data Group Company
Foster City, CA • Chicago, IL • Indianapolis, IN • New York, NY

In memory of My Sweet Mick, 1939–2000, my husband, who adored New York and could think of nothing better than to live in the city or visit the city and enjoy the restaurants, hotels, theaters, and even the stores.

IDG Books Worldwide, Inc.
An International Data Group Company
919 E. Hillsdale Blvd., Suite 400
Foster City, CA 94404

ISBN 0-02-863599-X
ISSN 1071-9725

Editor: Nicole Daro
Production Editor: Scott Barnes
Design by George J. McKeon
Staff Cartographers: John Decamillis, Elizabeth Puhl, and Roberta Stockwell

SPECIAL SALES
For general information on IDG Books Worldwide's books in the U.S., please call our Consumer Customer Service department at 800/762-2974. For reseller information, including discounts and premium sales, please call our Reseller Customer Service department at 800/434-3422.

Manufactured in the United States of America

5   4   3   2   1

CONTENTS

MAP LIST

An Invitation To The Reader from Frommer's

In researching this book, we discovered many wonderful places—hotels, restaurants, shops, and more. We're sure you'll find others. Please tell us about them, so we can share the information with your fellow travelers in upcoming editions. If you were disappointed with a recommendation, we'd love to know that, too. Please write to:

Frommer's Born to Shop New York
Frommer's Travel Guides
1633 Broadway
New York, NY 10019

An Additional Note

Please be advised that travel information is subject to change at any time—and this is especially true of prices. We therefore suggest that you write or call ahead for confirmation when making your travel plans. The author, editors, and publisher cannot be held responsible for the experiences of readers while traveling. Your safety is important to us, however, so we encourage you to stay alert and be aware of your surroundings. Keep a close eye on cameras, purses, and wallets, all favorite targets of thieves and pickpockets.

Find Frommer's Online

www.frommers.com offers up-to-the-minute listings on almost 200 cities around the globe—including the latest bargains and candid, personal articles updated daily by Arthur Frommer himself. No other Web site offers such comprehensive and timely coverage of the world of travel.

TO START WITH

Not only is this a new edition of *Frommer's Born to Shop New York*, it's also a newly reorganized edition. It has more changes than any other recent *Born to Shop* book, because of both the number of changes in the city and the shift of interest to the downtown area.

In previous editions, I always tried to second-guess the longevity of a store before I listed it—as books stay on bookstore shelves for about 2 years and there's nothing more irritating than going to a specific store address to find it closed. For this reason all the fun and funky stuff downtown had been ignored. No more. While I've still tried to be careful, I do ask that you call ahead if you are in search of a specific source.

I thank my New York correspondent Paul Baumrind, my New York hotel family, especially the team at the Warwick Hotel, and my late husband who loved to work on this book with me.

Chapter One

....

THE BEST OF NEW YORK

I certainly hope that you will be reading every word in this book (and underlining the good parts in pink felt-tip pen), but I understand that many people are truly living the New York Minute and are on a mad dash from here to there. You may simply find all the possibilities overwhelming. Or you may get confused finding your way from uptown to downtown.

I have created this at-a-glance chapter to help you get started; you can use these pages as a handy tip sheet. Each resource mentioned here is explained in greater depth in later chapters, and there are plenty more sources inside. These are just some easy-to-find shops where you can find what you need if you're short on time.

Jot down some of the addresses from this chapter (or the rest of this book) and put them in your "book," on your digital organizer, or on a card to keep handy. That way, whenever a free minute pops up between meetings, you know exactly how to maximize your time, seamlessly.

Addresses in all listings are given with cross streets so that you can easily jump in and out of a taxi. If you are indeed in a hurry, the subway may be your best bet—especially for long hauls, which can get tedious (and expensive) in traffic. Never take the uptown or downtown buses when you are in a hurry unless you use an express bus; crosstown buses can be worth the effort.

Because of the size of the city, and the new interest in all the hot offerings downtown, I have given both uptown and downtown options for most of the categories in this chapter. Please note that I'm using 34th St. as the dividing line. This is not a traditional dividing line between uptown and downtown (many people use 14th St. or 23rd St. as the official dividing point and consider 34th St. as midtown), but I find it very handy and use it throughout this text.

YOU HAVE ONE HOUR BETWEEN MEETINGS TO SHOP

If you only have an hour to shop, your choices really depend on what part of town you're in—and on how frequently you get to New York. Sometimes I'm willing to blow my 1 hour in town on something totally nontraditional. But let's go for location, since time is sooo tight here.

The Upper East Side

I can walk from 57th St. to 79th St. along Madison Avenue in about 2 hours, poking into whatever stores interest me (but not doing serious shopping). You can do this same stroll in an hour if you stick to window-shopping, and few districts of New York give you a better overview of why New York is so special.

Middle Fifth Avenue

Do you want an hour's worth of visual stimulation and excitement or do you want to do some serious shopping? If it's inspiration you seek (and maybe not that much in terms of durable goods), poke in quickly at **Henri Bendel** (712 Fifth Ave. at 56th St.). Bendel's was heading toward bankruptcy, then changed its focus to offer lots of hip and not-so-well-known designers. At Christmas, the tree is one of the best in New York. From there, walk to West 56th St. and hang a left, going west, just a few feet to a store (10 W. 56th St.) called **Felissimo,** filled with whimsy and wonder.

You really need something and need it fast? Do what I do: Spend an hour in **Saks Fifth Avenue** (611 Fifth Ave. at 49th St.). Saks in New York is a festival unlike any other Saks in the world, but it's also a bit of a cop-out. I want you to have your hour in Saks, but I do hope you've got another hour to do something wild and crazy.

Herald Square

One hour divided between **Macy's** and the new **Old Navy** store should get your creative juices flowing.

Lower Fifth Avenue or Chelsea

Take a taxi to **Jeffrey** (224 W. 14th St.) and step on it. Walk over to **Barney's Co-op,** if you have time.

SoHo/NoLita

Sure you can spend an hour breezily and easily in SoHo, but take time out and head for nearby NoLita! You'll only have time to window shop and then head back uptown, but you'll have a whirlwind tour of what's new and what's happening in New York retail. Head directly to **Janet Russo,** 262 Mott St., and then "do" all of Mott Street and Nolita.

Wall Street

If you are really downtown, in New York's financial district, get over to **Century 21** (22 Cortlandt St.) and don't think twice. One hour isn't much time, but it's doable if you hone in on one category of goods: men, head for the large first-floor men's department; women, get upstairs and into the designer clothing and the extra markdown room.

YOU HAVE ONE LATE-NIGHT CHANCE TO SHOP

Thursday night is traditionally the night that stores in Manhattan stay open late; most are open until 8pm or even 9pm.

However, with the amount of alternative retail in Manhattan and with all these new discount stores and superstores, hours are changing. Some stores now stay open late on other nights of the week.

YOU ONLY HAVE TIME FOR WINDOW SHOPPING

There's no question in my mind that **Hermès** and **Tiffany & Co.** have the best windows in New York. Thankfully, they are across the street from each other, on East 57th St.

If you're downtown, head to NoLita, which is fun for window shopping and just browsing. Start on Elizabeth at Houston, walk toward Spring, then cut over and try Mott and then Mulberry.

Magical Whirlwind Window Shopping Tour

Start at **Henri Bendel** (712 Fifth Ave. at 56th St.). Then move to **Takashimaya** (693 Fifth Ave. at 54th St.), **Felissimo** (10 W. 56th St.), and **Chanel** (15 E. 57th St.). Then it's on to **Hermès** (11 E. 57th St.), **Barney's** (600 Madison Ave. at 60th St.), and **MacKenzie Childs** (824 Madison Ave. at 63rd St.). Finish up at **William Wayne** (850 Lexington at 63rd St.).

YOU WANT TO MAKE SURE YOU SEE SOMETHING *VERY* NEW YORK

If you're visiting from Europe, much of American retail will seem new and fresh to you. If you're visiting from another big American city, you'll find that many Manhattan versions of your favorite chain stores are bigger and better but fundamentally the same. Therefore, visiting those stores that are the epitome of New York style (even if a few have stores in other cities as well) will give you supreme pleasure, whether you buy anything or not. Check out:

TAKASHIMAYA
693 Fifth Ave. at 54th St.

EILEEN FISHER
521 Madison Ave. at 54th St.

ABC CARPET & HOME
888 Broadway at 19th St.

YOU ONLY HAVE ONE DAY TO SHOP MARKETS

Manhattan is a great city for flea markets as well as green markets (farmer's markets). Market day has never been as good as a Saturday in Manhattan, when you can start with the flea market on Sixth Avenue and 26th St. and then bop through myriad antiques garages and junk shops in the neighborhood before heading east to the Green Market at Union Square.

Uptown flea markets are on the West Side. Try Columbus at 77th Street, where there's an outdoor and indoor portion to this Sunday-only market.

YOU WANT ONE NEIGHBORHOOD THAT PACKS IT IN

SoHo. No doubt about it, SoHo is changing and is bursting with new stores—some original sources, some branches of big names. Stores open late (beginning at 11am, some at 11:30am), so make a day of it. Add on a dinner at one of the hot restaurants nearby.

YOU WANT ONE NEIGHBORHOOD TO STROLL THAT IS REALLY EXCITING

If you're downtown, head straight to Bond Street, but not James Bond Street. Stirred and quite shaken and intoxicating.

If you're uptown, Bloomingdale's Country is your best bet. The area surrounding Bloomingdale's is a feast for the eyes.

SOMETHING WILD & CRAZY

Head for East 9th St. But before you start heading, a warning: This is not for everyone. East 9th St. is not for anyone who buys Chanel retail. It's funky, it's got an edge of the creepy, and it's not ready for prime time. But therein lies its charm. There are 2 blocks of new and funky stores, plus a very interesting branch of my beloved **Eileen Fisher** (314 E. 9th St.). If you have an open mind, come on down. The best 2 blocks begin at Second Avenue and stretch east to Avenue A.

If you did East 9th St. last year, try East 7th St. this year— same blocks, same area, but two down—more young and funky and lots of vintage clothing and just hip stuff.

YOU NEED SOMETHING FOR THE KIDS BUT FAST

There are a handful of **Toys "Я" Us** toys all over Manhattan, and more seem to be coming on a monthly basis. If you have no time for this kind of shopping or want something a little bit more New York, you have no option but to dash into **FAO Schwarz** (767 Fifth Ave. at 58th St.), Manhattan's most famous toy store, and shop at the quick pick desk where gifts are displayed and sold already wrapped. And, yes, there are a few affordable items.

There's also a **Warner Brothers Studio Store** (1 E. 57th St. at Fifth Ave.) and **The Disney Store** (711 Fifth Ave. at 55th St.). **The Metropolitan Museum of Art Gift Shop** at Rockefeller Center (15 W. 49th St.) has a wonderful kids department, and you can't beat the location.

THE BEST NEIGHBORHOOD FOR DOWN & DIRTY BARGAIN SHOPPING

Ladies Mile (Sixth Ave. at 18th St.). And no, it's not just for ladies anymore. You see, the mayor of New York rezoned this part of downtown and now discounters and off-pricers have moved in. Although **Loehmann's** (106 Seventh Ave.) is not in this stretch, it's only a block away and easily included as part of this neighborhood's whole—although since their financial woes they haven't had anything too special.

THE BEST NEIGHBORHOOD FOR SHOPPING FOR YOUR FIRST APARTMENT

You won't believe you read this here, and I can't believe I'm writing it, but here goes: The Upper East Side, mostly around the east fifties and sixties!

We'll forego the **James Robinson** silver and original artworks in tony stores on East 67th St. and still have a good time. Move over, instead, to Madison for **Crate & Barrel** (650 Madison Ave. at 59th St.). Or head straight for **The Terrence Conran** Shop at the Bridge Market under the 59th St. Bridge. Nearby, there's a big department store at 59th St. and Lexington Avenue called **Bloomingdale's** (yep, you have heard of it before!) that has a terrific bed linen selection that, when it goes on sale, equals discount prices. And for the final flourishes, head to Third Avenue (both sides of the street) at 70th St. and both branches of **Gracious Home** (1217 Third Ave. and 1220 Third Ave.).

THE BEST NEIGHBORHOOD FOR SHOPPING FOR YOUR FIRST CO-OP APARTMENT

Lower Broadway (LoBro) and Ladies Mile are your places. Start at **ABC Carpet & Home** (888 Broadway at 19th St.) and **Fishs Eddy** (889 Broadway at 19th St.). You can then wander the side streets east of Broadway and look for the upholsterers and quiet fabric and furniture sources nestled in and around 20th St. or just head straight over to Ladies Mile for **Bed, Bath & Beyond** (620 Sixth Ave. between 18th and 19th streets). Then, walk 1 block west and a couple of blocks south to **Williams-Sonoma** (110 Seventh Ave.), **Hold Everything** (104 Seventh Ave.), and **Pottery Barn** (100 Seventh Ave.), all right in a row on Seventh Avenue at 16th St.

THE BEST GIFTS FOR FRIENDS & LOVED ONES

Need to pick up a few quick gifts for friends? Here are a few ideas:

- A bag of gourmet coffee from **Bloomingdale's** ($13).
- Tripack of flower-shaped bath bombs from **Bendel's,** ($15).
- Hand-painted picture frames in bundles, **Zona** ($18 for three).
- Something from **Tiffany's.** You can still find small leather goods, scarves, and items in sterling silver that are reasonably priced. I like the leather case that holds Post-it notes for $30. Please note: Tiffany & Co. offers prestige and status to North American and Far Eastern shoppers, but Europeans are

still learning the name and thus might not appreciate the status or the gesture.

- Art or even folk art, from any of the museum stores.
- A gift for the pet—pet boutiques are the rage in all the major department stores.
- Salon de Thé is a unisex fragrance sold exclusively at Barney's ($55); it's a floral—very sophisticated and very New York.
- If you know what shades to buy, makeup from any of the international cult makeup artists is a great treat. MAC is one of the most famous and also reasonably priced ($14 for an eye shadow). Sold in department stores or in their own stores, but between Sephora, the new Bergdorf's and the downtown Lipstick District, you won't have a problem finding something.

THE BEST $10 GIFTS

Let's face it: All of us have $10 friends whether we like to admit it or not. Therefore, for those who fall into this category, consider:

- Notebooks, date books, note cards, and stationery items from **The Metropolitan Museum of Art** gift shops (in the museum itself, Fifth Ave. at 82nd St.; at the Cloisters, in Fort Tryon Park; in the mid-Manhattan branch of the New York Public Library, 445 Fifth Ave. at 40th St.; and at Rockefeller Center, 15 W. 49th St.) are in the $6.95 to $10.95 price range and provide useful, stylish gifts that also convey the message that you've been to New York.
- **Aveda** (509 Madison Ave. at 53rd St.) has some of the best aromatherapy products in the world—many of which are under $10. I'm big on their room sprays.
- **Sephora** sells a box of four packs of bath salts (scented) for $6.

- At **Bergdorf-Goodman** (754 Fifth Ave. at 58th St.), if you head upstairs to the housewares and home decor department, you'll find Venetian glass swizzle sticks at $8 each. Anything with Bergdorf's wrap is worth $10, just for the wrapping.
- Fakes. Nothing says "streets of New York" more than a fake Mont Blanc pen or a fake pair of Ray Bans. I'm opposed to major copyright violations but I do buy pens for $5 and sunglasses for $8. **Canal Street** has the best prices and selection; those street vendors selling the same items around midtown are con men.

THE BEST POSTCARDS

I like my postcards cheap so I buy in multiples from the tourist traps in the Times Square area, 10 for $1. If you're willing to spring for more expensive postcards, **The Metropolitan Museum of Art** has great ones and their shop in Rockefeller Plaza (15 W. 49th St.) is convenient for everyone.

THE BEST QUICKIE SHOPPER'S LUNCH

BURGER HEAVEN
7 E. 53rd St.

Try the Roquefort burger.

THE BEST HOTEL LUNCH

The day I discovered that fancy hotels in the world's biggest and best cities can offer a very competitive luncheon—not to mention restaurants that are true hidden gems—was the day I converted to eating lunches in hotels.

I now stop in regularly at several Manhattan hotels, depending on where I am. I think my favorite is **The Mark** (Madison Ave. at 77th St.), because it's in the heart of the Madison Avenue shopping district, has a great menu, and a fixed-price lunch for \$20. **The Pierre** (Fifth Ave. at 61st St.) also has a sensational full lunch at Cafe Pierre for around \$26.

THE BEST AFTERNOON TEA

THE PIERRE HOTEL, ROTUNDA ROOM
Fifth Ave. at 61st St.

THE BEST ONE-STOP SHOPPING DEPARTMENT STORE

SAKS FIFTH AVENUE
611 Fifth Ave. at 49th St.

THE BEST STORE FOR RETAIL AS THEATER

TAKASHIMAYA
693 Fifth Ave. at 54th St.

Runner Up

SEPHORA ROCKEFELLER CENTER
636 Fifth Ave. at 51st St.

THE BEST ONE-TRICK PONIES

If you've never seen one of these stores before, then New York can broaden your cultural appreciation of retail as theater. Most of these stores play in towns all over America and often in big international cities such as London. Still, if you've never seen one, now's your chance:

WARNER BROTHERS COMPANY STORE
Fifth Ave. at 57th St.

DISNEY STORE
711 Fifth Ave.

NIKETOWN
2 E. 57th St.

THE BEST SALE

Nothing beats **Saks Fifth Avenue** when the sale merchandise gets marked down an additional 30% to 40% off!

THE BEST OFF-PRICER FOR GETTING LUCKY

New York is suddenly teaming with off-pricers and discounters, so a new and better resource could pop up any time. However, for serious discounts, I go with **Century 21** (22 Cortlandt St.). Luck has to be on your side, but it generally is here (at least for me).

Now here's the good news and the bad news: Century 21 is located at the tip of Manhattan, so if you do business in the financial district you're lucky—otherwise, you're looking at a special trip on the subway or a $12 to $15 taxi ride. Parking is just about impossible, so don't count on finding a meter, even on a Saturday morning. Of course, this could be why God invented the Millenium Hilton Hotel, so you can sleep next door to Century 21 and not have to worry about transportation.

THE BEST RESALE SHOPS

ENCORE
1132 Madison Ave. at 84th St.

MICHAEL'S
1041 Madison Ave. at 77th St. (upstairs)

THE BEST PLACE FOR A WEDDING GOWN

Many a bride has come to New York in search of the wedding gown holy veil. Filene's Basement has its infamous Bridal Sale in Boston and in Chicago, but not New York, so if you have patience, the best thing to do is to shop the bridal wholesale buildings in the Garment District. Try no. 1375 and no. 1385 Broadway. Many makers have moved out recently, but those remaining usually sell to the public.

If you find that too stressful (you do have to move from one showroom to the next), but you still feel that you can handle some amount of stress, **Kleinfeld's** in Brooklyn (82nd St. at Fifth Ave., Brooklyn) is famous for wedding gowns, bridal party, and dress-up fancy.

Should you be willing to wear a used gown (of course you are), **Michael's** (1041 Madison Ave. at 77th St., upstairs) has one of the best selections in town.

If you time it right, you can get to the **Vera Wang Sample Sale**—last year it was held at the Hotel Pennsylvania. Call for the dates and details (☎ 212/628-3400).

If nothing but the full regalia will do, and your mom wants to sip tea while you try on your train, **Saks Fifth Avenue** (611 Fifth Ave. at 49th St.) has been doing this for years and remains the last of the full-service wedding belles.

THE BEST PLACE FOR CHIC MATERNITY WEAR

LIZ LANGE
1020 Lexington Ave., 2nd floor

Sort of the Kate Spade of the preggers group.

THE BEST DISCOUNTER FOR PERFUME

Getting perfume at a big discount in New York is not easy. Discounters exist, but few offer a wide range of brands and the discounts aren't particularly high. The duty-free shop at JFK Airport is no bargain either. (In fact, discount prices in New York's basic off-pricers are better than at the airport.)

For convenience sake, your best bet is **Cosmetics Plus,** with locations all over Manhattan. They discount brands by a mere 10% to 12%, but have a rather full selection including Chanel brands. They bill themselves as "The American parfumerie"; it's an accurate description. Each branch has a slightly different mix, so visiting more than one is a good idea.

THE BEST DRUGSTORE

Manhattan is dotted with drugstores. **CVS** and **Duane Reade** are fighting it out for the hearts and minds and dental floss of New Yorkers, even in the best business districts in midtown. Just about every place you wander you can find a branch of one or both. They carry all the basics from a small-sized bottle of water to health and beauty aids to condoms and anything else you might need in between. Please note that prices on sundries in Manhattan are more expensive than anyplace else in the United States, so that even using a discount drugstore like this, you may find that you pay less at home. Unless home is overseas.

So answer the question please, Suze. OK, for best in New York I am picking **Ricky's,** which is actually a beauty supply store-cum-drugstore. There's a handful of them dotted around Manhattan in your basic tourist areas such as Greenwich Village and SoHo.

THE BEST FANCY DRUGSTORE

CLYDE'S
926 Madison Ave.; ☎ *212/288-6966*

Wait here please, James.

THE BEST HANDBAGS

I'd head straight for **J. S. Suarez** (450 Park Ave. at 56th St.) where they sell either a variety of designer-style handbags made in the same Italian factories as the big names (Gucci, Prada) or factory direct on specific Italian lines, such as Desmo. We're not talking cheap here—there's probably little for under $100—but we are talking quality and less money than at big-name stores.

THE BEST ELECTRONICS & BOY TOYS

J&R COMPUTER WORLD
15 Park Row

J&R MUSIC WORLD
31 Park Row

THE BEST MUSEUM STORE

METROPOLITAN MUSEUM OF ART STORE
Fifth Ave. at 82nd St.

The flagship inside the museum itself is the best, but there are five other branches around town.

THE BEST NEW IDEA FOR A TRADITIONAL SHOPPING AREA

AVON CENTER
Trump Tower, 725 Fifth Ave. at 56th St.

Yep, Avon is calling. First store ever; with spa and special products created just for this space. Gorgeous to look at, yummy to sniff.

WORTH CHECKING OUT IF YOU LIKE IT HOT

JEFFREY
224 W. 14th St.

Trend-setting clothes in the meat-packing district!

THE TERRENCE CONRAN SHOP AT BRIDGE MARKET
415 E. 59th St.

Enormous lifestyle store similar to London and Paris, with giant eatery.

KIRNA ZABETE
96 Green St., SoHo

Two "fashionistas" do the eclectic rich hippie thing.

CREED
9 Bond St.

The French perfume house makes a splash downtown.

THE 10 BEST STORES IN NEW YORK

In alphabetical order:

ABC CARPET
888 Broadway at 18th St.

Even if you buy nothing, step into this beautifully dressed showcase for tabletop, linens, fabrics and, oh yeah, carpets.

APRIL CORNELL
487 Columbus Ave. at 83rd St.

Home furnishings and clothes for women and little girls in swirly printed Indian fabrics that feel like the South of France.

AVEDA
520 Madison Ave. at 54th St.

Aromatherapy, custom shampoo color, makeup, candles; very special particularly for the hair care line and the room sprays. Spa center in SoHo.

BARNEY'S
660 Madison Ave. at 61st St.

No matter who they offend, they still have a fabulous touch for makeup, tabletop (Chelsea Passage), and cutting-edge chic.

CENTURY 21
22 Cortland

If you crave the biggest designer names at discount prices, it's worth the trip downtown and maybe the trip to New York.

EILEEN FISHER
521 Madison Ave. at 53rd St.

Several branches around town offering droopy chic for women. Love those elastic waists! Silks and linens, boucle wools, soft color palette à la Armani but affordable.

KATE'S PAPERIE
561 Broadway, SoHo

Eye-popping choice of papers, craft items, wraps, and ribbons.

MACKENZIE CHILDS
824 Madison at 64th St.

Hand-painted table top in a world of wonder; cafe included.

SEPHORA
636 Fifth Ave. at 51st St.

Makeup forever in a dramatic setting surrounded by black scrim, *ooh la la.*

TAKASHIMAYA
693 Fifth Ave. at 53rd St.

Gorgeous flowers and drop-dead lifestyle designs to gawk at; no it's not Japanese style, it's just Japanese owned.

Chapter Two

....

NEW YORK DETAILS

BIG APPLE BITES CROISSANT

....

The American economy is booming and no place is booming more than New York City. New York is more than the Big Apple these days, it's the whole orchard. Hmmm, maybe that's why Orchard St. has had a renaissance. But wait, that's not the only place that's hot in town. You won't believe what's goin' on.

Nor will you believe how many area codes we now have, right here in Manhattan—it's a sign of the times. Sure, 212 is the old standard we all know, but now there's also 917 and 636—so don't freak. Just consider it one of the many new changes and a strong indication that everything you remember is being changed, updated, modified, and modernized.

Parts of New York that 2 years ago weren't considered ready for Prime Time now have some of the fanciest stores in New York. Parts of New York that were considered downright dangerous are now hip, hot, and chic. Parts of New York you never knew were parts of New York (like Alphabet City!) are now part of the scene. Uptown, downtown, East Side, West Side, New York has more new stores, more new neighborhoods, and more style per square inch than any other city in the world. The world is watching—and joining in.

European stores and European shoppers are on every corner, while discounters and off-pricers are on every other corner. We've been invaded by style-mongers from Charleston and Atlanta, from London, Paris, Stockholm—even from Russia, if the Russian Tea Room counts. The energy is contagious and the possibilities to buy anything are just about endless.

Big Apple bites croissant (**Fauchon** arrives), meatballs to come (Swedish meatballs, as **H&M** arrives). Chopsticks go uptown (**Shanghai Tang** moves to 714 Madison Ave.); sturgeon is back in town (**Russian Tea Room** reopens).

This is New York, New York: a very cosmopolitan, international city that, to me, anyway, is really the capital of America. The shopping capital. I welcome you to the city I chose when I was 21 years old and that still gives me a thrill, after all these years.

THE *NEW* NEW YORK

I must also welcome you to a town that is very much a living, breathing thing. It changes every day; it's changed enormously since the last edition of this guide. Note some of these ongoing trends:

- **SoHo** has turned out to be uptown in a downtown format. **Ralph Lauren** has gone for enormous space in SoHo. In fact, everyone in America and some of the crowd from Europe is now in SoHo, or about to be. Even **Creed,** a British firm from Victorian times that then moved to Paris and became one of the most famous French perfumers, has opened in SoHo. **Chanel** is about to announce; **Armani** is signing paper. SoHo has become mainstream (but not yet ho-hum).
- **NoLita** (North of Little Italy) has become the new SoHo, sort of, but it's real and small and intimate and fabulous. I'm ready to move there, to open up shop. Shhhh, don't tell

anyone. This is where the small stores are an art form and the retailer is the curator—and maybe the designer as well.

- **The Meat Packing District,** very far west on 14th St. (at Tenth Ave.) and into Chelsea, is still working on the smells—but has left everyone drooling for everything from **Jeffrey** to art galleries to warehouse space to the **Comme des Garcons** boutique that marries retail with a gallery feel and redefines the borders of Chelsea. I can't put a finger on the attraction, except maybe the raw-ness of it, but if you love factory districts in Hong Kong and your heart beats faster to the funk of reality, this part of town is for you. Martha Stewart has already bought in.

- **Fifth Avenue** has become one giant shopping mall with a wider range of retail than ever before—central Fifth Avenue in midtown right around Rockefeller Center and St. Patrick's is the center of a brave new shopping world.

- Many old faithfuls have given up their eye-catching real estate in order to either cash in (their real estate is worth a fortune these days) or to move to less pricey digs. **Bijan,** the store on Fifth Avenue that was closed to the public (you needed an appointment to get the doorman to let you in) has moved out to make room for progress—or democracy.

- Showbiz in the form of retail continues, with a more sophisticated refinement. The most dramatic, entertainment-centered stores have been **NikeTown** and **NBA.** But **Sephora** raised the ante when it opened on Fifth Avenue. You walk in the front door and find the place shrouded in black scrim, well my dear, we are not in Kansas any more.

- **Rockefeller Center** has reinvented itself. Say hello to a whole new scene, which includes the auction house **Christies** and the flagship **Sephora** store, live from Paris with more beauty and scent that you've ever seen before (and more black scrim). There's a new **Banana Republic** in the guise of a lifestyle store (this means home style too) and a branch of **J. Crew,** as well as a huge **NBC** store.

- Bookstores, one of Manhattan's best topics, have all but deserted Fifth Avenue to make room for even more big-name stores. Need a book? The library is closer to Fifth Avenue than any bookstores now.

- **Ladies Mile,** the section of Sixth Avenue where the first department stores in New York opened more than 100 years ago, has turned into superstore, discounter, and off-pricer heaven. Try the blocks from 18th to 20th St. for some rather amazing sights and discounts for all members of the family—yep, even kids.
- **Times Square** is finally happening. It took a while, but now that the *Condé Nast* editors are in their swanky new building, they can shop at **Virgin Megastore, Disney, Warner Brothers Studio Store, Gap,** and **Sephora.** Can Banana Republic be far behind? How about Manolo Blanhnik?
- West 34th St. claims it's been revitalized. I'm iffy on this claim, but I am knocked out by the new **Old Navy** store, which is across the street from **Macy's** between Broadway and Seventh Avenue, not off Fifth where you might be expecting it.
- The suburbs, and parts of New Jersey as well, have moved to Manhattan. You want details? Try these on for size: **Kmart** has come to town and moved into the Penn Station area as well as the East Village. Kmart is working on other Manhattan store locations as well. And Sears is looking for space like mad.
- The city is also becoming attractive for outlet stores, which have been kept out of town by regular retailers for years. Word has it that **Crate & Barrel** is looking for a warehouse space in the Meat Packing District for an outlet store and that many others will follow—all going into alternative retail neighborhoods, of course.
- Luxe is not a four-letter word in this town, which has seen discounters and off-pricers in trouble (both Loehmann's and Filene's Basement are under court-ordered bankruptcy protection). New York has opened its arms to an enormous **Moet Hennesy-Louis Vuitton** flagship (complete with **Christian Dior** boutique), a whole block of stores owned by the Vendome Group on a stretch of Madison Avenue, and all sorts of other

stores selling more cashmere, more pashmina, more big brands that any city has a right to need. Did someone say *need?* New York isn't about need.

- Stores have discovered they need two addresses, or more. Perhaps this is The Gapping of America. A few years ago, many established names felt they had to open a downtown store. Now, they are also opening a second uptown store, just as **Bulgari** did—to catch both the Fifth Avenue traffic and the Madison Avenue traffic. **Coach** has several stores. **Hermès** has two; **Prada** has three. **Sephora** has four, and plans to add three more. Remember the days when there was a Benetton everyplace you looked?

- Fur is making a big comeback; fancy restaurants are in, and many have a fixed-price lunch or dinner or well-priced tasting menu; limos are out, sedan cars or chauffeur-driven station wagons are in. Shopping at flea markets, thrift shops, and sample sales is chic. An army of resale shops has opened on the Upper East Side; vintage never went out of style but it's more in than ever.

So welcome to the place where you can enjoy the thrill of the choice along with the thrill of the chase; where you can get anything you want. If they don't have it, they'll make it up special. Welcome to the high end—the finest European designer boutiques, the kind of stores where children's shoes cost $250. Welcome to a bevy of the world's best department and specialty stores, many of which are fighting tooth and nail for your spending money and offer more razzle-dazzle than you've seen in years.

Welcome to the kind of place where you can hop on a bus at the Port Authority and be driven to some of the world's best bargain cities and factory outlet malls—in town or only an hour away. Or you can pull on your jeans and prowl the bargain neighborhoods for deals not seen this side of Bangkok.

Welcome to the world of flea markets, bazaars, street peddlers, fake watches, and everything in between. Welcome to the kind of city that has it all, sells it all, and doesn't tell you all. But I will.

THE NEW YORK RULE OF NATURAL SELECTION

New York offers more selection than any other marketplace in the United States, probably in the world, and that includes Tokyo. (Tokyo may have more merchandise, but it won't all fit you.)

What makes New York great is the fact that you can find things here that aren't available elsewhere or haven't yet been introduced in other parts of America. Shopping in New York offers the mental challenge of all times—can you bear to see this much stuff and not buy it all? Can you possibly choose the best thing for you at the best price? Shopping in New York is like living a game show.

In fact, let me just tell you this little shopping saga; it happened to me recently. I walked into **Saks Fifth Avenue** and bought one brassiere and one pair of panties for a total of $58.20. It was the first time in my entire life I'd ever paid full price for underwear, but I wanted this brand (Natori) and I wanted that flush feeling you get when you walk into a nice store and plunk down your credit card. The next day, I went to a suburban branch of **Filene's Basement** and there I found more Natori panties in the same color (different design) as the ones I bought. I bought several more pair, then a brassiere and selection of panties from Christian Dior and finally a pair of chinos—total bill: $68.10. The moral of the story? You can get anything you want in Alice's Restaurant. (Excepting Alice.)

Even though midtown is now populated by stores that you may have at home (even if home is Paris, France), the New York Rule of Natural Selection is simple: If it's new, it comes to New York first.

True, consumer products are usually test-marketed in more average American cities, but once a firm has decided to go with a product, it rolls out in New York. It builds a flagship in New

York. It decides to go for impact—in New York. The moral of the story: You can find things in New York that you can't find at home even if you have the same stores at home.

WINDOW SHOPPING 101

Actually, the best things in life *are* free. Even in New York. To me, the single biggest bargain in New York is the education you get; the high that comes from absorbing so much energy and so many creative ideas.

Look at the men and women who rush past on their way to work—study what they are wearing and learn from them. Look at the store windows and displays; stare at mannequins and even ads in the *New York Times*. If you want to buy a piece of the action (of course you do), you have choices, depending upon how much you want to pay and what style of retail best fits your mood or your pocketbook.

GETTING THERE

As the international hub city of the United States, New York serves just about every domestic and international carrier and then some. The trick is to realize that there are several airports and to know that you can avoid a traffic jam or even get a bargain by using a different airport than the one everyone else is using.

John F. Kennedy International Airport (JFK) is the most famous airport, especially for international flights, but it's not the only game in town. **La Guardia** serves mostly domestic flights, but it does offer action to Canada, Bermuda, and a few other destinations outside the continental United States. **Newark International** in New Jersey has grown dramatically as an international hub.

But that's not it. **Westchester** has its own airport and upstate New York has its own airport (**Stewart**), which wants to become an international hub to take some of the pressure off

JFK. To most visitors, the outer fringe airports might not be that convenient, unless price is a factor. Promotions are being offered to encourage traffic through them. Maybe you wanted to see Westchester after all?

GETTING AROUND

Public transportation in New York is not as civilized as in Tokyo or Paris, but there is a good network of subways and buses. Buses are safe and clean. Subway travel can be marvelous or horrendous; choose trains and routes carefully as well as the time of day that you travel.

Subways

You can ask for a free subway map at the token booth of any subway station or use our black-and-white map on page 27. Train routes change temporarily if repairs are being made to a line. Look for signs posted in subway stations regarding route changes. If you ask for directions to a specific shop (perhaps one that is out of Manhattan), ask if more than one train goes there.

Subways are not to be avoided at all costs, no matter what you hear. You just have to use them wisely. Travel during peak hours for safety's sake. No matter what train you take, use the same common sense you would use in riding the rails, be they in Paris or Rome. When you are on a subway, turn your ring into your palm and keep your necklaces inside your blouse— or wear no jewelry. Do not wear a fur coat on the subway. Keep your handbag across your body rather than just over your arm. Keep shopping bags between your feet or on your lap.

To use the subway efficiently, buy a **MetroCard,** which is a magnetic multitrip card that is used at each gate; a $3 card buys two trips. You can buy a card and then increase the value as you go; it's all done electronically. MetroCards allow you to transfer freely from subway to bus, and vice versa, within a 2-hour period.

You may also buy a bag of 10 tokens or several tokens at one time, so you don't have to stand in line at each station every time you need a token. Tokens can be used on buses as well.

Buses

Buses are easy to use and may feel safer than the subway. They are also much slower. It can take an hour to get from midtown to downtown on the bus; it will take 10 minutes on the subway.

Buses cost the same as the subway ($1.50 per ride as we go to press) and can be paid for with coins (exact change) or subway tokens or your metro card. You can get a free transfer good for travel within an hour. Ask the bus driver for a free transfer slip when you board the bus.

Bus routes are clearly marked on signposts, but always ask the driver to confirm that you are headed the right way. Buses can be very crowded during rush hours and are particularly slow at this time of the day due to traffic congestion.

By Foot

If you want to get someplace in a hurry, do what all locals do: Walk.

Taxi

If you just can't hack the walk, try a taxi. Taxis in New York can be flagged with a raise of the hand and a flick of the wrist. If the light on the top of the cab is lit, the cab is available. Get into the taxi and shut the door before you give your destination. This avoids the hassle of the driver telling you he doesn't want to go where you want to go.

You have to be a little bit lucky in the rain, but taxis are expensive and therefore not in the same demand as before. The flag drops at $2; taxi drivers expect a 15% tip. Note that the city has installed flat rate fees for taxi service from either JFK ($30) or La Guardia ($25) into the city but no flat fee out to the airport. These flat rates do not include bridge or tunnel tolls or a tip.

Manhattan Subways

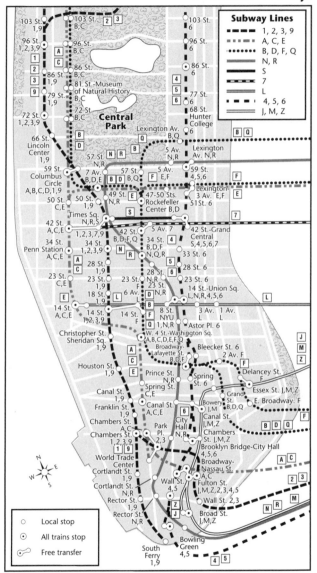

Now then, I have been talking about yellow cabs, official taxi cabs. There are gypsy cabs, some with meters and some without; some with TAXI on the top and some without. I just had a dreadful, dreadful, horrible, frightening experience in one so I remind you that you must agree on the price before you put your tush on the seat.

In my case, I went from a friend's house to Grand Central Station, a route I have often done in a gypsy cab (she lives uptown) for $10 flat. When we got there, the driver said $17. I said no way. He locked me in the cab. Nice.

Car Services

While limos are standard fare in New York, you can also get a sedan to drive you around for less than a limo. And frankly, who really needs a limo? Just be sure you book through a legit car service. I am now talking here about gypsy cabs that look like limos.

Car services can be booked by the hour, by the job, or for a standard run—such as going to the airport. Please note that on hourly jobs, the clock usually starts ticking the minute the car leaves its garage; if they are snarled up in traffic coming to pick you up, you still pay. All car services add tolls (this is most applicable to airport runs) and a tip. A 15% tip may be automatically added onto the bill, although some car services ask for a 15% tip for sedans and a 20% tip for limos. My friend and photographer Ian swears by **Tel Aviv Car Service.** They charge a flat $32 from Manhattan to JFK plus tips and tolls. Also, their phone number is easy to memorize: ☎ 212/777-7777.

EAST SIDE, WEST SIDE
....

You're hot to trot, but please, before you begin, study up on your New York neighborhoods before you pounce (see map on page 29). You'll also need a few tips that, once learned, will help to keep you from getting lost.

Manhattan Neighborhoods

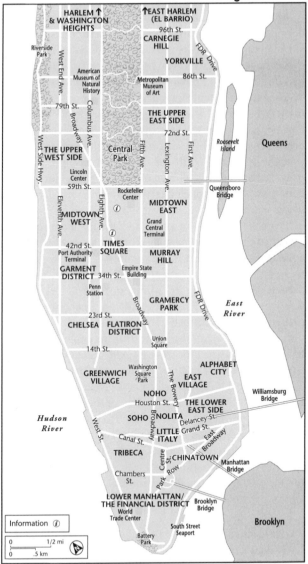

Most of Manhattan is laid out on a grid system with clearly distinguishable north, south, east, and west points. Look at any map to see the basics. Avenues run north and south, and streets run east and west. The East and West Sides are divided by Fifth Avenue, so the location of many addresses can be deduced from the numbers and the word East or West in front of them. North and south are not much used by visitors, or in directions, but locals will tell taxis to stop on the southeast corner of a certain block. If you care to learn this system, it's easy enough: Uptown is north and downtown is south. In many places in the world, downtown is a specific place. Not in Manhattan. In Manhattan, all directions are given in reference to where you are standing and where you are going.

If you are looking for a specific address on a numbered street (not an avenue), the even numbers are on the south side of the street; the odd numbers are on the north side of the street.

Generally speaking, each block of streets is divided by an avenue. The street numbers within each street block leap by 100 when you move to the next block. There are notable exceptions, however, such as when you advance east from Fifth Avenue to Madison Avenue (the street numbers only go to 50) and again when you move from Madison Avenue to Park Avenue (the next 50 numbers come before Park).

If you are at all concerned about where a shop or address may be, call first for directions. Ask for the cross streets and get the avenues and the street numbers to know exactly where in the grid of Manhattan you will be going. There are a few parts of Manhattan that do not work on a grid, but you can spot them on a map. (They're mostly at the tip of the island, but the Village can also be rather tricky.)

Finding Cross Streets

To figure out a cross street on your own, there is a system that really does work.

A *warning about the system:* It looks hard, elaborate, and confusing. You will take one glance at this information, curse, and turn to another page. Big mistake. The system isn't as hard as it looks.

Crosstown streets first, because they're the easiest:

- From Eleventh Avenue to Tenth Avenue, addresses run from 599 West to 500 West.
- Tenth Avenue to Ninth Avenue: 499 West to 400 West.
- Ninth Avenue to Eighth Avenue: 399 West to 300 West.
- Eighth Avenue to Seventh Avenue: 299 West to 200 West.
- Seventh Avenue to Sixth Avenue (Avenue of the Americas): 199 West to 100 West.
- Sixth Avenue (Avenue of the Americas) to Fifth Avenue: 99 West to 1 West.
- Fifth Avenue to Madison Avenue and Park Avenue: 1 East to 99 East.
- Park Avenue to Lexington Avenue: 100 East to 140 East.
- Lexington Avenue to Third Avenue: 140 East to 199 East.
- Third Avenue to Second Avenue: 200 East to 299 East.
- Second Avenue to First Avenue: 300 East to 399 East.
- First Avenue to York Avenue: 400 East to 499 East.
- Above 59th St., Eleventh Avenue becomes West End Avenue, Tenth Avenue becomes Amsterdam Avenue, Ninth Avenue becomes Columbus Avenue, and Eighth Avenue becomes Central Park West. Numbers on crosstown streets up to the top of Central Park, at 110th St., begin with 1 West at the corner of Central Park West, and go up as you head west (addresses from 100 West begin at Columbus Ave., from 200 West at Amsterdam Ave., and so on).

To locate the nearest avenue to an address on a street, follow this easy step-by-step process:

- Look at the address of the building where you are going—for example, 725 Fifth Avenue (the Trump Tower). If you are bad at math or can't visualize numbers, write down the number on a piece of scrap paper.

- Drop the last digit of the building's number. You are now working with the number 72.
- Divide this number in half. That puts you at 36.

Using the list below, add or subtract the number given. (Note that there are a few exceptions: You do not divide in half numbers between 775 and 1286 on Fifth Avenue. As this area is residential, it shouldn't pose a problem to shoppers using this system. Two other residential areas, Central Park West and Riverside Drive, do not fit into this plan at all, but again, this shouldn't inconvenience a shopper.)

First Avenue	Add 3
Second Avenue	Add 3
Third Avenue	Add 10
Fourth Avenue	Add 8
Fifth Avenue:	
Up to 200	Add 13
Up to 400	Add 16
Up to 600	Add 18
Up to 775	Add 20
From 775 to 1286	Do not divide by 2; subtract 18
Sixth Avenue (Avenue of the Americas)	Subtract 12
Seventh Avenue:	
Up to 936	Add 12
Eighth Avenue	Add 10
Ninth Avenue	Add 13
Tenth Avenue	Add 14
Eleventh Avenue	Add 15
Amsterdam Avenue	Add 60
Broadway:	
Above 1000	Subtract 30
Columbus Avenue	Add 60

Lexington Avenue	Add 22
Madison Avenue	Add 26
Park Avenue	Add 35

The Trump Tower, our example here, is at 56th St. by these calculations—and that's just where it is!

For Broadway addresses below 1000, this little chart will help:

1	Battery Place
100	Wall St.
200	Fulton St.
300	Chambers St.
400	Canal St.
500	Broome St.
750	East 8th St.
1000	23rd St.

BOOKING NEW YORK

If you are tempted to buy a lot of guidebooks about the city—don't. *Frommer's New York City* is a great tool to help you navigate the city. It includes hotel and restaurant listings and walking tours. The free package from the New York City Convention & Visitors Bureau is a good resource as well. Then, think about purchasing a *Zagat's* dining guide (the listings are based on readers' experiences, not those of restaurant critics) or one of the new Zagat Dining Maps.

In your search for up-to-date and basic information, check out **Where** magazine, which is distributed free in your hotel. *Where* is also handed out free of charge at the customer service desk on the first floor of Saks Fifth Avenue, near the side door across from St. Patrick's. Besides listing the expected tourist information, *Where* posts the big fashion shows, designer show houses, antiques sales, public sales, and auctions and is published each month. Sometimes there are coupons for discounts in *Where*. Don't panic if a favorite store or restaurant isn't included in *Where;* the magazine features only paying clients. Nonetheless, it's still a valuable source.

Want a guide to the area sample sales and warehouse deals? Try the *S&B Report,* which you can buy by the single issue if you write or call ahead. See page 276.

There's also a weekly column of sales and bargains in *New York Magazine,* and in *Time Out*—a sister of the British publication—does wonderful shopping coverage.

I just bought a book called *NY@tlas* published by VanDam Inc. for $10.95. I got it at Borders after seeing it at the airport. This handy square book is probably meant for drivers, but is great for shoppers because it shows you each and every tiny block in this city, where not every street is a square or is on the old fashioned grid system. All five boroughs are in the book. If you want to explore downtown thoroughly, the book will give you a boost.

SHOPPING HOURS

As the town that never sleeps, New York prides itself on having some retail services available on a 24-hour basis. Not at Bloomingdale's, mind you, but there are stores open whenever you may need them.

Regular retail hours are 10am till 5:30 or 6pm, Monday through Saturday. Regular retail means very little these days, especially now that the war of the superstores is on and Manhattan is looking more and more like the local mall or the village green. Here are some guidelines:

- Stores in business areas, such as Wall St., tend to open rather early in the morning to service locals on their way to work. Stores often open at 7:30 or 8am. These stores are frequently closed on Saturdays and Sundays.

- Power chains with enough money and staff often keep their stores open more nights of the week or later every night of the week. **Barney's** in midtown is open until 9pm, 6 nights a week. **The Wiz,** an electronics and gadget superstore, is open until 10pm 6 nights a week.
- Midtown stores that sell business apparel usually open at 9am. Beware, stores that open at 9am may close at 5 or 5:30pm.
- Mondays and Thursdays are traditional late nights for department stores, which stay open until 9pm. If a store has only one late night per week, it is Thursday night.
- Bookstores seem to have their own rules about hours, especially now that certain bookstores have become the substitute for the village green and have entire neighborhood social patterns revolving through their doors.
- During Christmas season, anything goes.
- In summer, a handful of stores close at noon on Saturday or don't even open on Saturday at all.
- Most stores close earlier on Saturday evening than during the work week, be it at 5 or 5:30pm, maybe 6pm. Few stay open until 9pm or later on Saturdays. There are exceptions, this is just a general rule for traditional retail.

Sunday Shopping

As for Sundays, I can't go so far as to say everything is open, but Sunday is a huge day for retail in Manhattan. Certain neighborhoods have a big social-retail-dining scene, like **SoHo** and the **Upper West Side.** You can go out for brunch and then go shopping.

Not only are all major department stores and chains open on Sundays, but the hours that they are open seem to be extending. While regular Sunday hours seem to be noon until 5pm, the opening times are creeping up. Many stores open at 11am now and a few open at 10am.

Religious Hours

Please note that stores owned and operated by religious Jewish people may have special hours; they will close at 2pm on

Friday and remain closed throughout Saturday. They open first thing on Sunday morning. This is true of many stores on the Lower East Side as well as specific stores here and there.

Holiday Hours

If it's a shopping holiday (like Christmas), look for extended hours. If it's summer, look for retracted hours—many stores close on Saturdays during the summer season. Not the big stores, but the little boutiques that give New York a lot of its special flavor.

Do note that as more and more stores need cash and will do whatever it takes to keep the electricity on, store hours become more flexible. I was shocked to see that all major New York department stores and many multiples were open last year on the 4th of July.

Seems that these days, anything goes.

Funky Hours

Now that so many funky neighborhoods have become chic, a whole new set of operating hours are coming into style. Most downtown stores open at 11am and stay open until 8pm at night. They may open at 10am on Saturday but they may not.

BAD BUYS OF NEW YORK

There are people who will tell you that anything you buy in New York that costs full retail is a bad buy, but I'm not one of them. I think the things to avoid are the things you can buy at home perhaps more cheaply, such as dry-cleaning services, makeup, vitamins, and pantyhose.

Computers, electronics, and cameras may be available for less in your hometown if you live in a major U.S. city. Before I did my electronics and camera shopping segment on "Good Morning America" from Hong Kong a few years ago, I got the newspapers from every major U.S. city to look at camera and computer superstore advertisements. Dallas had the best prices in America, and Dallas beat Hong Kong on the items we comparison shopped. Hook 'em horns, y'all.

I have done some rather extensive electronics research for this edition and have discovered the basic operating ploy for the Fifth Avenue and even Sixth Avenue electronics stores that seem to be offering such incredible deals in midtown: They all have a system. The system is that they do their pricing based on prices for those goods in Europe and Japan and in the world's most expensive duty-free stores where bargains don't exist. That way, to a foreign visitor, the prices seem like bargains. The visitors buy without realizing that there are several good and honorable firms in New York where you get good service, good price, and good value.

These stores survive because they are frequented by people who live out of town and may never come back to New York again to complain or who simply don't know they can do much better. Don't get taken.

In fact, any fake bargains are actually bad buys because they won't give you the pleasure of the real thing—this means anything from designer perfumes at cut rate prices to Prada handbags from a pushcart.

SPECIAL IN-STORE SHOPPERS

One of the things I find most staggering about New York is that there are free services to help busy people with their shopping. If you've ever been on one of those whirlwind business trips where you mean to get out for a few minutes in your favorite store but you never make it, a special shopper may work out for you. Every department store in Manhattan has a shopping service that will run errands for you and mail out your purchases (from that store only) or will pull together everything you want to look at and have it ready for you to peruse on an appointment basis at your convenience.

A special shopper will work the entire store with you, helping to coordinate your outfits or put together table settings for a dinner party or plan your wedding—although most stores have special wedding consultants for the bride-and-groom part. Or a special shopper will put together clothes for you and then invite you into the store to try them on. She can even bring them to your home, if you don't like to go to stores or have time constraints.

A special shopper is available with a store translator if you would prefer to work in a language other than English. Make an appointment and specify what language you will be speaking.

You should not pay extra for the services of a shopper, since she is an employee of the department store, but the shopper does not use outside resources for your buying, nor does she tell you where to get bargains or discounts. She may give you fashion tips and point you toward a good buy, but her job is to sell the store's merchandise. Men as well as women often use special shoppers.

CHARGE & SEND

If you are on a mad shopping spree, check with the concierge of your hotel about having someone pick up your purchases for you. Department stores will deliver for you, but they charge UPS rates and it takes a few days. Your concierge can get you a messenger to pick up and deliver your packages on the same day. The charges are computed by distance.

Stores will happily send a package to any address for you— but they'll probably pull out a zone chart and bill you a flat fee for the packing, wrapping, and mailing. Insurance is probably not included; ask specifically if you'd like to have it.

Technically, mail costs should be charged by weight and distance—but many stores guess at the weight and charge you a flat fee for the whole works. Snap it up.

Interstate shipping is also a good way to avoid sales tax, although New Jersey and Connecticut residents who shop in New York must pay a users' tax.

Most department stores have shopping services that will deliver to your hotel room for you, or your hotel concierge will send out for an item for you. Department stores will usually mail order any item you see advertised in the newspaper. Many of the more fancy boutiques (such as **Chanel**) offer a shop-by-phone system as well.

Although the U.S. Postal Service still works, you may prefer to rely on private mail services and 1- or 2-day delivery services. The U.S. Postal Service offers such a service, called **Express Mail,** which promises next-day or second-day delivery. There's also **Priority Mail,** which is good for small packages. You can use these services yourself through any post office.

Stores traditionally ship merchandise by **United Parcel Service (UPS),** which takes several days depending on your delivery zone. Many stores have a deal with **Federal Express,** a private courier company, and offer next-day or second-day delivery at less than regular Federal Express rates. Even if you pay full rates for FedEx, if it saves you tax, it can be a savings. If you are making a large purchase that will involve a good hunk of change in sales tax, consider FedEx if it is an option.

If you are an international visitor who will be in several different U.S. cities, consider using FedEx to get purchases to you in another state. On high-ticket items, this can save you money if there is a luxury tax involved or a sales tax on a luxury item.

Every now and then a store will provide free FedEx shipment. I bought a gizmo over the phone (to avoid sales tax) and they sent it to me via Federal Express for no charge. I'm impressed.

NEW YORK SALES TAX

Currently, shoes and clothing less than $110 are not subject to sales tax in New York City.

Note that some people shop in New Jersey or Pennsylvania specifically to avoid New York sales taxes.

MAIL ORDER & CATALOGS

Mail-order retailing can be a great way to shop the glories of New York without actually being here. Even people in New York, especially those too busy to make it to the stores, do this all the time. Also note that these days, when retail space is very expensive and it gets harder and harder for stores to make money, some places that had stores have gone down to just retail catalogs. If an old favorite of yours has closed shop, check to see if perhaps they now have a mail-order or catalog business.

Some department stores will put you on their catalog list automatically after a purchase, or you can pay for a catalog (usually $2, often redeemable toward purchase) and get newer editions if you buy something. Saks even has a special club of catalog and shopping offers for people who spend $2,000 per year.

In the months before Christmas you can make the rounds of the midtown retailers and put together a catalog collection. Usually, if you just ask nicely, you can get a free catalog. Many women's magazines have order forms for all the fancy catalogs, but you must pay for these.

I find that ads in the *New York Times* and catalogs often showcase merchandise that I simply wouldn't find on my own in a store. If you see the ad in the newspaper, call the mail-order number provided, supply a credit card, and get the item delivered to your hotel. I once browsed the **Crate & Barrel** catalog, saw something I liked, went to the store, and couldn't find it in person. It took a sales clerk to locate this item. Meanwhile, another sales clerk got out a calculator to see if the in-store price or the catalog price (promotional deal for set of six) was a better deal. Now that's service!

Should you see something you want in a store catalogue, most catalogs have 2-day delivery deals so that your order can get to you before you leave town.

The most difficult part of this, of course, is that if you do not visit the United States regularly, you may not know which catalogs are best. Ask any store you take a fancy to if they have a catalog; if so, ask for a copy—there should not be a charge. Most of the big companies do international shipping. And yes, they will take off the state sales tax on international mail orders.

There are some stores that are outgrowths of their catalogue business; a few of these even have European distribution deals. Check out J. Crew, Eddie Bauer, FAO Schwarz, Victoria's Secret, Hammacher Schlemmer, Brookstone, and Orvis.

Chapter Three

· · · · · · · · · · · · · · · · · · · ·

SHOPPING TIPS FOR FOREIGN VISITORS

COME SALE WITH ME

Every year I am the speaker on at least one crossing of the *QE2* when she heads from Southampton into New York. Usually this is the last crossing of the year, departing London around December 15 and filled with happy Brits who are crossing The Pond to scarf up American bargains and do all their holiday shopping. They are giddy with glee, especially since London is so expensive.

I've put together this short chapter for my passengers and for all my friends—and your friends—who come to New York for business or pleasure and to shop.

WELCOME TO DEAL CITY

Yes (*si, oui, ja, da*), in most cases, America is cheaper than Europe and many destinations in Asia. Europeans, especially Britons, are downright gaga for prices in New York—and I'm talking regular retail prices.

When French friends come to the United States, I know they come loaded down with shopping lists of not only wish lists from children and loved ones, but with style and model numbers of cameras and electronic gadgets so they can get the latest models at the best prices. *Vive la différence.*

British shoppers are all dying to get into The Gap and laugh and laugh to the top of their credit card limit.

If you are visiting from a foreign country, there are more tips throughout this guide, believe me. This isn't the only chapter to read. Of course, I want you to read the whole book, but be sure to see the chapter on bargains and all the information on factory outlet villages such as **Woodbury Common.**

Also note the size conversion chart in the back of this book.

ARRIVING IN NEW YORK

Most international travelers come to the Big Apple via John F. Kennedy (JFK) International Airport or Newark Airport, in New Jersey. The only international arrivals La Guardia Airport gets are from Canada.

Of these three airports, JFK has the most international traffic and therefore is the most congested and most likely to be confusing; also Newark is a lot newer and I think, easier to use. JFK has become infamous for its scams and for the variety of attempts made on innocents who do not know enough about New York to know they are being cheated. While police have cracked down to try to protect foreign visitors, often you don't know you're in trouble until it's too late. Therefore, a few tips:

Luggage Carts

In international terminals, they are free.

Skycaps

If you page a skycap to help you with your luggage, there is no predetermined fee as in many European airports or train stations. You tip at your own discretion. The norm is $1 a bag.

Getting a Taxi at the Airport

Ignore all drivers who approach you and offer a ride; this includes well-dressed limo drivers or people with "honest" faces.

Use only a yellow, licensed taxi. When you get into your taxi, take out a pen and paper and copy down your taxi driver's name, shield number, and the name of the cab company. Make sure he or she sees you doing this little ritual. The New York City Taxi and Limousine Commission states that a driver's license will be revoked if he or she is caught overcharging a passenger by more than $10.

There are now fixed prices for taxis into the city: $30 from JFK; $25 from LaGuardia. This fee does not include the tip or bridge and tunnel tolls.

Please note, the fixed-price situation does not work in reverse; you pay the meter in a taxi from the city to any of the airports.

Other Ground Transportation

There is public transportation from each airport into Manhattan and to the suburbs. Go to the Ground Transportation desk, located across from the baggage carousels or in the lobby outside of U.S. Customs after arrival. You have your choice of buses, subway, or private transport companies that take people into the city and suburban areas of the tristate area.

BUYING AMERICAN

For a comparison chart of U.S., Continental, and British clothing and shoe sizes, see page 301.

Also note that towels and bed linens in U.S. sizes may not match their Continental or British counterparts, but may work with some successful juggling or recalculating. My friend Ruth, who lives in London, says an American queen-size sheet fits two British twin beds together. King is 2 meters. Beware of an American size called California King; it's longer than a regular king and fits a European bed of 200cm.

Meanwhile, when it comes to clothing styles, a European cut is different from an American one and Far Eastern sizes are often scaled to the petite. I don't actually wear the same size that correlates on a chart between my official U.S. size and my official European size. To compensate, do what I do: Try many sizes; go by fit, not label.

Another different aspect to sizes in America is that they have many names and types of cuts. For example, size charts usually refer to women's sizes in even numbers—size 4, 6, 8, 10, and so on. They don't tell you that in America we also have junior sizes, sometimes called missy sizes, which are sizes 3, 5, 7, 9, 11, and so on. Missy sizes are usually a tad shorter, rounder, and bustier. They should not be confused with petite sizes, which usually have a P next to the size number.

Large sizes for women come with a variety of names, from queen size to plus to simply 1X, 2X, 3X; see page 189.

Men's sizes are found up to about size 44 in regular stores; after that you need a store for "big and tall men"; see page 189. Sizes that may be written as S (small), M (medium), and L (large) usually have XL for extra-large and sometimes XXL for extra-extra-large.

Also note that fragrance in the United States, even when labeled "Made in France," is made with denatured alcohol, not potato alcohol as in Europe. This may wear differently on your skin, but the scent in the bottle will smell the same. Huh? It all has to do with the U.S. Food & Drug Administration and what it will allow onto U.S. shores. For this same reason many shades of cosmetics are different in the United States and other parts of the world. They may or may not bear the same color name, number or designation.

PRICES IN NEW YORK

Most foreign visitors to New York are so dazzled by the price tags at regular retail that they fail to understand the concept of bargain shopping or to realize that there are places where you can get the same, or similar, merchandise for less money.

The first step toward getting a bargain is to bring from home a list of target acquisitions and their prices and availability at home. Begin by pricing at regular retail but also check out convenient bargain resources, alternative retail (such as resale shops), and factory outlets.

VALUE-ADDED TAX & SALES TAX

European shoppers may at first be shocked that the ticketed price on an item in the United States is not the final price: Once you go to the cash register, taxes are added on.

The United States does not presently have a value-added tax (VAT) or an export-tax program. We may get one, but we haven't got it now. Visitors from foreign countries are required to pay the state sales tax and cannot get a refund on this money when they leave the country. Sorry, I know that doesn't sound very fair, but that's the way it works.

Sales tax does vary from state to state. Some states have no tax on clothes (Pennsylvania) or no tax on clothing items up to $50 (Connecticut) or no tax at all (New Hampshire). New York happens to have one of the highest sales taxes anywhere in the United States, currently at 8.5%. But wait, someday New York is going to repeal or modify this tax on some items. We have been waiting now for politicos to work this out for the last 3 years. While they haggle, the state government grants us 2 or 3 tax-free weeks a year.

You can avoid sales tax totally by shipping your purchases to your home country. However, this may be costly in shipping fees and even more costly if it provokes duty fees. If you are buying diamonds at **Tiffany & Co.,** you may want to look into it, though.

Trick: If you are visiting a variety of states in your U.S. tour, you can send an item from a Manhattan store to your hotel in your final destination state (allow at least a week for delivery) and therefore avoid state tax. If you need fast delivery, you can pay for **FedEx** or 2-day **UPS Blue Label** delivery service to your next destination. Don't laugh. If it's a high-end item that could be small (such as a piece of jewelry or a small electronic gadget), it may even pay to have the item sent to you in another state. If the store sends it out, there should not be any tax, but ask first, because in some cases (when the store has a branch in the state to which you wish to mail something) tax will be added.

It is considered rude to ask a store to mail you an empty box to an out-of-state address. Years ago jewelers and furriers did it all the time. No more. Don't even think about it.

Some stores are very conscious of the fact that the United States has no VAT refund and go out of their way to give a discount to foreign visitors. **Conway's** does this; you must show your passport at the time of purchase. Ask at other stores.

MONEY CHANGING

Even if Europe converts to one currency, visitors coming and going across the Atlantic or Pacific will still need to exchange money. One of the best bets is to buy traveler's checks in U.S. dollars before you leave home. Although there is usually a fee for doing this, it allows you to freeze your rate of exchange at the time of purchase.

Some stores and businesses will accept Canadian currency at an automatic (and possibly unfair) discount rate; few stores will accept other foreign currency. **Bloomingdale's** has a foreign exchange office in the department store; it's right next door to its American Express Travel Services office, open Monday through Saturday from 10am to 6pm, Thursdays until 8pm; closed Sundays.

While you can change funds at airports and most banks, there are several services in midtown that specialize in money exchange and international traveler's checks. Most are open 7 days a week:

AMERICAN EXPRESS
Park Ave. at 53rd St.

CHEQUEPOINT
*551 Madison Ave. at 55th St.; 1568 Broadway at 47th St.;
22 Central Park South at 59th St.*

DEAK INTERNATIONAL
630 Fifth Ave. at 50th St.

THOMAS COOK CURRENCY SERVICE
630 Fifth Ave. at 50th St. (and other locations)

Global use of international banking systems is not yet here; a British friend who uses Nat West in London had no luck in a branch of Nat West on Fifth Avenue when trying to transfer dollars to his account.

If you travel to the United States frequently and stockpile cash, you may want to keep track of what you paid for your money. With currency fluctuations, you may find it smarter to sit on your cash and convert new funds or rely mostly on credit cards for a better rate of exchange.

INTERNATIONAL MAILING & SHIPPING

If you've bought more than you can carry home, you may want to send some packages overseas. The small-package airmail rate is the least expensive and has minimal paperwork. Once you get into big packages, it does get more expensive—even if you send surface mail, which is by sea. Airmail can get quite expensive, especially if something is heavy.

For surface mail to Europe or Asia, figure 6 to 8 weeks before your package will arrive; for airmail, about 1 week.

Various courier services carry overnight mail around the world, although with time changes and the international dateline, the service is rarely overnight. It will take 2 to 4 days, depending on the destination. (Too bad you can't fax yourself a sweater!) The U.S. Postal Service does have 3-day international airmail that is similar to courier service but less money.

The biggest problems with shipping are not American prices or laws but laws on the receiving end—many people cannot afford the duty on the gifts that you send them.

It is usually less expensive to pay for an additional piece of luggage as excess baggage when you fly home than to ship a package home.

POSTCARDS

Postcards are sold just about everywhere; the best prices are on those sold in minibulk from touristy electronics shops. Note that these stores sell cards at: three for $1 on Fifth Avenue in the 50s; six for $1 on Madison Avenue in the 40s or on Broadway; ten for $1 on Broadway in the 40s, on West 34th St. and on Fifth Avenue below the Public Library at 41st St.

Your hotel should have free postcards, featuring the hotel, of course. If you walk into the gift shop of the Plaza Hotel, you can buy a postcard of the hotel for 50¢.

Postage for an international postcard is 50¢; a letter (up to ½ oz.) is 60¢. A two-page letter may cost more.

E-MAIL

Most hotels have data ports in their rooms or they have separate business centers where you can send and retrieve e-mail. Note that most phone lines in Europe are digital, while they are analog in the United States; this will affect your modem settings.

There are also Internet cafes dotted around the city.

TRANSLATION, PLEASE

All major department stores will get you a translator if you will phone ahead, or more specifically, ask someone to phone ahead for you to make the arrangements. Your hotel concierge is a good bet to assist with the call.

Most of the big tourist stores on Fifth Avenue have salespeople who speak several languages; foreign designer boutiques often hire nationals who speak various languages. Walk into **Pratesi** and you will find someone who speaks Italian, and so on. I was at **Brookstone** where I noticed that various salespeople wear little buttons written in their second language. I spoke to Ed in French ("Hi. I'm Ed. Je parle français," said his button) and he answered me in the broadest American accent I have ever heard, but in perfectly fine high-school French. It wasn't like speaking to Voltaire, but it was good enough to do the trick.

SALE SEASONS

Sales are held much more frequently in the United States than in Europe. Because Americans think that a good sale is part of the American way, retailers look for any occasion to host a blowout or a promotion that will make shoppers think they are saving money. Most of these events are seasonal, pegged to holidays or once-a-year events; certain types of merchandise are sold. Yes, there are big January and July sales in New York as in every other city in the world, but there are also sales for things you may have never heard of, such as:

Thanksgiving: The Christmas season officially begins with this American holiday held the third Thursday in November. The following day, Friday, is usually the single biggest day in retail for the year. Sometimes stores begin their pre-Christmas sales on this date.

Pre-Christmas Sales: Recently created to goose Christmas shoppers with the warning that the store has less merchandise than usual so you better buy before they sell out.

Christmas Sales: Various stores have their own pattern for postholiday sales—some begin at 8:30am the day after Christmas. Some stores wait until after January 1 for the sale. It's rare for a store to wait until Epiphany, because it's rare to find an American who knows when (or what) Epiphany is.

January White Sales: Usually in January—a sale of bed linen, which is rarely white these days, with colors and patterns replacing traditional whites since the 1960s.

January Clearance Sales: While most department stores have their end-of-season sales right after Christmas or New Year's, most of the European boutiques in New York have their clearance sales toward the end of January, starting around the 20th. These events, even at stores as exclusive as Hermès, are announced in the *New York Times*.

Valentine's Day Sales: February 14 is Valentine's Day, a big day for lovers to express their feelings with traditional gifts such as flowers, chocolates, or fancy undies. These types of items, along with fragrance, jewelry, and anything with a heart-shaped motif, are promoted heavily.

President's Day Sales: Usually promotional sales for the entire holiday weekend in late February; a good time for winter clothes and ski equipment.

Memorial Day Sales: Geared for the last weekend in May, these are more promotional events for summer merchandise.

Fourth of July Sales: Bathing suits and some summer wearing apparel. Begin before the Fourth of July weekend. Also a weekend for blowout sales events, summer clearance sales, various specials offered for a day or two, and special-event sales. Outlet stores in the New York area often do big sales too.

Midsummer Clearance Sales: From late July throughout August, major summer sales on European brands. Sales on American brands usually begin right before July Fourth Weekend.

Back-to-School Sales: Last 2 weeks in August, promotional sales for school supplies, furnishings, and clothing.

Columbus Day Sales: Coats and early fall clothing.

Election Day Sales: Although there aren't elections every November, the sale is a good time to buy coats and fall merchandise that you can still wear.

HOTEL PROMOTIONS

American hotels are far bigger on promotional deals than European hotels, so there may be freebies and extras that you are not used to asking for or getting. Most frequently, these promotions are for weekends but there are hotels that offer upgrades at check-in, discounted parking, breakfast, or a free T-shirt.

PRIX FIXE & MEAL PROMOTIONS

Almost every famous restaurant in New York has a fixed-price lunch or dinner. The fixed price usually does not include wine and rarely includes tip.

There are also pretheater set-price meals (you must eat dinner before 7pm, which many visitors consider barbarian) that offer perhaps the best deals you can find. Even the most famous restaurants in Manhattan offer these promotions, including The Four Seasons and "21."

There are also times of the year when meal prices are fixed at the date, such as during a particular period in the year when the cost of the meal equals the date of the year. In 2000, a meal at a participating restaurant costs $20; in 2001 it will cost $20.01, and so on. With incremental increases of a penny a year, I think you can swing this one for many years to come. Many of Manhattan's most famous restaurants participate in this program; watch the newspaper for advertisements.

TIPPING

The basic tip in America is the $1 bill, although we may someday get a $1 coin, which will also do the trick. Just learn the size and weight difference between a quarter and a dollar so no one (on either end of the transaction) gets slighted.

When in doubt, give a dollar. Except **at meals,** you tip between 15% and 20% of the total bill *before* the tax was added on and; **in taxis,** you do not automatically tip your taxi an extra $1—taxis get a percentage of the meter, usually 10% to 15%.

Please pay attention to the fine print regarding tipping, especially in hotels. It is very common for a hotel to add the tip for room service and to then leave a second blank space labeled "gratuity" so that those people who are not paying attention will add in another 10% to 15%. Be careful!

Aside from hotels, it is rare for an American restaurant to automatically add in a service charge or tip unless you are part of a party of eight or more diners. Likewise, at beauty salons and spa you tip 15% to 20%.

BOOZE NEWS

This is a tricky category, so you may want to stay sober enough to take notes. Liquor in Manhattan, especially when sold from fancy liquor stores near the city's finest hotels, is outrageously expensive. Outrageously. I mean, liquor can cost 50% more than it should. Compared to these inflated prices, duty-free liquor is a bargain.

But wait, if you can get to a real part of America or even Manhattan (or New Jersey or Connecticut), liquor prices in regular old stores are less than in the duty free.

Now then, should you have the choice of buying a miniature bottle of liquor from your hotel minibar or a small bottle of liquor from an overpriced store, you have to figure out just how much you are going to drink. Miniatures in expensive midtown liquor stores are at least $4 each; a small bottle of Chivas costs about $20.

GADGET GURUS

Many a European visitor has come to the United States and planned his or her free time around the opportunity to go to some electronics shops, since electronics and small business machines cost about 30% less in the United States than in Europe.

Since there are many pitfalls awaiting you, please see below for more guidance. If you just want me to cut to the chase, here goes: Electronics are not as easy to buy as you think they will be. Proceed with care. I personally went through hell in order to fulfill an order for a computer for my friend Richard: It took approximately 20 hours of my time to research the buy, several transatlantic phone calls back and forth to make sure Richard understood the findings, and then a week of baited breath while we waited for a computer guru in Nice to install Richard's board to see if his memory would be wiped out. Throughout the research and the agony I kept screaming at Richard, "No amount of savings is worth going through this!"

Think about it.

Matching & Compatibility

Aside from the obvious basic difference in electrical and television systems, there are glitches to be found in the most mundane of purchases. You'd be surprised at what a wide window of unavailability exists within a certain brand. Various styles and models are made for U.S. or U.K. or Continental or Japanese markets and may or may not be available in New York. Likewise, what you buy in New York—especially in electronics—may not be compatible with what you have at home. And I'm not just talking 120 volts versus 240 volts— how about the businessman who bought a Sharp electronic Wizard only to find that he couldn't expand the memory because of incompatibility between his European model and U.S. memory boards!

Colors in fashions will usually match from same-season collections, but colors may not match if the goods were made, or dyed, in different parts of the world. In makeup, a certain shade can have the same code number throughout the world and yet be a different color in various parts of the world. Many cosmetics don't match up at all.

DUTY CALLS

All airlines have duty-free shopping on board; frequently they publish a beautiful color brochure that is in your seat with the other magazines. More important, in many cases the airline duty-free price is less than the airport duty-free price.

The best way to be sure is to look at the brochure (take it along with you) and price what you want on outbound travel. When you leave the United States, price the item in the airport duty free. Then look it up in your brochure to decide if you want to buy on the plane or not.

Speaking of airport duty-free stores, at JFK various terminals have different shops—some are better than others; some are downright sorry looking while others are more gorgeous than any U.S. mall. Many of them publish a price guide.

Duty-free stores in Manhattan are not real duty-free stores and offer no serious bargains. If you have the time to work on it, you'll do better at discount sources in New York.

EUROPEAN SHOPPING CHECKLIST

Many of my hotel manager friends ask me to take them shopping when they come to New York. Invariably they all want the same things. All Frenchmen seem to think about is Ralph Lauren and Estée Lauder! Italians want Oshkosh and Levi's.

Genuine Ray-Bans can be found at discount at a variety of sources (my best find was $39 for the Wayfarer style at **TJ Maxx;** these cost $49 discounted at **Nobody Beats the Wiz**).

Fake Ray-Bans are sold all over town. They are most easily bought on Canal Street near SoHo and Chinatown in the stalls that specialize in fakes.

I often give business acquaintances a fake Mont Blanc pen (and yes, I tell them it is a fake) with genuine Mont Blanc cartridges inside it (two in a pack; retail $8); you buy these at discount at any branch of **Staples.**

Everyone wants CDs. There are several large music stores in Manhattan that are so competitive that they have price wars. The usual policy is for one store to match the lowest price offered by the competition. Watch newspaper ads carefully, then pounce. **HMV** and **Virgin** are British companies that sell at American prices; **Sam Goody, Tower Records,** and **Coconuts** are American chains. There are branches of these stores in midtown and convenient to all business addresses.

Finally, for the Estée Lauder freaks—learn about "gift with purchase"—an idea that is beginning to catch on in Europe and Asia but with which most men are not familiar. Read the newspaper ads in whatever American cities you are visiting to see which department store is having an Estée Lauder promotion. Then buy the perfume and get a free gift from Estée Lauder. The gifts in America are always much better than the gifts in Europe or in duty-free stores at airports.

Please note: The duty-free stores of the world are rarely much less expensive than regular stores and can be more expensive—especially on imports such as American perfume sold in France. Also, Estée Lauder is not sold in all duty-free shops.

Chapter Four

....

EATING & SLEEPING IN NEW YORK

MORE TO EAT THAN APPLES

....

Even though we call it The Big Apple, we have more to eat than apples. Lots more. In lots of different price ranges. In fact, Paris has nothing on New York. New York has it all; eating in New York is part of the adventure and the fun of being here.

I've made my food choices for this chapter based on my personal needs as a shopper and visitor. Location and price play a big part in my choices, but so does atmosphere (not to mention the quality of the food and service). I'm looking for a special experience or some serious convenience; I am not Mr. or Mrs. Zagat so I give you the shopper's specials in assorted categories and styles or choices.

Hotel Dining Deals

One of the most important lessons I have learned as a traveler is that hotels are always looking for lunch business in their dining rooms, even when their dining rooms are famous, as many of them are in New York. As a result, you can often get the best lunch deals at the best hotels in town. Several of the city's snazziest hotels, and I'm talking from **The Pierre** to **The Mark** here, have fixed-price luncheon menus whereby you can be served three courses for a flat price that varies from $20 to $25 per person. You can pay that same amount for less food, less service, less atmosphere, and less quality at many places in town.

Pretheater Deals

Since Broadway curtain is usually at 8pm, most restaurants in midtown have a dinner special whereby if you eat early enough, you can get a fabulous meal at a fabulous price. You don't have to show your theater tickets at the door to prove you're going to the theater; you just have to like to eat dinner at 6pm. A three-course pretheater dinner at a good restaurant usually comes in at around $32 to $35 per person, which is considerably less than it would cost à la carte if eaten at 8pm.

Legends & Landmarks

Some cities offer dining experiences so sublime that I consider them "legends and landmarks." Just once in your life you'll probably want to try one of these:

LE CIRQUE 2000
Palace Hotel, 455 Madison Ave. at 51st St., ☎ *212/303-7788*

For those of you visiting from out of town who have a supreme need to see what's hot and be able to talk about it when you get home. Step no further than one block from your shopping spree at Saks Fifth Avenue. The atmosphere here is very different from the old Le Cirque, the crowd is much more mixed than before—you do get a lot of tourists and a lot of people doing birthdays or special events. The decor is so extravagant that all everyone can do is talk about how they love it or loathe it. (I love it!) The food is fabulous; don't miss dessert. Worth saving up for.

THE RUSSIAN TEA ROOM
150 W. 57th St., between Sixth & Seventh aves.,
☎ *212/974-2111*

It's possible that the Russian Tea Room is an old-timers kind of place, that it means something to me so I send you there with fond memories more than realistic expectations. Certainly the place has been redone in grand Warner LeRoy over-the-top dollar style. While the chef is said to be famous and fabulous, all I can tell you is that my meal was very disappointing. The black bread was great. Still, once in your life.

TAVERN ON THE GREEN
Central Park West at 67th St., ☏ *212/873-3200*

Despite the fact that tourists flock here, the beauty of Tavern on the Green (first built in 1870 for sheep, believe it or not) is that it's still used by celebs and beautiful people. The food is surprisingly good and the prices offer real value—they aren't too high and you may get dancing thrown in for free. Dancing in the garden with little golden lights twinkling in the trees, honest. There's a pre-theater fixed-price meal for $22. They also do lunch (all week) and brunch on Sundays.

Teen Legends & Family Fun

HARD ROCK CAFE
221 W. 57th St., ☏ *212/459-9320*

This international phenom is less sophisticated and more teeny-bopper-ish than Planet Hollywood. Boutique up front.

JEKYLL & HYDE
1409 Ave. of the Americas at 57th St., ☏ *212/541-9505*

My son discovered this when he was about 13; I take out-of-town visitors here if they have teenagers, although once they are into their twenties they usually feel too jaded for this Disney-esque "club" of spooks and tricks and gimmicks and gewgaws. Burgers, fried chicken, and more are served at moderate prices. You do not have one of these at home. You probably don't need a reservation, but you may want one if you are the plan-ahead type.

PLANET HOLLYWOOD
140 W. 57th St., ☎ 212/333-7827

While this firm is having financial difficulties, you wouldn't
guess it by visiting the New York venue. There's a huge menu,
prices are reasonable, and the place is like living inside a juke
box. There's cinema memorabilia everywhere with audiovisual
blasts on the walls and ceilings and it's just a hoot. I don't care
that it's owned by a gaggle of stars and that it's become part
of the international scene. The logo merchandise is sold from
a stand in the front.

In-Store Dining

All the major department stores have a place for you to eat;
some of them have several places to eat—and a variety of
styles of dining experiences. Such is modern retail. These in-
store dining out spots were not all created equal.

When I was growing up, my idea of heaven was to eat bar-
ley soup upstairs in Lord & Taylor and then finish off the meal
with apple pie—these were the only two things on the menu,
as I recall. It's all gotten much more sophisticated than that.

So sophisticated in fact that cafes have become really important to smaller shops where they have taken over the basements
or the mezzanines of just about every name brand in New York,
from **Old Navy** to **DKNY,** from **Armani** to **Frederic Fekkai** to
the **NBA Store!** Most of the cafes offer a gimmick (bagels and
health food snacks at DKNY; fifties-style diner at Old Navy).
Some of the stores have gone the extra step to offer fine dining, such as in the new **Nicole Farhi** shop on east 60th St., which
is noisy for a serious business conversation but lotsa fun with
really nice food (and great breads).

ABC Carpet has one of the best eat-in-the-store concepts
with a large restaurant, a bar for singles who just want a
quick bite or a coffee and a market. They even have a gourmet restaurant with one of the most famous chefs in America,
Jonathan Waxman. Sunday brunch is also a fun scene.

BARNEY'S
660 Madison Ave. at 61st St.

Fred's is the name of the stylish cafe in the basement level of Barney's uptown store; the restaurant is sort of moderne Milan in feel and is very much the place to be having a nosh. I'm not a big fan because it's simply too too, my dear. But you should do it once in your life. Without the kids, please.

BERGDORF-GOODMAN
754 Fifth Ave. at 58th St.

The Café has reverted back to the old style; but there's a brand new cafe in the basement in the new beauty portion of the store. I sometimes go across the street to Bergdorf Man where there's a tiny cafe with great salads and no tourists.

BLOOMINGDALE'S
1000 Third Ave.

Four different choices for four different styles: Le Train Bleu (a sit-down restaurant); 40 Carats (health food); Pasta Bar (pizza); and Showtime Café (a cafeteria).

HENRI BENDEL
712 Fifth Ave. at 56th St.

The tea room on the first floor serves a light lunch as well as tea. The view is of Fifth Avenue through Lalique windows. Teapots line the walls for decor; the tables have a shelf above your lap for your handbag. The food is adequate and midpriced—entrees are $15. Salads are nice.

LORD & TAYLOR
424 Fifth Ave. at 38th St.

Two restaurants and an espresso bar; it's worth a stop if you're shopping here.

MACY'S
Herald Square, 151 W. 34th St.

There are dining choices on every floor.

SAKS
611 Fifth Ave. at 50th St.

Cafe SFA is one of my favorite places for lunch in New York. It's elegant without being stuffy, they have that great raisin and walnut bread that costs a fortune if you have to buy it, and the menu has a good mix of light fare for those who only want a salad or so. And prices are moderate. Watch for special promotions—I went once when they had the pastry chef from The Ritz in Paris and were doing a French teatime—*génial!*

Snack & Shop

When I am into an intense shopping day, I do not want a 2-hour lunch, nor do I want to spend what is the equivalent of a pair of shoes for my lunch. I want quick, I want cheap, I want convenient. I don't mind good, but charm or chic is a bonus.

BURGER HEAVEN
9 E. 53rd St.; 804 Lexington Ave.; 291 Madison Ave.; 536 Madison Ave.; 20 E. 49th St.

Not only is this my regular haunt, but I dream of the Roquefort burger. I have brought many visitors to New York here, including foreign tourists.

While there is a menu and a variety of choices, I began here about 25 years ago with the pizza burger and moved over to the Roquefort burger about 15 years ago.

There are a handful of locations, but my regular is right off Fifth Avenue on East 53rd St., a great shopping location.

BURKE & BURKE
485 Madison Ave. at 52nd St.; 156 W. 56th St.; 416 W. 13th St.

Another chain dotted all over Manhattan, Burke & Burke is a gourmet sandwich shop. They do deliver, so you can actually order in to your hotel. Few of the shops have table service; this is gourmet takeout. Again, there is a large selection, but I fall for the same old sandwich, time after time. Make mine the turkey and brie on a baguette with honey mustard. When you pass a Burke & Burke during your wanderings, get their menu, which also lists all their addresses, so you're prepared wherever you may be.

OLLIE'S NOODLE SHOP
2315 Broadway at 84th St.; 190 W. 44th St. (Times Square), 1991 Broadway (Lincoln Center)

This is a noodle shop that actually has a full Chinese menu as well as dim sum and then some. I like the one on Broadway and 84th St. for a break while shopping in that area, but the business has grown and opened up all over town, even in the theater district as an attractive before or after possibility.

TUSCAN SQUARE
Rockefeller Center (enter W. 51st St. or through lower level of 630 Fifth Ave.)

Italian food and Italian shopping, mamma mia what will they think of next! Market downstairs has food to go. Note this is located right behind Sephora, the beauty supermarket, and may be why Sephora has no cafe in it. They are open downstairs for early morning coffee; enter through Rock Center.

Teatime

Although tea is a British tradition, it's especially welcome in New York, where you can get exhausted by a hard day on your feet or you may be going out to theater and not having dinner until 11pm. There are only a few specialty tea houses in New York, but all the major hotels do a big business in tea.

I tested some of the big names for this section and was quite disappointed in some of the most famous ones that are generally associated with afternoon tea in big hotels on Fifth Avenue. So if I don't mention your favorite, it might be that I wasn't wild about it.

FELISSIMO
10 W. 56th St.

Japanese tea service as well as herbal teas, old-fashioned teas, French infusions, and much more. Sensational store, so browse then plop down in their upstairs tearoom.

THE PIERRE
Fifth Ave. at 61st St.

Rotunda Tea is what they call it. I've never seen anything like this in my life—I came for tea and wanted to stay for retirement. And I don't mean bedtime. The Rotunda is a small and intimate space, with incredibly painted murals and drop-dead decor in the middle of the Pierre Hotel. A pot of tea is a mere $5. You can also get snacks or a light bite.

SoHo So Great

You'll have no problem getting something to eat in SoHo: They have grocers, kiosks, fast food, takeout, and cutting-edge chic. I have three regulars that I visit, depending on ability to get a reservation.

BALTHAZAR
80 Spring St., ☎ *212/965-1785*

Just half a block over from Broadway and the most commercial part of SoHo shopping, Balthazar is the "in" spot of the minute, a Parisian-style bistro with a great crowd, affordable prices, and a cute story. Not only do they have a takeout department adjacent and a bread shop, but at the end of the evening, they put out all the unsold bread so you can take it home with you (free) since it won't be used the next day. You'll never be hungry again! Make note, Marie Antoinette! Reservations can be hard to get although lunch is much easier to do than dinner. You can also go for morning café au lait.

BAROLO
398 W. Broadway, ☎ *212/226-1102*

Before Balthazar, this was my regular. Still great for pasta; there's a garden for al fresco dining. I do it for a late lunch, beat the crowds, and can usually escape calling ahead if I come at 1:30pm.

MONZU
142 Mercer St., ☎ *212/343-0333*

My beloved T Salon, in this basement space previously, moved to the twenties and this French-Pacific Rim bistro has come to SoHo. Tables are crammed in there but the feel is industrial French chic. One of the chefs trained with the famed David Bouley so foodies are talking.

SLEEPING IN NEW YORK

There seem to be two completely different schools of thought when it comes to booking hotels. Some people say, "Hey, I'm only sleeping there," and want the least expensive room they can get in a safe neighborhood. Not me.

I usually want my hotel to be part of my whole travel experience. I travel to make my life something it isn't when I'm at home. I live simply at home. I want to live divinely when I travel. And I want service and location and pretty flowers and sheets made of very crisp, real linen.

Since the kinds of hotels I like are generally very expensive, I am constantly looking for value at these hotels—or at least the little extras that make luxury a smart choice. Also, for me,

New York is different from any other city, because I live nearby and if I spend the night it's usually for convenience not glamour. I'm looking for a *find* in New York more than in any other city.

The hotels I have chosen for this chapter all have a location that is convenient for shoppers. I've spent less space on the glam hotels and more on the specialty hotels. Prices are also pegged to be at $200 to $250 per night at promotional rates and $250 to $300 in season, which in any big city, is a deal these days. Rack rates tend to run high, of course. But there's no reason for anyone to pay rack rate (the published rate).

Parking Concepts

If you have a car with you, pick your hotel with parking needs in mind. I don't want to sound discouraging, but some hotels charge up to $50 a day for parking! This is unusually high, but the norm is about $25 per day. And a day is not a 24-hour period; it's a calendar day, so you can get stuck for 2 days within one 24-hour period.

I often pick my hotel based on whether it has a parking package or offers free parking. Wouldn't you rather spend $50 on a new pair of shoes? One of the reasons we are devoted to The Warwick is that when you stay at the hotel, the lot next door charges $18 for overnight parking!

New York Hotel Deals

You may want to keep in mind a few standing promotions for which you might qualify:

Convention Rates: Professionals visiting New York for a convention should be aware of special rates offered by certain hotels that cater to conventions or to visitors on market weeks. Even Garment Center buyers coming to work the market qualify.

Corporate Rates: Most hotels offer corporate discounts, a 20% discount off rack rates. Since the rack rate can be outrageously

Hotel Tax Alert

While New York's occupancy tax has been lowered, it's still high at 13.25% and can add a shocking amount to your total bill. If price is a consideration, you might want to ask a few questions before you book. If you are staying for 5 days or more, the tax can be quite hefty.

high, this may not be the best rate the hotel has. Ask and compare. At some chains you can fill out a form to become a corporate member. Leading Hotels of the World has such a policy and then offers a fine corporate break in all of their hotels.

Weekend Rates: Weekend visitors should check the Sunday Travel section of the *New York Times* for the various weekend rates and special promotions—note that some are per room and some are per person! Don't be misled by headlines; read the fine print. Also ask what days are weekend days as some hotels include Sunday as part of the weekend, others do not. Usually a weekend is only Friday and Saturday nights.

Consolidators & Discounters

If you crave the deluxe hotels that I do but aren't quite ready to ante up top dollar, give a call to a few consolidators and see if they have bought block space. This doesn't work during heavily booked convention times, but can work out on a you-never-know basis. Please note: Sometimes a consolidator gets you a room but at no discount! Try:

Hotel Reservations Network: ☎ 800/964-6835; www. 180096hotel.com

Accommodations Express: ☎ 800/444-7666; www. accommodationsxpress.com

Weekend Deals & Steals

Because there are so many business people visiting The Big Apple during the week, hotel prices are steep and climbing every year. However, when those guys go home, weekend rates make the city attractive. Obviously the rates vary with the time of year and with availability, but so do the choices. The Waldorf-Astoria often offers weekend rates at under $200 per night as does the Helmsley Park Lane. Both are luxury hotels. The Rihga Royal Hotel, a terrific hotel, has weekend rates starting at $229 and this is an all-suite hotel. All three of these hotels are very different, as are their locations—you really need to do some thinking and chatting with reservationists before you pounce on a deal.

New Concept Hotels

Because of the interest in selling rooms at lower rates, hoteliers have begun to try out new concepts in Manhattan to try to offer a good product at a less expensive price. This usually means under $200 per night. The compromise is usually on the size of the room and then the decor. Among those more interesting new choices are The Time (224 W. 49th St.; 877/NYC-TIME); W Hotels (see below), and Ian Schrager Hotels (ISH) which range from The Paramount to his suggested new property, The Henry Hudson, where rooms will be less than $100 per night. Watch this space.

Luxury Shopping Hotels

Luxury hotels are New York's middle name; I was having tea in the lobby of the Four Seasons recently and in 20 minutes I saw (live! in person!) Oprah Winfrey, Jeff Goldblum, and Donald Sutherland. The fancier the hotel, the more chance your added bonus will be a little star-gazing in between arrival and departure. Certainly between The St. Regis, The Pen, The Four Seasons, The Sherry, and the hotels listed below, you can have all the luxury you crave and still be a few feet from a fine shopping district. Many luxury hotels are Leading Hotels of the World and can be booked by calling ☎ 800/223-6800.

My husband and I recently spent 2 different weekends in New York, a week apart. The first one was spent in one of our favorite four-star hotels; the next one was spent in a five-star hotel that we save for special occasions. There was only a $50 difference between the rate on the two hotels because there were weekend deals at each. From check-in to checkout, every moment in the five-star hotel was superlative and surely worth the $50 a day difference—to us. Sometimes you have to make that decision for yourself.

NEW YORK PALACE
455 Madison Ave. at 50th St., ☎ 800/NY-PALACE or 212/888-7000; fax 212/644-5750

This hotel kind of looks like a palace. It's a tower hotel built right over an existing landmark building that once housed a papal archdiocese and remains grander than thou. Right in the heart of midtown shopping, The Palace has a special shopper's package promotion with Saks Fifth Avenue. The package includes 10% off on weekend purchases made at Saks; complimentary delivery of the packages to the hotel from Saks; a massage; tea or coffee in the Cafe SFA; and more. If you qualify for the hotel corporate executive program and you book a Towers room, you will get all of the Saks shopping bonuses that come with the weekend package, except instead of a 10% discount on all purchases, you will receive a coupon worth $10 off any purchase.

There are some apartments in the hotel as well, complete with kitchens. They are ideal for those who are traveling with the whole family. Meanwhile, if you aren't cooking, you may want to note that the hotel restaurant is none other than Le Cirque 2000, which is worth staring at even if you don't eat there. If you do eat there, and perhaps eat too much, note that there is a new health and fitness center in the hotel, which also has antistress workshops!

The room rate is $199 per night on weekends, about the best you can do at a top-flight deluxe New York property in a prime location. The Palace is a Leading Hotel of the World.

THE PIERRE
Fifth Ave. at 61st St., ☎ *800/743-7734 or 212/838-8000; fax 212/826-0319*

I once thought The Pierre was one of those upper-crust places that would make me feel uncomfortable. I had no idea it was part of the Four Seasons chain or that it had an old-fashioned elegance that would make you feel as if you had truly arrived.

Furthermore, you want to talk about a great shopping location?

Aside from the location and all the attention to details and services they offer, The Pierre has dinner-dancing on the weekends; the Rotunda Tea must surely replace The Plaza as the most famous tea in the area and the cafe is a great pit stop for shoppers.

This is a luxury hotel that can be prohibitively expensive, but it does offer special rates and packages, so it pays to inquire. Don't make the mistake I did and assume this hotel is beyond you. I think you are going to be happily surprised when you discover this hotel is everything you wanted and can handle.

Four-Star Shopping Hotels

A four-star hotel is not a five-star hotel. Don't laugh; this is a profound distinction. I find myself amazed at the huge difference between the two. These days, it's very common for a four-star hotel to call itself a "businessman's hotel," add a business center and maybe a health center, and hope for the best.

I've never found any four-star hotel in New York that compares to the luxury five-star hotels the city boasts. And I'm not just talking about fancy rooms or better bars of soap: A luxury hotel functions in a manner that a four-star hotel simply can't quite get down pat.

It may not seriously offend you and the price difference may be worth the inconvenience, but never confuse a four-star property as being a close cousin to a five-star property. Four-star properties are simply for those who don't mind the difference and do like saving the cash.

THE BENJAMIN
125 E. 50th St., ☎ 888/4-BENJAMIN or 212/320-8002; fax 212/715-2525

This is another Manhattan East Suites property; it was The Beverly Hotel, which was one of my secret finds in New York. Now it's been redone, renamed, and repositioned. Rates are between $229 and $299 depending on what kind of promotional deal you can get; sometimes continental breakfast is included. I got a super promotional offer in the mail through the American Express card for a one-bedroom suite at $249.

THE DRAKE SWISSÔTEL
440 Park Ave. at 56th St., ☎ 800/DRAKE-NY or 212/421-0900; fax 212/688-8053

The Drake's fine reputation has been built on price and location and is considered a secret find by many Ladies Who Lunch, as well as by businesspeople who use this hotel during the week. Both sets know that this was once a residential hotel, so it has an intimate and plush feeling with rooms that aren't cubicles. The newly renovated rooms and suites are decorated in faux Biedermeier, which is a novel idea. There's a new spa and Fauchon will open soon.

Call ahead to ask about special promotions for the dates you will be visiting. A member of the Swissôtel chain.

MILLENNIUM BROADWAY
145 W. 44th St., ☎ 212/768-4400

This is one of my new secret finds, although it's more of a general all-purpose great location hotel than just a shopping location hotel. This new, modern high-rise is not only in the middle of the theater district, but it's across the street from several of my favorite places to eat (Osteria del Doge, Virgil's), is near Times Square, and is still walking distance to all your basic shopping places. Moreover, they have fair rates, great promotions, and are anxious to please.

THE SURREY HOTEL
20 E. 76th St., ☎ 800/ME-SUITE or 212/288-3700; fax 212/628-1549

I found this hotel by accident while I was shopping on Madison Avenue; you certainly can't beat the location! It seems that it was once an apartment building and is now part of the Manhattan East Suite group. The lobby is simple but swank; you can get daily rates or monthly rates as well as special weekend and promotional rates. A studio begins at $250 for one but goes up to $290 for two.

THE WARWICK
65 W. 54th St., ☎ 800/203-3232 or 212/247-2700; fax 212/957-8915

The Warwick is the kind of find every smart shopper wants to know about mostly because the price is about half that of a five-star hotel and the rooms are large. If price is paramount, you'll be thrilled with this choice.

The Warwick is an old, very famous New York hotel that went downhill for a while and therefore may have fallen off your list. The hotel has been completely refurbished and has enough good things about it for me to mention this to you as a viable choice. I stay here often.

I'm not going to tell you this is a quaint little perfect hotel, that the lobby will make you fall in love with the entire Warwick chain, or that the front desk people are always brilliant. Quite simply, this hotel has a fabulous location, a lot of promotional rates, and a parking deal so that if you drive into the city, your parking will be either discounted or included in your room rate.

The Warwick offers a special Born to Shop rate of $240 per night on availability, of course. This package is available for Fridays, Saturdays, and Sundays and on holiday weekends. The package includes breakfast or parking (you pick), a welcome drink at Randolph's Bar (named for William Randolph Hearst, who built the hotel), and an MTA MetroCard.

Unusual Locations (Great for Shopping)

HILTON MILLENIUM
55 Church St., ☏ 800/HILTONS or 212/693-2001; fax 212/571-2316

I know how to spell millennium but Hilton doesn't, don't blame me! This hotel is downtown, great for people working in Manhattan, as well as those going to Cirque de Soleil. And it's across the street from Century 21, my favorite discount source! All sorts of promotional events and rates and Hilton specials, they boast that rates fluctuate with availability, but figure about $250 to $290 for two adults.

HOLIDAY INN WALL STREET
15 Gold St. at Platt St., ☏ 212/232-7700

Can't tell you this is the shopping location of the world, but this hotel is one of many big names to open in this area. This hotel claims to be the most technologically advanced hotel in Manhattan; guests probably shop online.

SOHO GRAND HOTEL
310 W. Broadway, ☏ 212/965-3000; fax 212/965-3200

Located on the edge of SoHo, making it convenient to never go uptown, the SoHo Grand is swank, moderne, and in keeping with the cutting-edge nature of the neighborhood. Rooms are stark, small, and very chic; rates begin at $150 per night.

Chains for Deals

APPLE CORE HOTELS ☎ 800/567-7720

This is a group of three hotels, in the three- to four-star category, that are in great Manhattan locations and keep prices below $200 per night—some are even $150 a night!

They include Quality Hotel and Suites Rockefeller Center at 46th St. near Avenue of the Americas (formerly the Wentworth Hotel); Best Western Manhattan at 32nd St. off Fifth Avenue; and Quality East Side at 30th St. and Lexington Avenue. Rooms have the usual luxuries we expect including voice mail and even data port; the rooms are nice but not extravagantly decorated.

EAST SUITE HOTELS ☎ *800/ME-SUITE*

A group of nine hotels converted from apartment buildings; most in excellent east-side locations, although I find Beekman Place too far east for my personal convenience. You get lots of living space, much elegance, and fair rates.

W HOTELS ☎ 877/W-HOTELS

W is a concept hotel—moderne and minimal but high chic at low price. They have taken over several older Manhattan hotels, redone them, and created a whole new hotel picture with very realistic prices, often under $200 a night if you get a promotional deal. When I booked in, it was $269 per night but that was a weeknight. Since they keep taking more and more properties, you need to call and get the lowdown on which property has the best location for you and the best deal. I admit to not being wildly impressed by the Lexington Avenue hotel, but I'm extremely impressed by the W Tuscany. Call ahead for the latest deals.

Chapter Five

....

UPTOWN SHOPPING NEIGHBORHOODS

THE BRONX IS UP

New York is a city of neighborhoods. If you deal with each neighborhood as a small city, you will never feel overwhelmed. Just about every 10 blocks, the neighborhood seems to change. While certain neighborhoods are more residential than others, and certain areas more dangerous than others, wait 10 blocks and the scene will change again. Besides, what was dangerous last week is chic this week and gentrified next week. The city has totally recreated itself in the last 2 years.

What was once distinctly New York style is now found in Norwalk and New Jersey in ready abandon. What in my youth was "a bad neighborhood" is now the last word in downtown chic. SoHo has given rise to a million SoHo wannabes so that adjacent areas of lower Manhattan all have funny little abbreviated names (NoLita, NoHo, NoBo); ethnic delights fill the boroughs surrounding Manhattan. One weekend we went to Brooklyn but found Russia and Greece. The ethnic neighborhoods of the five boroughs are in flux; the real Untied Nations is all over town. And I haven't even begun to discuss the meat-packing district!

Or the fact that Rockefeller Center, which was so traditional you would hardly call it hot or trend setting, has also reinvented itself and has some staggering changes.

Uptown is downtown, downtown is uptown, everyone's on first. Or no one's on First and many are leaving Fifth.

Almost every place in Manhattan has become interesting; almost every place has some great shops. Every nook and cranny of New York (well, almost) is jam-packed with just the kind of stuff you came here to buy. Tourists seem to travel in a certain few circles and like their shopping also to be in these areas; locals like to avoid the tourist crowds and prefer their shopping to be close to home, office, or public transportation. As a result, no one place is the must-see, end-all shopping district of Manhattan.

Even when you are talking about discounts, there are several enclaves of discounters that serve the same metropolitan area. So people in Manhattan can choose to go to upstate New York, Pennsylvania, New Jersey, or Connecticut for certain types of bargains, but they needn't go to all of them. To put your shopping base camp in New York is to shop for convenience as part of the equation.

Many, many stores sell the same things. You can never shop it all, so there is no need to feel you must. Look at these next two chapters to get a better idea of the little towns that make up our town, and plan your shopping accordingly. There's no reason to be overwhelmed if you've planned your day carefully: You can have it all by limiting yourself to a few well-chosen neighborhoods, streets, or outlet cities.

I also think it pays to consider the personality of the various neighborhoods in Manhattan and your own interests—some people don't even want to waste their time looking at fancier-than-thou European designer boutiques (others want to do nothing but). If you have teens or tweens with you, there are certain neighborhoods that they may enjoy more than others. If your time is limited, you may want to hone in on those neighborhoods where you'll find what you need and be comfortable searching for it.

DIRECTIONALLY SPEAKING

There is no other city in the world that I know of where the directions depend on where you are standing. There is no center of town called "downtown" in New York. Downtown is down from where you are standing, unless you are in the river and then it's all uptown.

Since this is all so ephemeral, we are going to make some arbitrary map lines in these pages, especially important now that downtown Manhattan has become so vital to the new shopping scene. Therefore I am taking 34th St. as the divider between uptown and downtown. (For the downtown chapter of this book, see page 100.)

MOVIN' ON UP

Please note that in one of the most unusual trends in reverse snobism recorded, some of the hot new downtown stores have become so successful that they are opening branches uptown! Perhaps the best example of this is **Sephora,** which first opened in SoHo, then moved a branch into Times Square in its march uptown, and finally opened its flagship store in Rockefeller Center.

If you thought that was predictable, then check out **Calypso,** 935 Madison Avenue at 74th St., which came uptown from Nolita! **Face Stockholm** came uptown (687 Madison Avenue) from SoHo.

In a slightly different version of this same game, **Shanghai Tang** moved just 3 blocks but claims it's a world of difference. The store was on Madison Avenue at 60th St. and is now on Madison at 63rd St. Why? They claim north of East 61st St. is a whole different market.

I have used 34th St. as the dividing line between uptown and downtown. Old-fashioned types will tell you that 34th St. is clearly midtown. Not me! With all the new neighborhoods springing up downtown, I find that 34th St. is the downtown of uptown and the uptown of downtown. (This is also one of the reason to consider hotels in the enclave of hotels on Park Avenue in the upper 30s.)

WEST 34TH STREET

....

The West 34th St. neighborhood is actually a zigzag stretch from Penn Station to Fifth Avenue by way of a lot of shopping real estate—much of it new. The addition of **Kmart** and **Sports Authority** right near Penn Station has extended the shopping district and given everyone a reason and a season for one-stop shopping. The real energy comes from the new **Old Navy** across the street from **Macy's.**

You can take a bus from Fifth Avenue to Penn Station and then walk back, or just prowl on your own. There is a branch of **Daffy's** (one of New York's most famous off-pricers—although this is not my favorite branch); there's Macy's, Toys "Я" Us, The Gap, and a really terrific branch of The Limited Express (one of the few left in the city). A big Banana Republic just joined the team.

To get the most out of this neighborhood, you really have to consider the Garment Center and Lord & Taylor (Fifth Avenue at 38th St.), as well as the row of stores in that area right there on Fifth, as part of the 34th St. neighborhood.

The retailers and businesses in this area have banded together and founded an association dedicated to making things bigger and better and keeping shoppers happy. Real people who have no need for the highfalutin fashions of upper Fifth Avenue may find everything they want right here, although again, some of it is a lot like your mall back at home.

The whole big block from Fifth Avenue to Macy's is packed with fashion chains and discount stores and a whole lot of shopping. Don't forget that this is a great neighborhood to shop for kids, teens, and tweens—you've got tons of cheapie shoe shops such as **HMV** and **Contempo.** There are also discounts to be found in the various **Conway** stores (off-pricers); these are the kind of stores you have to be strong to take—but I love 'em.

There are a few street vendors and stalls here; many sell fake designer perfumes or big-name perfumes from the Caribbean. Let the buyer beware. Postcards in this part of town go 10 for $1, best you'll do in Manhattan!

Finds

CONTEMPO
55 W. 34th St.

This is a chain store with branches in many American malls, so if you've been to one already, pardon me. I like this source for affordable cutting-edge chic; they sell knockoffs of the latest trends that will possibly fall apart in 5 years, but by then they will have been out of style for 4 so it won't matter. Great for teens and tweens, but a serious possibility for anyone who ever wanted to look with it but didn't want to pay for expensive designer clothes.

KMART
One Penn Plaza

Maybe Kmart isn't your idea of a find, but let me just list the store's hours so that you know you can shop when everyone else is closed. Monday through Friday, 8am to 9pm; Saturday, 10am to 9pm; Sunday 11am to 8pm. The pharmacy is closed on Sundays.

OLD NAVY
636 5th Ave. and many more locations around town

This is the new Old Navy flagship in Manhattan and all I can say is "wow." The store is much further west than I had expected (it's almost at Seventh Avenue) and is huge, with tons of energy and displays and doodads that make it almost a science museum. There's a Joe's Diner in the basement, but I was not impressed with my meal there.

This is retail-entertainment at its finest.

THE GARMENT DISTRICT

....

The Garment District is the name of a neighborhood on the west side of Manhattan where most, but not all, of the needle trades have their showrooms, offices, and sometimes cutting rooms. Although the different kinds of garments are clustered in different parts of the Garment District, the main area where you see the racks whizzing by with their dozens of brand-new fashions is on Seventh Avenue around 40th St. Broadway bisects Sixth Avenue at 34th St., so this part of Broadway, which is very close to Seventh Avenue, also houses much of the trade. Many buildings have entrances (and sometimes two different addresses) on Broadway and on Seventh Avenue.

Seventh Avenue, in the Garment District, was officially renamed Fashion Avenue in 1972, and signs to that effect have been duly posted, although we don't know anyone who calls this Fashion Avenue.

The best thing about the Garment District is that it is different things to different people: Some salivate, others shudder. For the person who has *shmatte* in the blood, the Garment District is one of the most exciting places on earth—the hustle and bustle of the pipe racks, the screaming and swearing of the workers, the unglamorous workrooms contrasted with glamorous showrooms, the part-Yiddish way of speaking—all send shivers of ecstasy up the spine. To others, these very same conditions are cause for severe headache, stomachache, nausea, and bad nerves.

Some people like to wander around the Garment District buildings on a Saturday to see what vibes (and bargains) they can pick up. The big Broadway buildings (1407 and 1411) are totally locked up; the smaller buildings have one elevator man on duty who will take you to a specific floor for an appointment. A note to the crafty: These elevator operators are savvy professionals; they can spot a tourist a mile away. Don't try to fool them. Simply ask if any of the showrooms do business on Saturday. Many sample sales are posted on the elevator or building doors in the lobby; doormen and elevator men know everything.

If you're not keen on wandering around this area blindly, get a copy of the *Sales & Bargains* newsletter, which lists sample sales, many of which are in the area. See page 275 for more.

TIMES SQUARE

I wish I could tell you that the new Times Square was a must-do neighborhood and a shopper's heaven (or haven). The truth is, it works, it's enormously cleaned up, it's a vast improvement, and those sex shows and girlie joints are on the way out. Yet despite the addition of **Disney Store, Warner Brothers Studio Store,** and **Virgin Megastore**—and a group of snazzy hotels—this is not shopping paradise.

The electronics stores remind me of the ones they have in Hong Kong and make me fearful; some of the tourist kitsch is fun to giggle over. There's a lot of fast-food places, major cafes, movie theaters and legit theaters, and some Broadway souvenirs, but mostly this is a junky area that is far from classy.

ESPN ZONE
4 Times Square

This is so incredible I just had to include it, especially for you guys. ESPN Zone is run by Disney and is a sports-entertainment center with food and retail.

SEPHORA
1500 Broadway #304, (Times Square)

The Sephora at Rockefeller Center is the one that will change your life; still, it has also joined the renovation project in Times Square and is right near the ABC studios. There's another Sephora opening in the Flatiron at 119 Fifth Avenue, at 19th

Sample Sale Venue

Parsons School of Design is in this neighborhood. There are frequent sample sales here. Call ☎ 212/229-8959 for further information.

St. See page 196 for more on Sephora if you are unfamiliar with this French makeup chain.

EAST 42ND STREET

For the most part, East 42nd St. is not much of a neighborhood. But wait, there's action on two fronts. Maybe more. First off, we have finally unveiled our new **Grand Central Station** (42nd St. between Vanderbilt and Lexington avenues)—it is sublimely gorgeous and filled with great stores. Then, at the corner of Lexington and 42nd St., is a little anomaly I can't explain. For some reason, Ann Taylor decided to open its first official **Loft** store right here, 150 E. 42nd St.—as you know, Loft is its discount brand heretofore reserved for outlet malls. It's the Old Navy-is-to-Gap theory of retail, except that most of the clothing here looks cheap.

Across the street is a small branch of **Forman's,** 145 E. 42nd St. Forman's used to be a Lower East Side discounter, but it has moved up in the world and even onto Fifth Avenue. It doesn't discount so much anymore; it just gives the impression that it does. Then when the merchandise gets old, it's marked way down. Forman's carries brands like Jones New York, Ellen Tracy, and Ralph Lauren, so it's a good source to know about.

Speaking of discounters, **Dollar Bill's** is also on East 42nd St., closer to Fifth Avenue; see page 263.

If you think I am going to comment on that cheapie tourist souvenir mall with the inflated prices that's on the corner of Fifth Avenue and 42nd St., then you don't know me very well.

MIDTOWN FIFTH AVENUE

What locals refer to as midtown is what visitors sometimes consider downtown—the main shopping guts of the central city. The main shopping area of Manhattan also is in the main business area—between 57th St. and 34th St. Main Street USA in this case is Fifth Avenue, which is a legend in its own time. Fifth Avenue is not really a neighborhood, it's a street. It's not really a street, it's a mall that allows traffic to transverse it in a downtown direction. For my purposes, I have dubbed midtown Fifth Avenue as a neighborhood because it has a whole personality of its own.

Fifth Avenue is changing dramatically. There are specialty stores like **Bergdorf-Goodman** (two stores; one for men and one for women across the street from each other on Fifth Ave. between 57th and 58th streets) and **Takashimaya** (693 Fifth Ave. at 54th St.), a drop-dead fancy elegant store that despite its Japanese name and ownership is not particularly Japanese. This is the glitter end of the scale. But there are real people stores too.

There are plenty of places for people with average incomes, from **Liz Claiborne** (650 Fifth Ave. at 52nd St.) to **Façonnable** (689 Fifth Avenue at 54th St.) to **Oshkosh B'Gosh** (586 Fifth Ave. at 47th St.). There's **The Museum Company** (673 Fifth Ave. at 53rd St.) and the **Metropolitan Museum Shop** (15 W. 49th St.), which are not related to each other, despite the similarity in concept.

Begin your tour at Fifth Avenue and 58th St., the General Motors Building, home of some corporate offices and **FAO Schwarz.** Walk down Fifth Avenue all the way to 34th St., noting the changes in the crowds, the types of stores, the way the people are dressed, and the very feel of the air. You did notice, didn't you, that **Bijan,** the by-appointment-only retailer to the rich and very rich has moved off Fifth Avenue and been replaced by **Club Monaco?** There's democracy in action. **Steuben** has also moved from Fifth Avenue and is now on Madison.

I'm not certain which is more a tribute to the human spirit and imagination, **The Disney Store** (711 Fifth Ave.) or **Gianni Versace** (647 Fifth Ave.). Certainly the new **Gap** store and the new **Brooks Brothers** stores are terrifyingly alike, while the **NBA Store** is in a class by itself. Even if you don't buy anything in stores like this, go in and stare—this is the kind of extravagant detail that has made New York the Big Apple. This is what sizzle is all about. And *then* you can conquer Rockefeller Center, which, although in this area, has been listed separately (see page 85) because it is a universe unto itself.

Finds

H&M
640 Fifth Ave. at 51st St.

This new H&M store is the signal to the world that Fifth Avenue has changed, that New York retail has changed, and that power goes to the people. H&M stands for Hennes & Mauritz, a Swedish retailer, known for teenybopper clothes for men, women, and even kids. They can knock off the latest trends from the catwalks faster than you can say "Hennes & Mauritz are here at last."

THE NBA STORE
666 Fifth Ave. at 54th St.

From the sublime to the ridiculous, perhaps, but this store is unlike anything in the world—a new generation of retail entertainment that owes its inspiration to NikeTown and Warner Brothers Studio Store, but has more bells and whistles. To say nothing of WNBA Barbie! Most of the store is belowground; walk down the ramp—don't be lazy, just do it. The merchandise is inventive and creative, there is a snack bar, there are plenty of activities; the prices on some of the team merchandise are outrageous, but there are plenty of affordable items.

Takashimaya
693 Fifth Ave. at 55th St.

If you only have time to see one store in Manhattan and you may not even have time to buy, let me make life easy for you—speed through Takashimaya. The store is a museum to good taste; every little detail is breathtaking to behold. It all looks incredibly expensive, but some of it is actually affordable. The point, however, is not to buy. Feasting your eyes and your soul is the most important thing.

If you think that because this is a Japanese store they are only going to sell Japanese merchandise or designer items that Japanese tourists want to buy, you're wrong. The store artfully blends Oriental inspirations with country French and sophisticated Continental looks to provide one smooth international arena of finesse and magic. The florist is Christian Tortu, the toast of Paris.

ROCKEFELLER CENTER

Rockefeller Center sits in the center of Manhattan's big-time retail Fifth Avenue district and spreads over a 2-block area from Fifth to Sixth Avenue. It is a series of office towers that happen to be connected underground by pathways (filled with stores). The best real estate, aboveground, is also filled with stores. In the last year, the turnover in tenants has been almost complete. **Christie's** has moved into the area, while **Sephora**—the French makeup chain—opened its U.S. flagship store (630 Fifth Ave.); **Banana Republic** opened a lifestyle store (amazing) and **J. Crew** even took space inside the NBC building (50 Rockefeller Center). NBC expanded its retail space (also at 50 Rock), while **Tuscan Square** (5 W. 51st St.) glistens like a new-found gem, even though it was the first to move into the area more than 2 years ago.

Note that because of the crowds that come to watch *Today* live at NBC, some of the stores open at 9am. Now that's smart selling.

MIDDLE MADISON AVENUE

I call midtown Madison Avenue (from 57th St., south to 42nd St.) Middle Mad. The lower end of the stretch, in the 40s, is very geared toward haberdashery. If you are looking for the older version of **Brooks Brothers** (346 Madison Ave. at 44th St.), you'll still find it, all right, along with many other big-name haberdashers who serve men and women; there's **Joseph A. Banks** from Boston (366 Madison Ave. at 46th St.); **Paul Stuart** and **Thomas Pink** (520 Madison Ave. at 54th St.). But the stretch beginning around 56th Street has filled in with a mélange of big names from malls and up-and-coming talents that deserve to be found, including my darling **Eileen Fisher.**

The venerable **Concord Chemists** (425 Madison at 49th St.) is not in the same league as Boyd's (see page 92), but serves this stretch quite well for cosmetics, health, and beauty aids. And speaking of drugstores, I should also add that Middle Mad is headquarters to several health and beauty stores and salons (see chapter 10) as well as a branch of the discounter **Cosmetics Plus.** And speaking of discounters, **Daffy's** has a store here too. The area is also good for camera shops offering good deals on postcards; I wouldn't buy a camera here if I didn't know what I was doing, but postcards are fine.

In Middle Mad, **Lacoste,** the French polo shirt maker, has opened up a freestanding store to take advantage of its recent fashion and status comeback. **Eileen Fisher** and **Talbots** are on one side of the street and **Mary Quant** (no, she's not dead!), with a few other retailers, are all grouped together too.

Finds

COACH FOR BUSINESS
342 Madison Ave. at 45th St.

If you're addicted to Coach handbags, then you'll immediately understand this new offshoot of the business. Coach now offers a separate store geared to businesspeople, specializing in brief-cases, wallets, and other small leather goods in addition to its usual preppy fare. The store is located right in Middle Mad in the heart of traditional preppy uniform land. The uptown store remains open for m'lady.

CROUCH & FITZGERALD
400 Madison Ave. at 46th St.

Famous for its leather goods, this store sells luggage, handbags, and even Louis Vuitton. A staple for fine leather goods for as long as I can recall, this is where I bought my first briefcase. The firm also sells Italian-made handbags, many of them in the style of Judith Leiber. The luggage consists of the usual big-brand names at top-of-the-line prices and the house brand of luggage crafted from canvas and belting leather. It is handsome, practical, and well made. Each August it has a handbag sale that is worth trying to catch: Every handbag in the store sells for $69!

DAFFY'S
335 Madison Ave. at 44th St.

This is my regular Daffy's because it is a block from Grand Central Station. If you can't get to the bigger Daffy's downtown on lower Fifth Avenue, you make do here just as I have. The store isn't as big but you can bump into some bargains for men, women, and children. Men's clothing is upstairs in a small space; there's a large selling space down the escalator where women's and children's clothing, as well as underwear and accessories, are sold. Sometimes you find the big names, sometimes you don't. The discount is hard to measure because you rarely find current merchandise here. Never mind. The escalator only goes down, but there is a way out. You may not want to leave, however. (There's an elevator located in the corner of the children's department.)

EILEEN FISHER
521 Madison Ave. at 53rd St.

I consider this my own personal find and success story; I actually once worried that Fisher wouldn't make it in the big time.

Silly me! Positioned as a way-of-life dress style, Fisher's clothes are moderately priced yet high on fashion, chic, and comfort. Colors are the selling point: They are always high fashion and new, with an almost European palette. Clothes are pull-on styles, mostly in solids—all you do is mix and match—but because of the quality of the fabric and the fabulous colors, they make a great fashion statement. There are other stores around town. Shop them all.

57TH STREET

No one street in Manhattan represents the new retail scene more than 57th St. In the space of a couple of years, it has changed from one of the fanciest addresses a store could boast to a street with two divergent personalities: the original one, drop-dead chic, as typified by **Chanel, Escada, Hermès, Louis Vuitton,** and **Bergdorf Goodman.** There's also the "real people" and shopping-as-entertainment chic, the mass-produced style that has kept America affordably clothed and furnished for the last few years, from such stores as **Levi's, Swatch, Warner Brothers Studio Store, NikeTown,** and, my God, have you seen the **Tourneau** watch store?

Fifty-seventh Street is both a state of mind and a neighborhood. Traditionally, it's been a high-ticket address for residential and retailing real estate, especially where it bisects Fifth Avenue. Although the street does stretch across the island, as a shopping neighborhood, it begins on the east side at Park Avenue and it ends on the west side at Carnegie Hall (887 Seventh Ave. at W. 57th St.).

In these 3 or 4 blocks you'll find a few expensive antique shops (many are upstairs) and art galleries, quite a few clothing shops representing the best of Europe's retail elite, as well as America's own retail landmark **Tiffany & Co.** You'll also find a few shocking surprises.

Daffy's has arrived on East 57th St., to bring stylish discounting right to the upper crust. **Borders,** a very good bookstore, has invaded The Ritz Tower (Park Avenue at 57th St.) and **Louis Vuitton** built a building that is meant to totally eclipse the sun (21 E. 57th St.), which will house **Christian Dior** and maybe even **Celine.**

The feel of the whole neighborhood has been lowered further by the addition of some decidedly touristy attractions for the shop-weary or the lunch bunch. If you have teens or tweens, you don't want to miss Jekyll & Hyde Club, a Disneyesque version of a club-cum-burger joint with a horror theme (1409 Avenue of Americas at 57th St.) that will thrill you to death. It's my son Aaron's favorite place in New York. Also try Planet Hollywood (149 W. 57th St.); or Hard Rock Cafe (221 W. 57th St.). Grown-ups may prefer their teen thrills via the Disneyesque Russian Tea Room, just reopened after a hiatus.

Don't forget **Sony's Wonder Technology Lab** either (550 Madison Ave. at 56th St.), which is a virtual reality amusement park. Here, you can listen to music, watch videotapes, or pretend you are in a Nike store that doesn't have any shoes. They do sell CDs, cassettes, and other merchandise.

I don't want all of these details to muddy the waters too much—despite all the changes, 57th St. has not become retail poison for the rich and famous. *Au contraire.* **Chanel** is still chic after all these years; Italian hotshots such as **Bulgari** and **Laura Biagiotti** show no sign of being disappointed with the location; nor does their neighbor **Brookstone!** Note: If the new **Gucci** rehab of its Fifth Avenue store isn't completed when you get this book, check out its temporary headquarters at 10 W. 57th St.

Finds

DANA BUCHMAN
65 E. 57th St.

Owned by the Liz Claiborne people but operated as a separate and more upscale bridge line, Dana Buchman's clothes are available in department stores and now, in her own store—the designer's first freestanding store. The line is mostly for working women and hovers between moderate and moderately expensive; some looks are boring, others are classics. There's a selection of petite sizes and special orders for plus sizes. This is a good standard for the working woman to know about.

DEMPSEY & CARROLL
110 E. 57th St.

This doesn't look like much from the outside, but it is one of the most elegant suppliers of stationery to debs and their moms. They will keep your die on file.

FREDERIC FEKKAI
15 E. 57th St., upstairs

Talk about hidden! This salon-cum-spa doesn't even have frontage, but because it is a division of Chanel, no one cares. Fekkai was the star hairstylist of Bergdorf-Goodman who was snapped up by corporate France and forced to open an incredibly chic villalike series of spaces in the Chanel high-rise here. Not only can you have your hair done, you can also get all sorts of spa treatments, or simply have a coffee. They sell their beauty and hair products and makeup line as well as handbags and headbands. There is a freestanding accessories store on upper Madison Avenue.

GHURKA
41 E. 57th St.

Despite the exotic-sounding name, which conjures up Gunga Din and colonial India, this is a luggage and leather goods store. It sells a fabulous line of canvas and leather items made in a very specific look, which I have to call "Ralph Lauren Fisherman Meets Isak Dinesen on Safari." The items are outrageously expensive, very statusy, quite chic, and there is an outlet store in Norwalk, Connecticut. Prices in Norwalk, even when discounted 50%, are also outrageous. But it's a great store with beautifully made goods.

HAMMACHER SCHLEMMER
147 E. 57th St.

I'd become such a jaded New Yorker that for years I have forgotten to mention this unique source of pleasure and inspiration as one of the most exciting stores in New York (although there are branches in other U.S. cities). This store does have a fabulous catalog, so don't go home lonely. Although they don't call themselves a toy store, this place is heaven for gadgets and gimmicks and gifts that no one else has. Their collectibles are very expensive but their cutie-pie gadgets are sensational.

HOLLAND & HOLLAND
50 E. 57th St.

In keeping with the horsey-woodsy-fishy-chic shops sprouting up here, Holland & Holland has opened its first shop in America after being bought by the same company that owns Chanel. A famed British gun maker, the store has surprisingly chic women's clothing that's more weekend oriented but still worth mooning over. It has a hot French designer and is opening stores on all the best streets in the world-shopping cities; it's really getting a lot of attention, especially in Europe.

WATHNE
4 W. 57th St.

Ghurka and Wathne come together in the same breath for me since there is something very similar to their look and to their customer. Wathne has a little more fishing, camping, and Hermès outdoorsy touch to it, as if they really compete with the French line rather than anyone else. I find their goods, which include everything from leather goods to silk vests to riding clothes and scarves and weekend wear, to be very special and quite wearable in that "I'm rich and you're not" kind of a way. They have a catalog and an outlet store in Liberty Village in New Jersey. A sensational look to have and to hold. Marry money. Spend weekends in the country. Get a horse.

UPPER MADISON AVENUE (57TH STREET & BEYOND)

....

The average visitor to Manhattan perceives Madison Avenue as the dream shopping stretch that actually begins at 57th St. and works its way uptown. Although the street has changed its personality many times, it's still a great place to shop and enjoy stores representing the big names not only in European fashion and style, but also in international creativity. Many designers have moved into different stores on the street; some, like Givenchy, have given up their stores making room for new tenants. As much as the street evolves, it is still a marvelous stroll worthy of an afternoon.

Note that there's been tremendous change and activity most concentrated around 60th Street with **Shanghai Tang** moving uptown a tad, **DKNY** moving in, **Stueben** taking Shanghai Tang's real estate, and **Barney's** continuing to thrive (to the surprise of many).

There is another interesting aspect to Madison Avenue: Many very successful middle-of-the-road retailers and designers are now opening their own shops on Madison. I'm talking the kind of resources who are not ranking members of the Great American Designer Club like Calvin Klein or Ralph Lauren. The range spreads from midpriced fashion houses in women's wear names like **Tahari** and **Nicole Miller** with shoes by **Via Spiga** to mass shoe merchandisers like **Unisa** and **Nine West** and even home furnishings and style giant **Crate & Barrel**. These stores offer a wonderful environment, a great selection of gear, and the opportunity to find something moderately priced in a high-priced area where you might otherwise feel uncomfortable.

Finds

BOYD'S
655 Madison Ave. at 60th St.

Boyd's is a Madison Avenue pharmacy that has evolved into a mecca for makeup, hair accessories, foreign bath products, and hard-to-find specialty items. It is very much the kind of place that is related to its location on Madison Avenue as the commercial resource for some of the wealthiest residents in New York. First developed to serve the people who lived in the neighborhood and now a thriving business as its own destination, Boyd's provides lots of service, plenty of makeovers, testers and spritzes, and the mom-and-pop atmosphere that makes you feel rich and pampered. No bargains, but then, price isn't the point, is it?

CLYDE'S
926 Madison Ave. at 73rd St.

Geographically positioned between Boyd's and Zitomer's, Clyde's is newer, fancier, more sophisticated, and neat. They carry an enormous number of lines from Europe that are hard to find in the United States as well as many American brands that you've never seen before. The clients are also fun to stare at or eavesdrop on.

H2O PLUS
650 Madison Ave. at 60th St.

While this is a branch store of a multiple, if you don't know the line I think you will enjoy shopping here. As the name would imply, it sells goodies for the bath—gels, shampoos, toys for kids, travel kits, and some aromatherapy items. You can find great gifts to take home as souvenirs for just about every age on your gift list. The kiddie bath toys and products are the best. You can indeed find gifts here in the $10 price range.

RALPH LAUREN
888 Madison Ave. at 72nd St.; 867 Madison Ave. at 72nd St.

I realize that you don't need me to tell you about Ralph Lauren or to explain to you that there are now not one but two shops right here on Madison Avenue, but here goes anyway: You absolutely must visit these stores just to get a look-see. The Rhinelander mansion is one of the most beautiful stores you will ever visit in your life. And then there's the new store across the street that specializes in active sporting gear and the Double R line. Both could be tourist sights; they could sell tickets for admission and I would certainly pay up. Latest addition to Ralph gear: toddler and infant clothing. From cradle to grave.

ZITOMER
969 Madison Ave. at 76th St.

I list Boyd's and Zitomer back to back because they are spiritually related, although they are rather different from each other and are about 10 blocks apart. The crossover between them serves two different parts of the Madison Avenue residential scene. Zitomer also began as a pharmacy and might have become Boyd's, but instead they went several steps past Boyd's in terms of size, stock, selection, and sphere—Zitomer is really a tiny department store.

Every nook and cranny of this store—and it has many, so don't be deceived when you first walk in—is filled with American and European beauty, bath, health, and luxury items. If you are European, or if you travel a lot and cannot find your European favorites in regular U.S. stores, this will be better than a high school reunion. When I stroll the aisles of Zitomer, tears come to my eyes. Seeing these packages is like visiting with old friends.

Zitomer also carries a wide range of costume jewelry, hair accessories, and a cashmere shawl or two in season. They are expanding into a full department store of luxury and whimsy.

BLOOMINGDALE'S COUNTRY

Last millennium, when I was a girl, there was an advertising campaign that identified the trading area around Bloomingdale's as Bloomingdale's Country. I can think of no better label, so let it stand. There are actually good stores on Lexington Avenue leading to Bloomingdale's and on Third Avenue leading away from Bloomingdale's (in the uptown direction).

On the Lex side, marching from 57th St. right past Bloomingdale's, the stores are mostly teen oriented, but do include the city's first **Zara** shop. On Third Avenue, you get more upmarket chains, such as **CP Shades** and **Club Monaco.**

Finds

DIESEL SUPER STORE
770 Lexington Ave. at 60th St.

Italian jeans headquarters for the lifted bottom fit; washing machines in the windows. Important trend setters beyond jeans wear—if you're 15 to 25, that is.

URBAN OUTFITTERS
127 E. 59th St.

Retro hippie store of cheapie fashions created by the man who went on to found Anthropologie, one of my favorite stores. This is the poor woman's Anthropologie with clothes made in faraway places at lost cost. Two levels; mostly for teenagers.

CARNEGIE HILL

So there it was, the basic Carnegie (as in Andrew Carnegie) mansion, which has since been converted to the Cooper-Hewitt Museum, a branch of the Smithsonian. The Carnegie name still influences this neighborhood on upper Madison Avenue, which, in recent years, has been slowly developing into a hot retail area partly because several private schools are in this area. You've never seen so many retailers of either kids' clothing or notebooks.

A residential area of grace and refinement, Carnegie Hill, in the low 90s, has a few select shops clustered on Madison Avenue (sometimes called Upper Mad). Some are branches of European stores (**Jacadi, Bonpoint**); some are original retailers. **Penny Whistle,** the innovative kiddie store, began in the neighborhood because its owners live here. **J. Mclaughlin** has one of its shops here, and because the owners are also neighborhood residents, it's one of their prize stores.

The neighborhood gets less European and more midtown Manhattan-like as you walk downtown, so by the time you get to 86th St., there are branches of big chains—from discounter **Bolton's** to mall faves such as **Williams-Sonoma,** the kitchen and cookware mavens from San Francisco. If you haven't yet caught up with **Eileen Fisher,** there's a store at 79th St. (1039 Madison Ave.).

Adrien Linford is a great little gift shop in the neighborhood. Visit its uptown and original branch at 1339 Madison Avenue at 93rd St.

Mixed in with the specialty stores and the branches of the mall stores are several resale shops—most of them have upstairs addresses, so don't be afraid to climb a flight of stairs; see page 278.

UPPER WEST SIDE

This is one of the few areas of the city that became hot during the recession— but has morphed enormously now that we have the boom. Broadway is singing while Columbus is drowning. Go figure.

Broadway has become the home of numerous superstores, discounters, and lifestyle resources, while Columbus Avenue is more the mall with a branch of everything you may need and then a few specialty retailers. Amsterdam has been slower to develop but has a few funky stores, some antique shops, and resale shops. For some reason, Columbus has lost its energy and just doesn't have "it" any more.

Broadway

Upper Broadway is full of high-rise condos and trendy restaurants these days, but still has many of the old staples clustered from the high 60s to the mid 80s. There's **Talbot's** (2289 Broadway at 81st St.), and an **Ann Taylor** (2017 Broadway). Choose from two of the many **Gap** stores that abound in this area (2109 and 2373 Broadway). There's also a **Gap Kids** (2373 Broadway). Check out The **Body Shop** (2159 Broadway). **Bolton's** (2251 Broadway) offers discount designer women's wear; **Filene's Basement** does, too.

The area has become very residential so there's stores for real people who live here, ranging from **Barnes & Noble** to a branch of **Fishs Eddy** (2176 Broadway) for dishes. **Fairway,** the grocery store, has redone itself and competes more than ever with **Zabar's**.

Amsterdam Avenue

Amsterdam Avenue may surprise you. If you decide to stroll along the whole avenue, you may think we've sent you to the wrong neighborhood to do any shopping at all. So aim high; head straight to the blocks in the 70s through the 80s to discover craft and design stores, some antiques shops, funky shops offering wear for children, the city's wildest second-hand clothing resource, and plenty of restaurants and cafes, should your shopping spree leave you famished. Don't miss our favorite spots for browsing and buying:

ALLAN & SUZI INC.
416 Amsterdam Ave. at 80th St.

If you're looking for an eye-popping ensemble at a real bargain price, look no further. Grab a cab and head for this store with an international reputation for "retro fashion." Don't stop to stare at the silver glitter 8-inch platform shoes in the window, but dash right in and start trying on "gently worn" items from designers. Some of the merchandise is too funky for me, but with prices that run from $10 to $8,000 there's guaranteed to be something here for everyone's taste. Warning: I saw a fake Chanel scarf here and it made me very nervous. Make sure you know what you are buying.

RUE ST. DENIS
376 Amsterdam at 78th St.

Another vintage clothing shop—it's not to die for, but while you're in the area, take a look.

Columbus Avenue

Welcome to the mall. There's no single area in all of Manhattan with a greater concentration of the stores you're familiar with from any suburban shopping mall. The unique stores that are retailing gems are still around. It's just that you have to look past all the big chains to find them. But since all the shopping giants are so handy, why not check out the whole scene. Weekends are jam-packed and now that they are tearing up the center of Columbus Avenue, traffic is a nightmare. Please note that many of the stores in this neighborhood do not open until 11am. My favorite finds include:

APRIL CORNELL
487 Columbus Ave. at 83rd St.

One of my 10 favorite stores in Manhattan; one of the most likely places for you to find something you don't see that often but that you will love for you, for your home or even for a little girl.

This small, home-style shop actually has multiple personalities. Some of the stores are now known by the designer's name (April Cornell), a few are still called Handblock, the old name of the store. Who cares what the place is called; memorize all the addresses. The look is unique, colorful, and I think sensational.

Remember those paisley and madras bedspreads from the 1960s? Now the prints (that look surprisingly like some from Pierre Deux) have been pieced together and sewn into bedspreads and quilts. Tablecloths and napkins are a sea of color swimming with flowers in contrasting shades with leaves and vines and swirls of dizzy delights. There're also jewelry and some nighties, and a lot of accessories for the home. Refreshing and unpretentious, colorful and quaint, charming and delicious. Not cheap but worth saving for.

There's an excellent sale rack in the back (for clothes); twice a year there are half-price sales that are worth flying in for. Last sale season, I bought four tablecloths, $12 each! These were marked down from $85 (each).

BETSEY JOHNSON
248 Columbus Ave. at 72nd St.

Teen angel, are you with me? I never met a teenage girl who didn't crave to be dressed by Betsey. So here you go, moms and teens alike—have a look. As wild and wacky as ever, Betsey has stores throughout Manhattan, and continues to make waves in all of them. She's always the first in the neighborhood with something new—if slightly on the cutting edge without being too outré. Lots of the clothing is clingy, which is why my young teenage girlfriends like it so much. With a dress costing over $100, you might want to save up if you're buying for a young girl.

Chapter Six

. . . .

DOWNTOWN SHOPPING NEIGHBORHOODS

DOWNTOWN IS A STATE OF MIND

You've heard of Uptown Girl? Forget her. Manhattan has gone Downtown crazy. Downtown has become so complete that hotels are opening up left and right and tourists don't even want to venture north of Union Square. Downtown has become so uptown that limos pull up to districts that once gave people the creepy-crawlies; Martha Stewart has bought in (with her pickup truck) and the scene has taken root. A tree may grow in Brooklyn, but this is a garden. It's a good thing.

DEPARTMENT OF SILLY NAMES

SoHo seemed to make sense and we accepted it easily enough, but now, as James Bond might say, enough is enough. Every downtown district has a name; most of them are made from geographic abbreviations of where they are located (south of Houston; north of Little Italy, north of Houston, and so on). Only Alphabet City makes sense—this is the part of New York that is so far east that the avenues have run out of numbers and have taken letters of the alphabet.

LOWER FIFTH AVENUE/SOFI

Hop off the Fifth Avenue bus at the Flatiron Building (23rd St.) and begin the prowl so that you can check out the scene on lower Fifth Avenue, South of the Flatiron, which I like to call SoFi. You are walking downtown on Fifth Avenue headed toward 14th St. Don't worry, I'll stop you before you actually get to 14th St. and it's perfectly safe here. In fact, it's so safe it's almost a mall.

Lower Fifth was the start of something big years ago; now it doesn't have as much energy as when it was first getting going, but it's still so well situated and worth a visit. You are walking distance to the **Union Square Greenmarket,** to **ABC Home & Carpet,** to all the discounters and big box stores on Sixth Avenue and even to SoHo. If you are really up for a walk, you can even make it to **Jeffrey** (14th St. at Tenth Avenue).

Plan your day accordingly and take time to look up listings, or use a map to see how all these other neighborhoods interconnect. You haven't got a second to waste, as there's more here than can possibly be done in a day.

Finds

B. SHACKMAN & CO.
85 Fifth Ave. at 16th St.

This is a novelty broker who sells to the public and offers Victorian reproductions such as valentines, stocking stuffers, cards, and other small gifts.

CLUB MONACO
156 Fifth Ave. at 26th St.

This is a Canadian chain now owned by Ralph Lauren with about 150 stores dotted all over the world and a new flagship going into Fifth Avenue in midtown. This was the flagship, complete with cafe, of course. The resource is great for

Downtown Manhattan

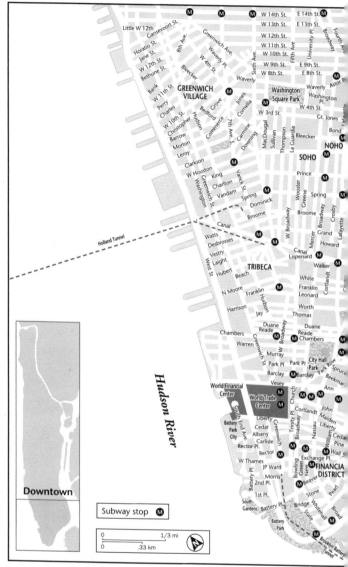

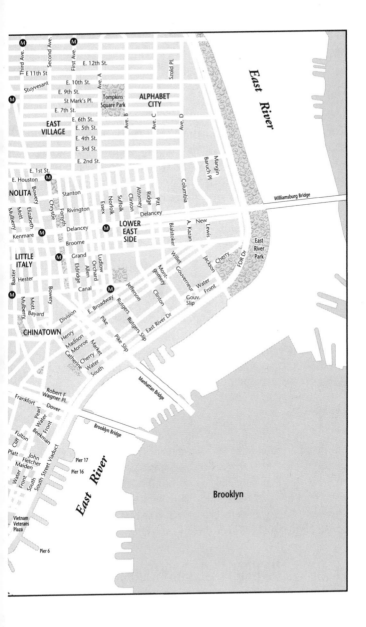

cutting-edge fashion at affordable prices; trendies may do well here. There is even a makeup line.

DAFFY'S
111 Fifth Ave. at 18th St.

This is one of New York's best bargain basements—35,000 square feet on two levels, jammed with bargains for men, women, and children. Stock varies tremendously—a lot of it comes from big-name department stores after they've taken it off the floor. They even sell luggage here. I've done very well with designer men's sports jackets on the markdown rack; I rarely find much in women's wear. There are other Daffy branches in other parts of the city.

EILEEN FISHER
103 Fifth Ave. at 23rd St.

There are a few of Fisher's boutiques in the best shopping districts of New York. Like the others, this store features the comfortable, easy to wear, droopy-Japanese chic that Fisher is famous for. Her color palette is sublime; sale prices are fabulous because the regular retail price is quite affordable.

PAUL SMITH
108 Fifth Ave. at 16th St.

Smith is a London designer known for his inventive ways with quality clothes that appear to be traditional but have a tiny twist to them—like unusual colors or fabrics. While he makes menswear and women's wear, many items in the store can be worn by either gender. Much of it is very hip. Prices are high to match the quality. They do have sales.

FLATIRON EAST/UNION SQUARE

Running alongside SoFi to the east is a neighborhood that's just as hot as SoFi, although not quite as smooth. The main drag is Broadway, which runs on the east side of New York once you get this far downtown and is now called LoBro by some shoppers.

The stores take to two different themes: funky (**ABC Carpet & Home** rules the roost, but **Anthropologie** has now moved in) and hipsters of the New Age. Union Square is the uptown for the new downtown crowd. The Green Market (page 106) has been attracting hordes from all over (even the burbs) and the superstores (such as **Barnes & Noble, Bradlee's, Toys "Я" Us**) are definitely for the locals, but this is the beginning of the Downtown Sensibility.

If you take Broadway further downtown (from Union Square), you'll hit **The Strand Bookstore** (828 Broadway at E. 12th St.) for discounted books (including current bestsellers) and **Forbidden Planet** (840 Broadway at 13th St.) for comics galore. By the time you get to 12th St., you are in an antiques neighborhood (see page 249).

By East 9th St., you've hit a territory of stores so hip and hot that they've been written about in the *New York Times* and now attract busloads of Japanese tourists. Head east on East 9th St. to get to the heart of this area—see page 111.

So don't even consider a dash for SoHo without exploring this little den of delights. From here you can head for SoHo, NoLita, and so on.

Finds

ABC CARPET & HOME
888 Broadway at 19th St.

Be still my heart. If I were making a movie of New York's best stores, this would be the star. Years ago it was a carpet store, then it expanded into bed linen, and at one point in time it tried to pass itself off as a semidiscounter, although everyone who knew really knew that what they offered was selection, not price.

Now the store has been redone and again we have a story of selection not price, but we also have a story of theater, of charm, of visual pow and wow and impact and excitement. The kind of store where you want to touch everything and then just move in and stay forever. Prices tend to be fair and there are affordable goods. Mostly I send you here not because of the price issue but because the store feels like Aladdin's chic cave and I know you are going to swoon and go to heaven. Explore each floor seriously and then there's more across the street.

ANTHROPOLOGIE
85 Fifth Ave. at 16th St.

I wanted to name this one of the 10 best stores in New York, but then I decided no chains or branches of multiples could go on that list, so you're on your own. It's certainly one of my favorite stores in New York. Anthroplogie is the brainchild of the man who created Urban Outfitter—the store sells a lifestyle of clothes for men and women, home furnishings and gift and style items. It's all very warehouse-cum-touch-this-and-that-store; I love it.

FISHS EDDY
889 Broadway at 19th St.

Stop sweating, palms! Please, take my credit cards away before I do it again! Did someone say dishes? If you know me well, you know I am bonkers for dishes. And thus for Fishs. The store's original concept was to buy up and resell restaurant supply and hotel has-beens, but the store has become so popular that it now casts old molds and sets its own trends. You'll find prices vary from the what-a-deal category to what approaches the limit for a not-yet-ready-for-the-big-time collectible. (Dinner plates from a fine London hotel go for about $50 a pop—not cheap.) But you will have a ball as you explore this small, crammed museum of old dishes and hotel services. Amen and pass the gravy boat.

UNION SQUARE GREEN MARKET
16th to 14th sts. at Broadway

I don't care if you're a tourist or a local, you do too need a green market. This one has a very special New York feel about it, especially in fall when the whole city celebrates the change in the air. The best apples I've ever eaten in my life came from this market; there are vendors selling farm-grown greens and farm-made cheeses and wines and ciders and juice and fruits and veggies and even flowers and it is simply heaven. Although I'm not sure if heaven is this crowded on a Saturday.

While this market is a regular event (Monday, Wednesday, Friday, and Saturday), it is a tad sparse in winter months; March is downright bleak. Saturdays are always the busiest day. There's not that much in the way of prepared foods, so it's not like you can go to the market and walk away with "le picnique."

CHELSEA

The dimensions of Chelsea are changing enormously, as this is one of the "hot new" neighborhoods in New York. Chelsea is considered the area from the west 20s all the way to 14th St., and from Seventh Avenue to Eleventh Avenue.

Primarily a residential area, Chelsea began to make news when many art galleries from SoHo relocated in this district. Then **Comme des Garcons** became the first must-see clothing boutique—and you must see it: part gallery, part boutique, part museum of modern art.

Chelsea has expanded so much that the best flea market in New York is in danger, word is that the parking lots where these weekend events are held, on Sixth Avenue and 23rd St., might be sold at any point for high-rise buildings.

The real problem with Chelsea is that the area is huge and the distance between the avenues is so large that you cannot stroll and shop the way you can in SoHo and NoLita. If you have a car and just want to look around, that's great. This is relatively impossible to do on foot.

Also note that like every alternative retail district, the hours are alternative—consider noon to 7pm as the regular hours.

Finally, I consider Ladies Mile to be a totally different area, although that can be argued. Technically it is part of Chelsea, but I have given it a separate entry. Why fight? See that section on page 109.

If you want to do the gallery scene while in Chelsea, try a few of these addresses:

Gagosian Gallery, 24th St. & Eleventh Avenue
Kasmin Gallery, 293 Tenth Avenue at 27th St.
Andrea Rosen Gallery, 525 W. 24th St.
Cacciola Gallery, 501 W. 23rd St.
John Stevenson Gallery, 338 W. 23rd St.
John Weber Gallery, 529 W. 29th St.
Metro Pictures, 519 W. 24th St.
Paula Cooper Gallery, 534 W. 21st St.

Finds

COMME DES GARCONS
520 W. 22nd St.

It's worth a taxi trip directly to this address; don't miss it if you need to discuss avant-garde retail, architecture, creativity, or chutzpah. Many of the products sold here are only available in this store and in the Tokyo flagship.

CHELSEA MARKET
75 Ninth Ave. (at 15th St.)

This monster building, which I think was once a bread factory, takes up a city block and serves mostly as a cutie-pie renovation turned wholesale/retail space. It's mostly related to foods, although I just read about a design sample sale being held here. (Honest.) Great for one-stop shopping or snacking. Truly exciting visually.

BARNEY'S WAREHOUSE/THE CO-OP
225 W. 17th St.

Make no mistake about it: Barney's Warehouse is a warehouse and is not located where the store used to be. It's around the corner from Loehmann's, if Loehmann's is still there when you read this. Make no never mind, taxi directly to the address listed.

Once the home of a twice a year sale, this building is being turned into a branch of The Co-op with trendy clothes. Look out, Jeffrey!

LADIES MILE

OK, I promised you a separate listing. As noted, Ladies Mile is in the district some people call Chelsea. I'd say it's borderline and a thing unto itself. You be the judge.

You see, around the time of the Civil War, when department stores were just catching on and ladies were allowed to go shopping without chaperones, the great names in New York retail stood in a row along Sixth Avenue and stretched from 14th St. to 23rd St. Remember that the world of New York was built from the bottom up and 14th St. was sort of the edge of civilization at that time, so this was an exciting area to be in. Most of the department stores of the time were along Sixth Avenue, although the original WJ Sloane department store was on Broadway, where ABC Home & Carpet now is. You can see that the whole area was the shopping mecca of New York.

Although some of the retailers who had stores here have stayed in business, they moved uptown as trade moved uptown. Thereafter, most of the buildings were empty and abandoned, especially those on Sixth Avenue. For almost 100 years Ladies Mile was a wasteland of gorgeous, empty, hulking cast-iron beauties. Then, voilà, they were rediscovered and have now been saved and occupied by famous retailers; others have been replaced with new structures that house what the trade calls "big box" stores or superstores.

Most of the tenants are value oriented. Stores include everything from The Gap's low-end line **Old Navy** to **Filene's Basement,** a branch store of the famous Boston off-pricer. If you're looking to furnish your first apartment, there's **Bed, Bath & Beyond.** There's something for everyone. Weekends are a zoo. Mind the strollers.

Finds

ALCONE
235 W. 19th St.

Beauty supply store selling theatrical makeup brands and professional makeup.

BARNES & NOBLE SUPERSTORE
675 Sixth Ave. at 21st St.

While there are several Barnes & Noble superstores in Manhattan, this one is special because it helps round out the personality of the neighborhood and is a great pit stop. If your feet are swollen from too much shopping, simply plop down here for a coffee and a book. It's also rumored to be a great pick-up place. I bring Euro visitors here for the discounts and the selection and they love it.

BURLINGTON COAT FACTORY
116 W. 23rd St. at Sixth Ave.

I used to hate this store and was slow to warm to this branch, but it does have the world inside its doors—discount on clothing for the whole family. You cannot ignore that it's here and widens your selection.

THE FAN CLUB
22 W. 19th St.

Vintage clothing from Gene London, one of New York's most famous theatrical costumers. Most of the donations come from Hollywood. Very casual atmosphere, dig for treasure.

OLD NAVY
604–12 Ave. of the Americas at 18th St.

If you like The Gap but can't wait for its sales, you may want to try its line of clothing at Old Navy, which is 30% less expensive than the regular Gap line. God only knows what sale prices are. There are Old Navy stores all over the country now, but this one's a beaux arts beauty in New York's new super-store district. A cafe-cum-diner is included.

Don't think Old Navy sells used clothing or an army navy or surplus kind of look. This is pure Gap basics, mostly of the unisex variety: T-shirts, khakis, easy clothing for weekends, and so on.

THE EAST VILLAGE

The area that I call the East Village extends east of Broadway from 14th St. down to Houston. Independent designers and artists take advantage of the relatively lower rents to open store-front shops and galleries; there are a number of wonderful and unusual choices for the adventurous shopper.

But first a warning: Shopping in the East Village is not for the faint of heart. You'll have to push past bikers in leather, kids with brightly colored hair and safety pins in their noses, a crush of students from nearby NYU, and panhandlers who compete for sidewalk space with vendors. It's not overly cute, it is funky. You must have a spirit of adventure and like to find the finds before they are found by Barney's or Bergdorf's. If you can brave it, you're in for a unique shopping experience.

If you're out with teenagers, a trip down St. Mark's Place (East 8th St.) will immediately establish you as the coolest grown-up around and give you a taste of the East Village. If you like what you see, take off on your own and wander and explore the other streets between Third Avenue and Avenue A.

Begin your tour at St. Mark's and Third Avenue, the corner of the busiest block in the East Village. There is an eclectic mix of stores and restaurants crammed onto this short block. You'll find CD and record stores, bookshops, and clothing shops advertising "Rock Star Clothing"; check out St. Marks Comics for a huge selection in comic books and T-shirts. If skin-tight leather jeans, microminis, or vinyl clothing are your teen's style—or yours—don't miss Trash and Vaudeville for the best in punk gear. If you need to stock up on inexpensive goodies, you'll pass street vendors selling scarves, sunglasses, earrings, socks, and the like at cheap prices.

As you cross Second Avenue and continue east, the crush of shops gives way to residences, hipper-than-thou cafes, and cutting-edge boutiques. Take the time to stroll East 9th St. between Third Avenue and Avenue A to check out the newest trends in everything from home furnishings to lingerie. There is a branch of my beloved Eileen Fisher here that will have you whispering the secret to your nearest and dearest.

And for those academics among you, yes, I have trolled the Kmart here, waiting to be impressed. I like the Kmart at Penn Station, but this one is not as good. Win some, lose some. You didn't come to this part of town for Kmart, now did you?

Finds

DEMETER
83 Second Ave. between E. 4th and E. 5th sts.

A fragrance line that is certainly one of the most original you'll ever encounter at any counter—this line sells about 30 different scents that are more like flavors and include things like the smell of fresh-cut grass. Unisex products. Quite unique, also sold in some department stores uptown.

EILEEN FISHER
314 E. 9th St., between First and Second aves.

You can't read too much of this book without noticing that I am wild for Eileen Fisher, a local designer with a handful of shops around town who also sells around the United States and who will make it in the big leagues for her easy-to-wear comfort chic (if she hasn't already). She doesn't have an outlet store in Manhattan (there is one in Secaucus, though), but this strange little store in the East Village has samples, markdowns, and odd little rejects in bins and baskets along with regular merchandise so that you can just enter and go straight to heaven.

I bought a silk blouse from a bin on the floor for $25 and a dress for $62 that was in stores for $139. Even though my dress has a slight defect, the savings makes it invisible to me.

As far as I'm concerned, if you shop nowhere else on East 9th St., a visit to this store is worth the trip.

KIEHL'S
109 Third Ave. between 13th and 14th sts.

It's hard to call Kiehl's a find since it's been around for well over 100 years, is sold in many uptown department stores, and has a cult following that includes just about everyone in New York. But if you are from out of town, you might not know that the original Kiehl's store—home to all sorts of natural beauty lotions and potions—is right here, and has been since 1851.

TG170
309 E. 9th St.

The hottest rage for the trendies; showcase for up-and-coming designers. I am too old for this.

SOHO

SoHo has become more than the Village ever was because real estate prices have risen—and so have the stakes. Plain old funky doesn't cut it anymore. Expensive funky is the mood and mainstream funky is quickly approaching. They say **Chanel** is looking for space; meanwhile everyone from **Louis Vuitton** to **Yves Saint Laurent** to Brazilian jeweler **Hans Stern** has taken space down here. You also find your chicer-than-thou types, such as **Vivienne Westwood, Helmut Lang, Marc Jacobs,** and **Anna Sui.** Sure, there's some mass merchandisers already (OK, all of them are here), but the neighborhood hasn't really been ruined. Yet.

SoHo stands for South of Houston (say "*HOUSE*-ton") and is one of the most interesting neighborhoods in New York. Art galleries compete for space with trendy restaurants and boutiques and even trendy grocery stores, and although it's a part of town I once thought most likely to go bust, it has continued to thrive.

In fact, it's spawned two new subneighborhoods—one at its northern border that I call LoBro (it stands for Lower Broadway); the other (as yet nameless) at its eastern border, consisting of the 1½ -block stretch of Lafayette Street just below Houston. Then there's NoLita, which I am sure will merge into SoHo within the next five years. They are adjacent and NoLita is growing fast.

So far, LoBro (Lower Broadway) seems to be the place to find snazzy, larger versions of upscale mall home furnishings stores, such as the **Williams-Sonoma**–owned **Pottery Barn** (600 Broadway at Houston St.) and its new concept, Williams-Sonoma **Grande Cuisine** (580 Broadway at Houston St.), a 15,000-square-foot store devoted to cookware, expensive olive oils, and more. Williams-Sonoma is trying to compete with those elegantly funky independently owned home furnishings stores (like Portico Bed & Bath, and Wolfman Gold & Good) that have helped to make SoHo such a happening retail scene.

Before those of you in the know start thinking this means SoHo is going to the dogs, shuffle over to Lafayette Street. This is where much of the new excitement in SoHo is coming from. Lots of little home furnishings boutiques are opening up here in the cheaper real estate to the east.

You see, home furnishing is really what SoHo excels at. Check out the section on home decorating in chapter 9 before beginning your explorations.

Uptown & Midtown Manhattan

To show you the diversity of names, styles and talents that are here, get this: There's **Patagonia** (101 Wooster), **Laundry by Shelli Segal** (97 Wooster), not to be confused with **Laundry** from Amsterdam, 2 blocks away; **Todd Oldham** (123 Wooster) and **Vivienne Tam,** also on Wooster. And, hey, that's just 1 block of Wooster, so you get the idea of what is going on down here!

Then there's **Marc Jacobs** (163 Mercer St.) and **Dolce & Gabana** (434 West Broadway); **Zara** (the Spanish retailer) opened at 560 Broadway; and **Old Navy** at 503. **Coach** is coming to 447 West Broadway in spring 2000. Are you dizzy yet?

Don't let the scant number of listings below throw you. I could do a book on SoHo alone. Just about every store has arrived, each is fun; many stores are flagships or showcases.

To simplify things, for example, I have not listed Eileen Fisher below since there are many pages of this book devoted to her work, and yet, the Eileen Fisher store is SoHo is three times bigger than any other single Fisher store in Manhattan, so look at everything (**Eileen Fisher,** 395 West Broadway). Also note that this part of Manhattan is sometimes called The Lipstick District because of the number of beauty and makeup stores as well as day spas. For listings on those, see chapter 8.

SoHo is a day trip; this is an event, a time to wander and to celebrate retail at its best. And do bring your credit cards. There's a guide to SoHo that has ads and all sorts of listings, if you want comprehensive directions and goals, it costs $2.95 at local bookstores (*Streets of SoHo Map & Guide*) but then, so many new things open at a constant pace, that you do best to just wander and enjoy.

There are several different subway lines that will get you to SoHo. Since I discovered the E train, it has made my life in SoHo so much easier to understand. SoHo is also an easy walk from many other neighborhoods (Chelsea, the Village), so you have no excuse not to visit. Yes, you can even walk here after you stock up on fake pens and sunglasses on Canal St.

To get to Canal St., simply take the subway to the Canal St. stop (three lines will get you there, N is the best bet), then walk east on either Broadway or West Broadway (two different streets). I suggest Broadway.

Finds

ANTHROPOLOGIE
375 West Broadway

See "Lower Fifth Avenue" section, above.

BLUEFISH
150 Green St.

You'll have to go out of your way to find this store since it's on the corner of Houston Street and your zigzag explorations may not lead you this far over on each street. BlueFish is a New Mexico design force known for a very specific type of baggy and droopy chic, usually with hand-printed or -stamped motifs done with wooden block printing. Note the handmade dog water bowl at the front door; that really says it all.

CATHERINE
468 Broome St.

Her name is Catherine Malandrino; she is the new best friend of the moment of every fashion editor in town; she has grown so much that I even got invited to her sample sale. This is her own store and her own vision; her day job is to lend a helping hand at Diane Von Furstenberg. Very Gallic, whimsical, *et charmant.*

5S
98 Prince St. (Mercer-Greene)

The "S" stands for Shiseido, the Japanese brand that has invested heavily in SoHo. This is a concept store with color makeup and skin care; most items cost $10 to $15. The ideas are color coded and themed; there are tons of testers. This is a really unique source probably not available elsewhere in the United States.

HARRIET LOVE
126 Prince St.

Chic vintage clothing and new retro styles from one of the premier dealers in used or worn, plus droopy chic; don't miss it. Prices are not inexpensive. When I'm rich I can waltz into this shop and pay full retail. And I won't even blink. Not once.

HOTEL VENUS
382 West Broadway

Patricia Fields has long been one of the most famous names in downtown fashion; this is her SoHo shop with affordable funkiness. Think color and disco.

KATE SPADE PAPER
59 Thompson

This venue is the original Kate Spade store, which she left on her march to stardom. The space is now used to sell her paper goods line. Because this particular store is a bit off to one side from SoHo, you should look at a map and find your way to the outer limits. This isn't a great part of town, but Thompson has a number of stores on it and is a link street that connects SoHo with the West Village. Kate Spade's store is itsy bitsy tiny.

KATE'S PAPERIE
561 Broadway

This SoHo shop sums up all that SoHo was ever meant to be, so step into my parlor. Kate's sells assorted handmade and art papers by the sheet, various paper products like notebooks, all sorts of paper toys and goodies, stationery, note paper, artsy fartsy this and thats, rubber stamps, and even papier-mâché. It's sheer heaven. Not cheap, but great fun and very sophisticated. You haven't seen the best of Broadway if you don't come to Kate's.

KIRNA ZABETE
96 Greene St.

This is the other must-do, hot boutique space with flag flying outside and editors drooling inside. Many of the Euro designer names are unknown in the United States, some are known by "fashionistas," but hard to find in uptown sources. The store owners were fashion editors; the store display is very gallery-esque. The downstairs space sells lotions, potions, and aromatherapy notions. The store is a full-service look with everything from clothes to shoes to jewelry and accessories.

MORGANNE LE FAY
151 Spring St.

I saw the dreamiest chiffon dresses in the world here, even some in white that would have made magnificent wedding gowns. I found the prices inconsistent—things I loved were $180 and others were $630. Ouch. Still, the shop is pure heaven in terms of it being everything you want a stylish, secret, SoHo source to be. There is a Madison Avenue shop, by the way, for those of you who are too uptown to call my name; the line is also sold in Bergdorf's now.

YASO
62 Grand St.

This is another favorite shop with a completely different look, although consistent with my love to Harriet Love and yet I find this a very SoHo source. Yaso specializes in one-size droopy dresses and charming hats; there's a new home-style line. The droopy dresses cost close to $200 (half-price sale twice a year!) and are usually made of luxurious fabrics. Yaso, if you must know, is the daughter (Yasmeen) of the owner and designer.

Some Recent SoHo Arrivals

CLUB MONACO
121 Prince St.

EMPORIO ARMANI
410 West Broadway at Spring St.

HELENA RUBINSTEIN
135 Spring St.

MANRICO CASHMERE
140 Wooster St.

MAX MARA
450 West Broadway at Prince St.

PRADA
116 Wooster at Prince-Spring

RALPH LAUREN/POLO
370 West Broadway

VIA SPIGA
390 West Broadway

VIVIENNE WESTWOOD
71 Greene St. at Spring

WOLFORD
122 Greene

YVES SAINT LAURENT
88 Wooster

CANAL STREET

While you're in SoHo, you might want to wander a few blocks over on Broadway and find yourself at the corner of Broadway and Canal Street, where all the fake designer goods in the world are sold. This is at the edge of Chinatown and a few blocks from SoHo, so it's not really inconvenient.

I don't actually suggest you buy any of this junk unless you are looking for joke gifts, but friends from Europe love it here and teenagers seem to think these items are must-haves. Trust me, very little down here will fool anyone much more sophisticated than a teenager. On the other hand, now you know where it's at.

But wait, before I toss you out on your fake Chanel earrings, let's talk about **Pearl River** (227 Canal St.), which is a Chinese department store. Let's get honest here, I go to Hong Kong once a year. I don't need to come to Chinatown for a Chinese department store and I am not that impressed with this resource because I've seen better in San Francisco and much better in Hong Kong. That said, let me warn you that every fashion editor in Manhattan loves this resource for cheap thrills.

NOLITA

Although the name of this area is derived from the term North of Little Italy, the area is adjacent to SoHo. My guess is that the two will merge within 5 years. Right now, of the streets in the area, the best are Elizabeth and Mott, on the blocks from Houston to Prince. The storefronts are very tiny, you can feel the energy of all the creativity in the air, and it's absolutely charming to browse around here. No big names or big chains are here—hmmm, well **Lucien Pellat-Finet** is a big name in France, but few in America know this couture cashmere brand. Just as there are independent films called "indies" in the industry, these little shops without benefits of big brands or big budgets are also called "indies."

The point of the whole neighborhood, other than the fact that the rents are much lower than SoHo and it's walking distance from SoHo, is that the store owner can make a personal statement, much as if his or her boutique were an art gallery or a personal show-and-tell lesson in school. The store owner is the star of the show, and often the sole employee.

If you're thinking low prices, forget it. If you're thinking cutting edge chic, you've come to the right place.

Finds

CALYPSO
280 Mott St.

One of the most famous of the jewels in the area and one of the crown jewels of retailer-entrepreneur Christiane Celle, who has been so successful at her BoHo hippie chic look that she has also opened up a store uptown. Note that the same woman also owns Jane and Calypso Enfants (284 Mulberry) as well as Calypso in SoHo at 424 Broome St. between Crosby and Lafayette.

HEDRA PRUE
281 Mott St.

This store has tons of color, some of a Caribbean resort Mexicana feel, but mostly creative stuff for those who love to look like themselves and wouldn't be caught dead in black.

JAMIN PUECH
242 Mott St.

From the Calypso people, this is a handbags and accessories store; the brand is also found in France. Very funky, somewhat cher. If you like the unusual, the one of a kind, the Fendi baguette, this is your source.

JANET RUSSO
262 Mott St.

Nantucket regulars will remember that Russo had one of the island's most charming boutiques there for years. She closed that but found herself in NoLita where she sells the same whimsical blends of vintage clothes and home style. No one does the look or captures the spirit of downtown better than Russo.

LANGUAGE
238 Mulberry

Small selection of lotsa brands, interesting decor, and enough fun stuff to make you realize you're not in Kansas any more. One of the best resources in the area for understanding what it's all about, Alfie.

SEIZE SUR VINGT
243 Elizabeth

This is a men's store; the name refers to a grade in the French school system. They do both off the rack and custom, it's sort of preppy rich chic with an edge, not too downtown at all.

ZERO
225 Mott St.

Icon hero to the street fashion chic crowd, Maria Cornejo who, with her partner John Richmond, used to have tons of stores in the global marketing trip, has edited herself down to one where she controls everything and calls it conceptual fashion. Worship here and tell people you've been here; it's part of the downtown schtick, you can't talk the talk without visiting this store.

NOHO

NoLita borders on Houston Street, so you have to cross over to get to NoHo or North of Houston. This area almost runs into the East Village, lying west of Alphabet City. The most developed street is Bond Street, but Lafayette is also movin' on up. In fact, Lafayette is almost a movie set and is the most perfect little retail area that you could dream up; you must do it, even if it means taking a taxi directly to the new Creed store and then exploring here before wandering into the new downtown districts.

To get here from NoLita, cross Houston and take Bowery to Bond. Not that development on Lafayette is on both sides of Houston, there are plenty of stores in the stretch between Houston and Grand, which is part of NoLita.

Finds

BOND 07
7 Bond St.

While this store takes its name from its address, I'm certain it's also a play on James Bond and 007. This is one of the shrines to alternative retail which made the street what it is today.

CREED
9 Bond St.

Creed is one of the most extraordinary stores in Manhattan and certainly is the cherry on top of Bond Street. The brand, which many know because Prince Rainer asked the house to create a fragrance especially for Princess Grace as a wedding gift, has been hard to find in the United States before this date. Originally an English firm, Creed moved to Paris in the late 1800s and has since been considered a French brand. Not only do they have a slew of specialty scents (for men and women), but they do custom-order clothes.

All 200 scents are in the store along with information on the celebrities who have worn them; there's also candles and perfumed oils as well as a library—and a car that will take VIPs and big spenders home if their packages are too heavy to carry.

DARYL K
21 Bond St.

The granddaddy of downtown and the first tenant to really make Bond Street worth the trip, Daryl K is known to dress celebs and rock stars. Daryl K also wholesales and is sold in a few hip SoHo boutiques.

KATAYONE ADELI
35 Bond St.

One of the newest entries to Bond Street, Adeli has come here to show off her ready to wear, not just the pants she has become famous for because they grace the tushies of people like Gwenyth Paltrow. The sizes are so tiny they make me itch.

THE WEST VILLAGE

· ·

Also known as Greenwich Village, or even The Village, this is the area west of Fifth Avenue from 14th St. to Houston St. There are actually several neighborhoods woven into this warren of little colonial streets. There's teen heaven on West 8th St. (very touristy!); there's the gay and lesbian part of town around Christopher and West Fourth streets; and the funky antique store part of town stretching mostly on Bleecker for 2 or 3 blocks up until Christopher.

Anyone over the age of 15 who thinks that West 8th St. has good shopping is not someone I particularly want to shop with. There are a number of shoe stores selling cheap junk and some jeans places and former head shops where you can now have body parts pierced or tattooed, but I mean, really.

Deeper into the West Village, it gets better. I could spend days wandering and shopping the maze of streets with names like Bank, Perry, Charles, Christopher, West 10th, and West 11th streets. This is one of the most tranquil neighborhoods in all of New York City. Perfectly kept brownstones on calm tree-lined blocks are companions to an eclectic assortment of well-appointed shops selling everything from antiques to clothing to crafts. There are any number of charming restaurants and cafes, should you need a break from shopping. This is a wonderful neighborhood for wandering, getting lost, and discovering your own special places.

I suggest spending an afternoon strolling around to become familiar with the neighborhood. But if you have limited time, a short walk down Bleecker St. provides a microcosm of West Village shopping. Begin where Sixth Avenue intersects Bleecker St. As you head downtown, turn right off Sixth onto Bleecker and begin walking. You'll begin in a very commercial area, but once you cross Seventh Avenue, you'll be in strolling and shopping heaven.

Second Childhood (283 Bleecker St.) is a must for anyone who collects antique toys. Once you cross Seventh Avenue, the neighborhood becomes more residential, but you can still make a big haul at Village Army Navy (328 Bleecker St.), where neighborhood residents stock up on Levi's, Lee, and other brand-name sportswear. At Pierre Deux Antiques (369 Bleecker St.), I once saw a very elaborate *panitierre* from Arles for a mere $9,500.

If you prefer resale and vintage, there's Dorothy's Closet (335 Bleecker St.). The most famous vintage and used clothing shop in the Village, however, is Antique Boutique, 712 Broadway, at West 4th St. Stella Dallas (218 Thompson St.) is another source for resale; these clothes aren't as vintage as they are fashionable.

If you're into paper and whimsy, can't make it to SoHo, its Kate's Paperie, 8 W. 13th St. There's some famous resources for coffee, like McNulty's, which is so old-world charming you won't believe you are in this century or even the last century (109 Christopher) and Porto Rico, 201 Bleecker.

Don't forget New York's most famous condom shop, Condomania, 351 Bleecker, loaded with gifts, party favors, cheap laughs, and more. Much more.

MEAT-PACKING DISTRICT

I think this is one of my favorite parts of the new New York not because everyone says this is the spot, but because it still feel's, uh, raw. Yes, there are wholesale butchers and sights to unsettle you and its very, very real down here, especially on 14th St. itself, right around Ninth and Tenth avenues.

The talk of the town, of course, is **Jeffrey** (449 W. 14th St.), who has done his own version of Barney's in a great big space here in what was the middle of nowhere. Not any more. For more on Jeffrey, see chapter 7.

Even before Jeffrey arrived, there were signs of the times: clubs, galleries, restaurants, uptowners slumming it with a smugness that bordered on glee.

Note that while Jeffrey is considered the outer reaches of Chelsea these days, it's a pretty big schlepp from here to Comme des Garçons.

SOUTH STREET SEAPORT

I count this as a neighborhood even though it only consists of two malls and a strip of stores. On a clear day, you can shop forever. South Street Seaport is built around the old Fulton Street fish market, and is wedged against the water on the east side of lower New York. If you ever want to believe in urban renewal, take a look here at what money and talent can do.

There is a maritime museum here, and it's very interesting, especially for your kids (make this a family trip). There are also three buildings full of shops—many are branches of famous stores, such as Liz Claiborne, Ann Taylor, J. Crew, and Brookstone. Abercrombie & Fitch is here, as well as lots of restaurants and food stands. The Wall Streeters are particularly dense during lunchtime; tourists can take over on weekends. The singles scene is fabulous after work hours.

The best news? **Antique Annex Flea Market,** Burling Slip, South Street Seaport (☎ 212/243-5343).

WALL STREET

Although I'm not crazy about a lot of subway rides in Manhattan, one of my favorites is to hop on the downtown no. 4 or 5 from Grand Central Station and exit some 7 minutes (or so) later at Wall St., where all the excitement of Manhattan's financial and downtown districts converges in a neighborhood with some surprising shopping highlights. And most of them are discount.

It's not gorgeous down here. There are a few pockets of very old New York, some beautiful churches, and some patches of atmosphere. Not many.

The interesting new architecture is reserved for the big new skyscrapers and housing developments, not the stores, but there are branches of many uptown stores and of some big national chains as well. **Brooks Brothers** (1 Liberty Plaza) has long held forth in a smallish store as you step from the subway station. But now **Alfred Dunhill** has joined up (60 Wall St.). **Alan Flusser,** the menswear maven, has kept his uptown penthouse open but has moved himself and his headquarters down to 50 Trinity Place. Choose from bespoke, made-to-measure, or off-the-rack.

More and more visitors, mostly businesspeople, are interested in staying downtown, and this really is downtown. As a result, several hotels have just opened or are about to open: everything from the new **Holiday Inn Wall Street** (15 Gold St., at Platt St., ☎ 212/232-7700) to **The Regent Wall Street** (55 Wall St., ☎ 212/845-8600)

With a booming Wall Street, of course Wall Street is booming.

Finds

CENTURY 21
22 Cortlandt St.

The best discount or off-price source in New York, maybe the world. Men's, women's and housewares. See page 260.

SYMS
42 Trinity Place

Syms does have an uptown store, and a few suburban stores, but its lower Manhattan store is jammed with clothes (and luggage) for the whole family—at discount prices, of course.

Sym's is sort of an old-fashioned warehouse discounter; nothing snazzy here; Century 21, on the other hand, is almost as fancy as any department store. Still, the store is worth visiting and is especially good on men's clothing and tuxedos.

"An educated shopper is our best customer" is the house motto.

LOWER EAST SIDE

A million years ago, when I first lived in Manhattan, Sundays on the Lower East Side were a shopping treat—there was little else open on Sundays in those days, and discounters (except for Korvettes) were hard to find. All that has changed now. I've spent a great deal of time exploring the Lower East Side, and while its history is fascinating, I cannot in good faith send you shopping there. But wait, there's something new and hot brewing on Orchard Street, so if you want (or need) to be up on the latest, that might be your next destination.

Remember that the area is jammed on Sundays. Come during the week when it's empty. Jewish retailers still maintain most of the stores; they observe the rules of the Sabbath. Stores close at sundown on Friday—which may be 3pm in winter—and are closed all day Saturday. Sunday is a full working day. (You can wake up and go shopping!) All Jewish holidays are observed.

This is a great Sunday adventure, but if you tend to get claustrophobic, or hate crowd scenes, you may prefer the middle of the week. On Sunday, Orchard St. is completely closed to traffic and becomes a pedestrian mall. If you've ever complained that a city was closed up on Sunday morning (most are), come down to the Lower East Side, where stores open by 10am. Since SoHo is nearby, you can walk or taxi from one neighborhood to the next.

The main fashion street on the Lower East Side is Orchard St., which stretches some 5 blocks north and 5 blocks south of Delancey St. To see it all best, walk up one side of the street and down the other. Grand St., where the home textiles and linen dealers are, is 2 blocks below Delancey—this is all in easy walking distance.

Although there are several ways to get to the Lower East Side, I usually take the F train to Delancey St. Or you can ride one stop past Delancey on the F to East Broadway, walk up the stairs leaving the station, turn around, cross Canal St., walk up Essex to Hester (for bakery goods) or Grand (for pickles), walk west (left) a few blocks to Orchard, then proceed to explore the Lower East Side from here by walking up Orchard St. You can even visit the Lower East Side Tenement Museum (97 Orchard).

Finds

ALIK SINGER
168 Orchard St.

This is the epitome of the New Orchard St. A Russian designer—along with his son, who also designs a line—has set up a fancy store selling the two lines, one very expensive and the other, moderate. It's all in the fabric and the drape.

BRIDGE ONE
100 Orchard St.

Leather for men and women including the very hottest and newest trends.

DDC LAB
180 Orchard St.

Indie boutique selling the creator's own looks; open till midnight on weekends. Yep, this is where the sneakers cost more than $2,000 a pair.

FINE & KLEIN
119 Orchard St.

OK, let me blurt this out and get it out of the way. Fine and Klein is one of the most famous stores in the area and generations of women have been coming here for, well, generations. I find it singularly boring. It took me 20 minutes to find a bag I would even consider buying. It does have a huge stock of Sharif, which is one of my favorite brands, and if you are buying at the beginning of the season, then maybe a 20% to 25% discount is worth the trip to you.

They will order something for you; the walls are plastered with ads from magazines and newspapers showing bags for sale in this small but well-stocked outlet.

KLEIN'S OF MONTICELLO
105 Orchard St.

The classiest store on the Lower East Side and one of the best stores in Manhattan. If you are a Barney's shopper, this is your kind of place. How they make do down here, beats me.

The store is small, chic, and filled with drop-dead gorgeous, high-end, elegant, exquisite, low-key designer clothes that are for movie stars and high-profile moguls who know how to dress in quiet style.

Its specialty is European looks, its color palette is very sophisticated. You're going to pay several hundred dollars for anything, but you'll never look better in your life.

Chapter Seven

....

NEW YORK RESOURCES A TO Z

ACTIVE SPORTSWEAR

....

I refuse to list every major chain in Manhattan. However, there are some specialty retailers that are fit for a king. They're even fit for Ralph Lauren and Prada. Also note that the various athletic shoe companies have snazzy shops and we now have our own **NikeTown**. **Speedo** came to town with great success with multiple locations; **Reebok** grows. Even **Nordic Track** opened a store on Madison Avenue to sell its equipment and its exercise/workout clothing. Give me a break.

If you need a quick overview, and you don't have a **Sports Authority** store in your hometown, there is one in New York, across from Penn Station, 401 Seventh Ave. at 33rd Street. This is a superbig-box store for all sorts of things and was incredibly useful to a group of foreign visitors I took shopping who needed all sorts of equipment at bargain U.S. prices.

I have left out of this category what you might call active sportswear chic—stores such as **Wathne** and **Holland & Holland** are listed elsewhere in the text. Fabulous as they may be, they are for the fashion conscious—and the rich.

EASTERN MOUNTAIN SPORTS
611 Broadway; 20 W. 61st St.

Part of a larger chain of active outfitters, EMS has one of its largest stores on the edge of NoHo and the cutting edge of fashion—this is the place to go for both price and selection. They bill themselves as "The Outdoor Specialists." You can get your skiwear, camping gear, or fishing or hiking supplies at this well-stocked, one-stop sporting-goods mart.

HUNTING WORLD
16 E. 53rd St.

If you think shooting and hunting are sports, then you probably already know about Hunting World. I used to like the store because I thought its handbags, totes, and safari jackets had a nice cachet. Now I find it a tad touristy and very expensive. If you avoid the items that have become status symbols, you can still outfit your safari here.

MILLER'S HARNESS CO.
117 E. 24th St.

A dazzling store for the Mr. Ed crowd. Everything from Hermès saddles to boots. Don't miss the sale racks in the basement.

ORVIS
355 Madison Ave. at 45th St.

If L. L. Bean came to Manhattan, he would probably check into Orvis, a small store in midtown not far from Grand Central Station. You can get your fishing supplies here, and that's what Orvis is famous for. You can also get gifts for fishers (ties and pillows) and clothes rather suitable for weekending in the country or for visiting Balmoral. This store offers fishing chic with a name that is famous, although the fashion pales when compared to L. L. Bean.

PARAGON
867 Broadway at 18th St.

One night a madcap friend kidnapped me to take me to his favorite store in New York. Was it Barney's? No way. Macy's? Guess again. It was Paragon, a sporting-goods supermarket not far from Union Square and part of the new Lower Broadway hoopla. This is the kind of store you whirl through with a shopping basket—it truly has everything you can imagine.

PATAGONIA
426 Columbus Ave. at 81st St.

Active outdoor clothing for men, women and kids—a status brand on the Upper East Side. Technical products for specific sports make up most of the inventory.

BEAUTY & BEYOND

See chapter 8 for beauty sources.

BIG NAMES IN FASHION

Manhattan is packed with showcase shops that feature the creations of the world's top designers. For those who shop in these stores, the names, the faces, the looks, and the prices stay more or less the same—depending on the season, the styles, and the fluctuations of currency. Therefore, I only list addresses for these sources in this section. Please note that many of these designers are in the process of opening stores in SoHo. Also note that because of the amount of available real estate, especially on Madison Avenue, the names have been moving around like mad. Since the last edition of this book, roughly half a dozen shops moved within 2 blocks of their previous locations. Others have announced a move in works. When the new address is known, I have listed both and put the year in which the new location is expected to open in parenthesis.

American Big Names

It's only recently that the biggest and most successful American designers have gone into retail. The leader of the pack was Ralph Lauren; Calvin Klein talked about opening his own stores for more than a decade before committing to Madison Avenue, where he opened in fall 1995. After opening in London and other cities first, Donna Karan finally got her Manhattan store opened.

The best place to see the breadth of American design is still in any good department store. If this list doesn't have the address you are looking for, there is another list of big-name chain stores on page 155.

CALVIN KLEIN
654 Madison Ave. at 60th St.

DONNA KARAN
655 Madison Ave. at 60th St.

GEOFFREY BEENE
783 Fifth Ave. at 59th St.

LEVI STRAUSS
3 E. 57th St.; 750 Lexington Ave. at 60th St.

LIZ CLAIBORNE
650 Fifth Ave. at 52nd St.

MARC JACOBS
163 Mercer St., SoHo

NIKETOWN
2 E. 57th St.

OSHKOSH B'GOSH
586 Fifth Ave. at 48th St.

RALPH LAUREN
867 Madison Ave. at 72nd St.

ST. JOHN
665 Fifth Ave. at 56th St.

English, European & Japanese Big Names

ALMA
820 Madison Ave. at 69th St.

GIORGIO ARMANI:
ARMANI COUTURE
754 Madison Ave. at 65th St.

ARMANI EXCHANGE A/X
645 Fifth Ave. at 54th St.; 568 Broadway at Prince St.

EMPORIO ARMANI
110 Fifth Ave. at 16th St.; 601 Madison Ave. at 58th St.;
410 West Broadway at Spring St., SoHo

BALLY OF SWITZERLAND
628 Madison Ave. at 59th St.

BENETTON
666 Fifth Ave. at 53rd St.

BOTTEGA VENETA
635 Madison Ave. at 60th St.

BURBERRYS
9 E. 57th St.

CAROLINA HERRERA
954 Madison Ave. at 74th St.

CÈLINE
667 Madison Ave. at 61st St.

CHANEL
15 E. 57th St.; 139 Spring St. (SoHo—opening in Spring
2002!)

CHLOE
830 Madison at 70th St.

CHRISTIAN DIOR
19 E. 57th St.

DOLCE & GABANA
434 W. Broadway, SoHo

EMANUEL UNGARO
792 Madison Ave. at 67th St.

EMILIO PUCCI
24 E. 64th St.

ERMENEGILDO ZEGNA
743 Fifth Ave. at 57th St.

ESCADA
7 E. 57th St.

ETRO
720 Madison Ave. at 64th St.

FENDI
720 Fifth Ave. at 56th St.

FOGAL
680 Madison Ave. at 61st St.

GIANFRANCO FERRE
845 Madison Ave. at 70th St.

GIANNI VERSACE
647 Fifth Ave. at 51st St.

GOLDPFEIL
777 Madison Ave. at 68th St.

GUCCI
585 Fifth Ave. at 54th St. (temporary: 10 W. 57th St.)

GUY LAROCHE
36 E. 57th St.

HERMÈS
11 E. 57th St.; 691 Madison Ave. at 62nd St.

HOLLAND & HOLLAND
50 E. 57th St.

ISSEY MIYAKE
992 Madison Ave. at 77th St.

JAEGER
818 Madison Ave. at 69th St.

JIL SANDER
484 Park Ave. at 56th St.

KENZO
805 Madison Ave. at 66th St.

KRIZIA
769 Madison Ave. at 66th St.

LA PERLA
777 Madison Ave. at 67th St.

LAURA ASHLEY
398 Columbus Ave. at 79th St.

LAURA BIAGIOTTI
4 W. 57th St.

LES COPAINS
801 Madison Ave. at 67th St.

LLADRÓ
43 W. 57th St.

LOUIS FERAUD
3 W. 56th St.

LOUIS VUITTON
21 E. 57th St.; 116 Green St., SoHo

MAX MARA
813 Madison Ave. at 68th St.; 450 West Broadway at Price, SoHo

MISSONI
836 Madison Ave. at 69th St.

MONT BLANC
691 Madison Ave. at 69th St.

NICOLE FARHI
10 E. 60th St.

PRADA
*45 E. 57th St.; 28 E. 70th St.; 724 Fifth Ave. at 56th St.;
116 Wooster St., SoHo*

RODIER
610 Fifth Ave. at 51st St.

ROMEO GIGLI
21 E. 69th St.

SALVATORE FERRAGAMO
663 Fifth Ave. at 54th St.

VALENTINO
823 Madison Ave. at 68th St.

YVES SAINT LAURENT
855 Madison Ave. at 70th St.; 88 Wooster, SoHo

CASHMERE

The thought that anyone would walk into a cashmere store and pay regular retail is a joke to me; I'd do it during a sale period—of course. Or I'd use my regular discount sources, be they off-pricers or discounters. But pay full price? Eeeeek!

Cashmere is difficult to buy at discount because there are so many tricks to the quality that you may pay a low price, but get exactly what you pay for. You do better to pay more and get the best possible quality. If you take care of your cashmeres, they will last your lifetime—or longer. I still wear a sweater of my mother's that is easily 50 years old.

A crop of cashmere specialty stores has opened on Madison Avenue; most are Italian. Please note that some of these stores sell more than cashmere—in fact, they have to, just to stay in business. I once bought my husband a bathing suit at Malo!

Since the big-name makers sell different versions of the same thing, I merely list them. There are differences between Scottish, Italian, and Chinese cashmere. Note that the big English brands usually sell Scottish cashmere.

In no way does the $99 cashmere special at **Lord & Taylor** compare to what is sold in these stores.

By the way, when is the best time to buy cashmere my dear? July, of course. That's when it's on sale and mere mortals think of cashmere and get hot flashes.

The Big Names

BERK
781 Madison at 66th St.

CASHMERES ETC.
854 Madison Ave. at 70th St.

MALO
791 Madison Ave. at 67th St.

MANRICO
804 Madison Ave. at 67th St.

PEAL
5 W. 56th St.

TSE
827 Madison Ave. at 69th St.

Midprice Cashmere

Banana Republic has made a reputation for its fairly priced cashmeres, including pashmina. **J. Crew** also has cashmeres in their stores and at their outlet in Woodbury Common. **Jennifer**

Tyler is a brand with freestanding stores, 705 Lexington Ave. at 57th Street. Actually, Tyler can be rather pricey.

Discounters

ALBERENE CASHMERE
435 Fifth Ave. at 39th St., 3rd floor

Similar to Best of Scotland; I don't happen to think that a ruffled cashmere cape at $600 is a bargain, even though I know these capes sell for $900 to $1,000 and more at name stores. I'm cheap. It does offer free shipping; call ☎ **800/843-9078** if you want to comparison shop for prices or make an order. Of course, for $600 I could fly to Scotland; but then I'd still have to rent a car and drive to Hawick and get to the factories and pay for the shawl. Hmmm, decisions, decisions.

BEST OF SCOTLAND
581 Fifth Ave. at 47th St., 6th floor

The words *cashmere* and *discount* do not really go hand in hand. Prices are not low and there is little below $100. But if you like quality cashmere and those shawls with the little ruffles, this is your chance to buy at a slightly better price.

CHIC & SIMPLE

There is a trend in New York for women with money and style to avoid the big stores and concentrate on a single source or two that can supply a simple yet perfect style and maximum service. The clothing sold is not inexpensive, but it's classical chic—always refined, simple, elegant, and yet practical. Much of it is in the Armani style, but streamlined, and is almost always monochromatic in palette. I've listed **Eileen Fisher** in this text about 5 million times; she offers the baggy and less expensive version of this look (see page 104). The new Eileen Fisher flagship is in SoHo (see page 116). I've heard word in the fashion

trade that the catalog firm J. Jill will open a store in New York—
their look is very sporty, casual, minimal, chic, and the prices
are more than fair. Also, we can't ignore the fact that Banana
Republic's clothes are very Armani inspired these days and that
the new Rockefeller Center store is a masterpiece.

JIL SANDER
484 Park Ave. at 56th St.

I once visited Hamburg, Jil Sander's hometown, and I truly
thought that, at long last love, I could maybe afford to look
like this, minimal and chic and beige or gray and rich. Alas,
the store makes even Armani seems affordable. Still, if you must,
this is the ultimate. I buy the No. 4 fragrance and feel proud
of myself. It was recently acquired by the Prada people so that
the accessories business can blossom.

SHEN
1005 Madison Ave. at 77th St.

Sublime, body skimming, simple elegance in gorgeous fabrics. I
saw a fluttery, lightly layered froth of chiffon in a sleeveless tank
top that was the whisper of everything I always wanted to be. It
was almost $200, but this is where you put your money when
elegance is all you believe in. Usually solid colors with a monochromatic palette. If I could afford it, I'd shop nowhere else.

CHILDREN

Shopping for kids in Manhattan is a bit of a catch-22: You have
to be crazy to spend time in New York shopping for kids, but
you'd be crazy not to think about it. So think carefully. The
truth is that you can do better in suburban discounters, off-
pricers, and through mail-order catalogs if price or the combination of price and acceptable style are your main concerns.

   I am assuming that you have chains such as **GapKids** and
BabyGap in your neck of the woods; if not, they are great fun.
Sale prices are even moderate.

Should you be able to hit the outlet malls, please note that Carter's has outlets in Woodbury Common as well as the New Jersey malls that sell not only the Carter's line but also the Baby Dior line. In town, there's a kids' source for discounted everything at **Burlington Coat Factory** in Ladies Mile.

If you want to splurge, that's another story. Welcome to a city where people spend $200 for a pair of party shoes for their kids.

A few thoughts to help you past that notion:

- All the big department stores have excellent children's departments.
- The Lower East Side is good for bulk in layette at a 20% discount.
- Madison Avenue is dotted with fine and funky boutiques that sell unusual specialty items that no one has ever seen before (read: very expensive). Check out places like **Au Chat Botte** (1192 Madison Ave. at 88th St.) for the cat's meow in this genre.
- The area of upper Madison Avenue from 86th to 96th St. houses many private schools and is therefore jammed with boutiques catering to young ones—many are branches of international big names such as **Bonpoint, Jacadi,** or **Oilily.** A few are just simple little local resources such as part of the **Greenstone et Cie** family or the **Penny Whistle** family (no clothes at Penny Whistle).
- And then there's **FAO Schwarz,** which does not sell fashion, but has T-shirts, sweats, and a few items like that.
- There are some **Toys "Я" Us** branches dotted all over town.
- Some of the big names, especially in what I call conservative fashion, make kids clothes—check out **Brooks Brothers** and **Talbots.** Even **Ralph Lauren** now has a toddler line.
- **Daffy's,** the discounter, sells kids clothes at all its locations; see page 104.
- There are a few resale shops right in the tony part of the East Side, such as **Second Act,** 1046 Madison Avenue at 80th St., which is fabulous. Prices aren't at the giveaway level, but I found many cute dresses for my 8-year-old niece in

the $16 to $18 price range. It carries boys and girls clothing, lots of party shoes, raincoats and outerwear, some baby and layette items, and so on. **Children's Resale,** 305 E. 81st St. is part of the growing number of resale shops in that area, but this one caters to kids.

ENCHANTED FOREST
85 Mercer St., SoHo

A SoHo spot for the kids, filled with trolls and make-believe and magic in an honest-to-goodness forest that is populated by many handcrafted and one-of-a-kind items. Prices range from 10¢ to $2,000. No clothes.

FAO SCHWARZ
767 Fifth Ave. at 58th St.

FAO Schwarz is in the General Motors Building, in what used to be a car showroom. If you walk in from the Fifth Avenue side, you enter next to an elaborately built clock that has all sorts of wooden moving parts that sing and dance. Go up the escalator to see the life-size stuffed animals and the remote-control Ferraris that cost as much as the monthly payment on a Mercedes-Benz.

I rarely buy anything here (too expensive), but I love to visit. I give the store a lot of credit for being fun, inventive, colorful, and warm—especially when the prices are as high as they are. Every item in the store can be found cheaper somewhere else—but if you don't like to hunt, or if you want to be wild and crazy, you may actually enjoy buying here.

FAO Schwarz does have an assortment of logo souvenirs as well as a stack of prewrapped gift items; you pick the sample but pay for the already wrapped item.

Gift wrapping is free; rest rooms are clean. No trip to New York is complete without a visit here. I don't need to tell you this place is a zoo the day after Thanksgiving and thereafter throughout the holiday season. It does have a catalog.

Now here's the best part: You can rent out the store for an overnight slumber party for your kids ($17,500). If that isn't the last word, I have no idea what is.

GREENSTONES ET CIE
442 Columbus Ave. at 81st St.

GREENSTONES TOO
1184 Madison Ave. at 86th St.

One of the most famous and longtime residents of the reborn Upper West Side, Greenstones et Cie thankfully is not one of those cute kiddie stores that's as big as a closet with prices as high as a condo.

I mean, prices aren't low, but the range of looks is wide, from Chanel-style suits for your young miss to leather bomber jackets. There are almost a hundred different European lines sold here, as well as American standard faves such as Oshkosh.

Now on upper Madison as well.

MAGIC WINDOWS
1186 Madison Ave. at 87th St.

Expanded now to include the teenage debutante and party set, this store mostly features dress-up clothes because the clients all wear uniforms to school. Doesn't everyone?

PENNY WHISTLE
448 Columbus Ave. at 82nd St.; 1283 Madison Ave. at 91st St.; 132 Spring St., SoHo

A nice selection of European and American toys. Britain's toy knights are $1 and $3 each. Halloween items are well stocked. The store has high prices on some items, then surprises you by being reasonable on others. There are many run-in-and-buy-a-silly-something kinds of gifts and child-pleasers if you are out with your tots and need a sudden bribe.

OSHKOSH B'GOSH
586 Fifth Ave. at 47th St.

A brand long popular in the United States and with almost cult status in Continental Europe, this maker of clothing for tots has opened a store in Paris and even conquered Fifth Avenue with a good-sized store crammed with its line for boys and girls. I find the clothes expensive and prefer to buy them used, but Europeans are going nuts for the prices because this line is so pricey overseas that the store seems like a bargain basement.

OILILY
870 Madison Ave. at 71st St.

This is a Dutch chain with stores all over the world and prices that make my heart break. I wait for the sale when I splurge for my niece Julia, who loves bright colors, happy splashy designs, mixed patterns, and all the celebration a garment can take. Best news: They now have an outlet store at Woodbury Commons.

DEPARTMENT & SPECIALTY STORES

New York department stores open around 10am and close at about 6pm. They are often open until 8pm on Thursday. But wait: They frequently have other late nights as well, which may include a Monday night or even a Wednesday night.

And Barney's is open till 9pm every weeknight, so there seems to be a war at hand. Let's all eat early and then go shopping! Hours are getting more and more erratic, so for your convenience, I've included them in the listings below.

Delivery service is available at all stores, but you will be charged for it. Few stores have private delivery service anymore; usually they use UPS, except for large pieces of furniture.

All stores will provide free, simple gift wrap. Elaborate wrapping costs extra. Usually you can get a free shopping bag with handles by asking at a customer desk or wrap desk, although stores also have machines that sell outsize shopping bags.

All stores have buying services, personal shoppers, and translators, as well as clean bathrooms. Many have checkrooms for your coats and packages. Some even have spas. It's the latest thing. Now you really can shop till you drop.

A variety of credit cards are taken at all stores; some are still pushing their house credit cards and may even offer a 10% discount for purchases made when you sign up for the card. International customers are accepted.

BARNEY'S
660 Madison Ave. at 60th St.

BARNEY'S CO-OP
255 W. 17th St.

What becomes a legend most? Uptown Barney's. I don't mean uptown as an adjective as in Uptown Girl. I mean uptown in terms of location, but indeed, only tourists and uptown girls shop here, as this store is special beyond special. Newcomers may not even know the history of what Barney's was because it has re-created itself with the times and become one of the most exciting retail properties in Manhattan.

Indeed, no shopping trip to New York is complete without a visit to this store. Whether you buy anything or not is meaningless—you must see and touch and feel.

The store is actually two different eight-story stores that connect on the street floor if you know how to connect them—otherwise you may get lost or worse, miss the other half of the store. The amount of store for viewing (and shopping) combined with the power of the display and the fixtures is so staggering that you don't want to miss one square inch.

The most exciting part (to me) is Chelsea Passage, the home design department. I'm also keen on the fragrance division, which has a number of unique bath products, European favorites that I don't see elsewhere and cult makeup brands.

OK, about prices. While a lot of the merchandise is very expensive, a lot of it is not. It all looks expensive, but there are plenty of items, especially accessories, that are moderately priced and possibly better priced than in other big-name shops.

There is a small store at the World Financial Center that does not have as wide a range of merchandise.

The Madison Avenue store is also open 7 days a week and stays open until 9pm; hours that help to make midtown browsing a new evening sport.

Now then, here's the big news. Barney's has converted its Chelsea Warehouse space, where its famed sales had been held for decades, into a retail store called Barney's Co-op, which is the division of the store that sells the young, trendy, and really exciting stuff. This puts Barney's back into Chelsea, puts Chelsea deeper into retail, and puts you in the driver's seat. The fixtures in the store are outrageous and creative and artistic (to match the clothes, of course) and the space is meant to attract the Jeffrey's crowd and everyone else with style and moola. Taxi, please!

BERGDORF GOODMAN
754 Fifth Ave. at 58th St.

BERGDORF GOODMAN MEN
745 Fifth Ave. at 58th St. Hours: Mon–Sat 10am–6pm; Thurs evening until 8pm.

Holey moley! Bergdorf's has had a face-lift and a change of heart or a change of pace, or face, or something, they have done some dramatic things to this store to bring back some of its lost energy. If you haven't been here for a while, do stop in. And drop down under.

The big news is the lower level beauty floor. The other news is that hosiery has been moved off the street floor to make that space hotter and to expand for accessories that are what's selling these days. In short, they are shakin' up the joint.

The seventh floor of the store is perfection—gift department along with Kentshire Antiques; Christmas is a delight. Every day is a delight actually.

The rest of the store is coming along; they do have brands that no one else has, such as Voyage from London. On sale, you can do well in this store, so don't write it off as too blue for your blood.

BLOOMINGDALE'S
1000 Third Ave. at 59th St. Hours: Mon–Wed and Fri 10am–6:50pm; Thurs 10am–9pm; Sat 10am–6pm; and Sun noon–5pm.

A trip to Bloomie's is a trip to the moon on gossamer wings. You start off filled with energy and excitement and love everything you see, but as you wear out, you wear down, and suddenly you realize you're lost, the store is difficult to shop, and you can't remember all the departments. *C'est le Bloomie's.* Still, it's one of the best department stores in the world.

You must know the territory or go with someone who does if you like to shop efficiently. Otherwise, just take small doses, always remembering that no one does it like Bloomingdale's and that's why the store has become a legend in its own time. The designer boutiques are excellent; second markdowns can make you very happy.

I cannot tell you that Bloomingdale's lives up to its legend. I can tell you that for massive amounts of merchandise and for selection, this store is possibly the best in town.

This store does not carry size 11 in fashion shoes, which I find personally offensive, but it does seem to have something for everyone—including many logo souvenirs.

I buy my coffee here (Southern Pecan) and swear that it's worth the trouble and the $13.99 price tag.

Some tips: The store has many entrances. You can enter on Lexington Avenue, even though the official street address is Third Avenue. Also, there is a subway under Bloomie's, so you can coordinate your shopping tours properly. There are lots of lines.

HENRI BENDEL

712 Fifth Ave. at 56th St. Hours: Mon–Sat 10am–6:30pm; Thurs evening until 8pm; Sun noon–6pm.

I love to shop at Bendel's for the visual treats alone—the women who shop here belong on the pages of a novella written by Judith Krantz or Danielle Steel.

From a merchandise point of view, the store has changed dramatically recently. In fact, this store was tottering on the edge of disappearance and brought itself back by finding its own niche—that niche is undiscovered designers, new talents, and great brands that you've never heard of. This is where I became devoted to Yeohlee. Yep, Yeohlee.

Prices vary from outrageous to quite moderate. The home furnishings nook is fabulous. They sell Bobbi Brown and MAC cosmetics as well as Chanel and a few big brands, as well as their famous brown and white stripe logo travel cases.

Here's one of the best parts—this store does zillions of parties and promotional events, many of which are after hours. You usually get a goody-bag when you attend; at the last event I went to the goody-bag even had a $25 gift certificate in it for any purchase at Bendel's. These events are very much worth attending. Get on the mailing list and party like crazy.

JEFFREY

449 W. 14th St. Mon–Fri 10am–8pm (open until 9 on Friday); Sat 10am–7pm; Sun 12:30–6:00pm.

If I didn't know Jeffrey's family from Charleston, or what he accomplished in Atlanta, I might have laughed when I heard he was coming to New York to open a specialty store in the meat-packing district. Few laughed, because Jeffrey has an international reputation—even though he is not originally from New York. Make no never mind. Those Southern boys sure know how to treat a lady.

I'll spare comparisons to Barney's or even Colette in Paris (which is my least favorite store in Paris); I'll simply say that Jeffrey has done some very interesting things. Architecturally this is a temple of moderne set into the contrast of the surrounding district; there is a live DJ most of the time; the salespeople have been poached from the best stores in New York and are fabulous beyond belief. My personal person is Wendy; she calls me for sales, she tracks items I've paid attention to but couldn't afford, and obviously works "her book" of customers as well as she works me. Better perhaps, since I've never bought anything there.

Jeffrey carries shoes, accessories, some cosmetics, menswear, and several types of women's clothing for just about any look. Although some of the names are also sold uptown, Jeffrey's buy is in keeping with his taste and I find his taste much more exciting than uptown, he tends to be less safe and take more risks. This is one of the most exciting stores in New York if you know who you are. If you're just browsing and don't have a finely tuned understanding of the ironies of glamour, the store isn't worth the time it takes to get downtown. Let's pray there's enough people who "get it" to keep this store thriving.

LORD & TAYLOR
424 Fifth Ave. at 38th St. Hours: Tues–Sat 10am–6:30pm; Mon night until 8:30pm; Sun noon–6pm.

I think that Lord & Taylor will eventually take a place in the history of retail. Aside from deciding to create a specialty aura about itself—the store is known as the place for dresses—Lord & Taylor also is the first, and so far only, department store that has actually become a discount department store while still maintaining its somewhat upscale image.

Lord & Taylor is a very old-fashioned, traditional department store. The last of a dying breed. In order to stay in business, it has incredible promotions at the beginning of each season and various deals and sales throughout the seasons. Thus you can often buy new merchandise in pleasant surroundings and get a 25% discount. It beats the outlets many times. They also run a lot of coupon promotions in the *New York Times*, so you can often latch on to a deal simply by reading the newspaper each day.

Furthermore, the store is not nearly as large as Macy's; you won't be overwhelmed. Two lunchrooms for a quick pick-me-up while shopping; there's a coffee bar. All store services are available, including store shoppers and translators.

MACY'S
Herald Square, Broadway at 34th St. Hours: Mon, Thurs, and Fri 10am–8:30pm; Tues and Wed 10am–7pm; Sat 10am–7pm; Sun 11am–7pm.

Every time I shop Macy's I come away absolutely amazed: I'm not sure why there are other stores in New York or the world or how anyone can be strong enough to shop the whole store and even grasp what it has. It has everything. It's also so big you can get a headache.

Macy's is two stores joined together (an older and a newer wing), so you will definitely get the feel for the front and the back of the store, and they don't necessarily feel related. This is the largest retail store in America and one of the largest in the world.

The designer floor is pretty good; the kids' floor is great; and the choice in terms of selection of anything, from petites to juniors to cute but inexpensive clothes, is vast.

Don't miss the **Cellar,** the downstairs housewares and gourmet-food section—there's **Eatsi's,** which is a market space you will adore. Go early.

Check out the mezzanine shops, which you would pass by if you didn't know they were there—**The Metropolitan Museum of Art** actually has its own little gift shop up there. There's also a department on the mezzanine with bath and spa products.

There's a small shopping area in the basement next to Eatsi's that I find very interesting—great New York souvenirs, even ones that can be purchased from a vending machine. Also, in terms of innovations, there are "Price Check" stations throughout the store where you can scan a code yourself to find the price of an item if it happens to be without a tag.

SAKS FIFTH AVENUE
611 Fifth Ave. at 50th St. Hours: Mon–Sat 10am–6:30pm; Thurs night until 8pm; Sun noon–6pm.

Even though there may be a Saks in your hometown, try to visit the Saks in New York. They've expanded their space and glitzed up their store in the past few years to sail into the new century with a modern look that I think is just the right size—not too big, not too small.

In fact, if I personally need something and don't have time to try my bargain resources, or I just want to shop in one department store to get a feel for what's happening, I invariably choose Saks. Saks is my favorite department store in New York because it's easy and convenient.

While many of the New York department stores have changed dramatically in the past years as they try to juggle debt and style, Saks just keeps on keeping on. Yes, there are almost 50 Saks stores around the United States, but only a handful of them are tippy-top of the line and none of them compare to this flagship store.

The store has full services for gift-buying, personal shopping, translators, and so on. There's a wonderful desk on the first floor that provides free sightseeing information. I'm waiting for the free Saks Fifth Avenue postcards. Best of all, the ladies' room is large and clean, and possesses banquettes, facilities for the handicapped, tons of phones, a change machine, and everything except fax machine. You may find me there.

There's a wonderful cafe for lunch. The fragrance department is world renowned as the best in America and is trying very hard to keep that reputation now that Sephora is across the street. Saks has a special deal with most perfume houses so that it launches new fragrances first; it also has a variety of unique gift and purchase promotions. Discounts are available through the Palace Hotel and the Drake Hotel.

Frank MacIntosh, the home furnishing's table top guru, has left Henri Bendel to set up shop at Saks—the effect isn't what it used to be, but there's some nice merchandise.

FABRICS, NOTIONS, TRIMS & MORE

If you have nerves of steel, you might want to wander in the 200 West block of 40th St. where all the fabric stores are lined up on both sides of the street along with **Parsons School of Design**. The most famous of these is B&J Fabrics, but there are dozens of them; you can get a headache in no time at all. It's great fun. Can't get to the Garment District? Not to worry, 57th St. has more than enough to keep you in stitches.

B&J FABRICS
263 W. 40th St.

When I die and go to heaven I will be reincarnated as a bolt of fabric at B&J. Hanging around listening to the design students talk about their "critics" is enough to make your day. Touching the three floors of fabrics is also great fun.

And, yes, this is indeed where you buy your live Chanel fabrics; downstairs to the right—about $75 per yard, thank you.

A Garment District resource, this store can be overwhelming, but a good eye can find the best. I'm not sure these are bargain prices, but students get a 10% discount for cash and you get a discount if you buy 12 yards or more. Martha Stewart often lists this as a resource for her crafts projects as made up in her magazine.

HYMAN HENDLER
67 W. 38th St.

Ribbons so fancy, so special, so expensive, that I can't imagine who can afford to buy them. It's like a museum here and you will go nuts for the colors, the quality, and the possibilities. If you make your own headbands, you may want to splurge. There are less-expensive ribbon brokers on the same street, but this is the most famous.

I recently bought two pieces of French silk ribbon here; each one measuring a yard and a half (to tie around a hat). The total price for my purchases? Would you believe $60? Still, it's sensational ribbon.

M&J TRIMMING
1008 Ave. of the Americas at 38th St.

This branch of M&J specializes in buttons, gems, braids, and trims of all kinds, feathers, and all other sorts of fun gewgaws. The walls are lined with cards wrapped with yards of trim. If you buy the whole card, you get a 10% discount. This is where to find your Chanel-style braid.

TENDER BUTTONS
143 E. 62nd St.

If it's buttons you need, or even cuff links, this small but wondrous shop can occupy you all day. Even if you don't need buttons, you'd need your marbles examined if you didn't stop by. *Tip:* You can buy Chanel-style buttons here, but not any fake Chanel buttons or the sorts with the interlocking C's on them. (If you are missing a genuine Chanel button, take the garment to the boutique and they will give you a missing button if they have it in stock.)

I will also admit that this store can be very pricey. I collect buttons and rarely shop here, just because I simply can't afford it.

THE FASHION CHAINS & MULTIPLES

Note: Many of these chains have additional shops throughout the city. Check a phone book or ask your hotel concierge for a complete selection and for the store most convenient to you or your hotel.

ANN TAYLOR
645 Madison Ave. at 60th St.

Wow! This is specialized retailing at its finest, with private-label merchandise now leading the way for a solid career look and nice surroundings. There are weekend looks, accessories, shoes, and a complete fragrance and bath/body line, Destinations. Call ☎ 800/228-5000 for catalog or mail order. The address listed is the new store. There are other branches around town, but they pale in comparison.

Note that Ann Taylor has opened **The Loft,** which is their answer to The Gap having opened Old Navy—it's a less expensive line that mimics the thought of the real line but at lower prices, and lower quality. I am not impressed, but check it out yourself, Lexington Avenue at 42nd St.

BANANA REPUBLIC
626 Fifth Ave. at 50th St.

There was a time when we feared Benetton would conquer the world but they lost out and The Gap seemed to win. Now The Gap has let its sister company Banana Republic step into the limelight and into an enormous, and stunning, new store in Rockefeller Center.

Banana Republic has been a huge hit ever since the company rebuilt its image as the poor person's Ralph Lauren. Gone are the jungle stores and the fun atmosphere; you may not even remember that ancient history. This store is all brushed steel and deco details and marble floors and glorious lighting. Yes, the lighting helps.

I like Banana Republic clothes just fine, but I find that I am amazed at what the stores have become and sometimes just wander around the newer, larger stores, gaga.

There's a very nice big, full-range store on Madison Avenue, but the newest addition to the family is the flagship on Fifth Avenue. Yummy!

CLUB MONACO
699 Fifth Ave. at 55th St.

There are now several Club Monaco stores in Manhattan, and a handful of them dotting the major shopping cities in the United States. This is a huge Canadian brand, expanding now and moving into the limelight because it was bought up by none other than Ralph Lauren. The makeup line got its own boost when Monica Lewinsky wore their gloss on her TV special with Barbara Walters and phones were jammed with callers wanting to know the shade (it's "Glaze"). The makeup is sold also in Sephora stores.

The firm specializes in translating fashion looks into affordable clothing without doing the cheapie trendy thing. New merchandise comes in every month; the turnover is extraordinary. A firm, solid resource for conservative yet hip young things in the business community.

COUNTRY ROAD
335 Madison Ave. at 44th St.; 411 W. Broadway

This Australian chain has a few branch stores across America and would like to think of itself as a cross between The Gap and Dries Van Noten. The clothes are fashion oriented, the colors more muted. Good basics at upwardly mobile prices. I mention this store because you just might not have seen one and I think it's a great place to shop.

CPSHADES
1119 Third Ave.; 300 Columbus Ave.; 154 Spring St., SoHo

Since I am a fan of droopy clothes with elastic waists or big dresses or comfort clothing in fashion shades that are nice but neutral, I am a big CPShades fan. I especially go nuts when they have sales. The look is a little too Boho for normal business clothing in Manhattan, but it's great for weekends or suburbia. This is one of those lines that works for teens as well as their moms and grandmothers too.

EDDIE BAUER
578 Broadway, SoHo

Who would have ever believed that a store famous for its weekend gear could make it in Manhattan? Eddie Bauer has several stores in town, similar to ones in your hometown mall. The store has not only weekend clothes but also work clothes for those prepsters who like conservative clothing; it has gifts and novelty items, luggage, and some of the stores have their home furnishings department, which is sensational.

THE GAP
With stores too numerous to list, here are just a few: 1164 Madison Ave. at 86th St.; 527 Madison Ave. at 54th St.; 89 South St., South St. Seaport; 22 W. 34th St.; 250 W. 57th St.; Old Navy, 604–12 Ave. of the Americas at 18th St.

If you are British or French, you'll die laughing when you realize how much you've been overpaying for this merchandise. Furthermore, everyone should know that The Gap specializes in moving its stock, so it has very good and very regular sales.

Also, certain stores in Manhattan are holding points for dumped sale merchandise. I once searched five Gap stores for a specific tangerine orange linen skirt (perfect for Mexico); finally I found it on East 23rd St.!

The big news: A new chain is about to be launched: Gap Body—it's underwear.

H&M
640 Fifth Ave. at 51st St.

H&M stands for Hennes and Mauritz, a Swedish firm, that is just now opening its first store in New York—and what a location, not only on Fifth Avenue but right next door to Sephora. Look out, world.

If you've never been to an H&M, or if you have teens in your family, you need to rush over there and check out this company, which makes men's, women's, and kid's clothes but is most famous for copying the looks on the catwalks of the international fashion shows and having the copies in the stores in a month—and costing $30 to $50.

J. CREW
30 Rockefeller Plaza

Note that this address is Rockefeller Plaza not Center; that means it's in the NBC Building, behind the ice-skating rink. That understood, this is the store's new New York flagship, carrying 15 different collections. Men's clothing is on the street level; women's is upstairs.

THE LIMITED EXPRESS
7 W. 34th St.

The Limited Express stores, also written as Compaigne International Express, sell inexpensive versions of trend-setting looks meant for teens and tweens (and middle-aged moms like me!) They have really cute, fun-to-look-at spaces done as if they were silly French bistros. They sell inexpensive merchandise with panache and flair. The line has had terrible financial woes and has closed most of its stores in New York.

OLD NAVY
610 Sixth Ave. at 18th St.; 503 Broadway at Broome, SoHo; 150 W. 34th St. at Broadway

My goal in life is to take the Old Navy franchise to France and retire a zillionaire. One look at the new flagship on West 34th St. and you will forget that this brand started life as the cheapie line from The Gap. All the stores are good, the one on 34th St. is one of the best stores in New York.

TALBOTS
525 Madison Ave. at 54th St.; 2289 Broadway at 81st St.

Attention conservatives, preppies, and traditionalists: This New England company has gone from mail order to retail and now has stores all over the United States and Japan. They had a short period of financial trouble but their last few years have been dynamite. The twice-annual sales are the times to stock up. They have kids stores and petites areas and even Petites Stores.

FURS

The fur business has changed tremendously in recent years; things are suddenly looking up. Now that you're ready to come in from the cold, there are plenty of new facts you can snuggle up to.

I am here to state that I believe in ranched fur; I wear both ranched fur and synthetic fur. If you're ready to turn in your good Republican cloth coat, you should be ready for the thrill of your life—Milan and New York are the fur-wearing cities of the world. New York is the best place to buy and buy well.

Remember that the cheap coats, especially those cheap minks and the $995 specials, are made in Asia and are vastly different from a coat made in Europe or the United States. As Mother always said, you generally get what you pay for. As fur moves back into the spotlight of fashion, it is quality fur, not mass fur, that makes the grade.

However, as fur becomes big business once again, it gets trickier and trickier to find out what's going on since most of the big department stores are now advertising and selling what look like awfully nice mink coats in the $2,000 to $3,000 price range. Because we tend to trust department stores, we have no way of knowing if these coats are cheapies made in Asia and marked up for profit, or really good buys. Not knowing is reason enough to buy wholesale from a furrier you trust and avoid the big department stores.

Also avoid the mass producers; avoid the warehouse sales held in giant coliseums, hotel ballrooms, and stadiums (if you want quality, anyway), and go for a well-known furrier in the district—Seventh Avenue and west on 30th St.

Coats made in Asia are usually not as well made technically as coats made in the United States. Collars are usually not turned as well; sleeves may be set in very tightly. The skins themselves are not as fine.

European skins are not as fine as U.S. skins. By European, I do not mean Russian (Russian sable is the best). There are only a certain number of minks being ranched in the United States; the rest have to come from somewhere else. You need to know where they are coming from.

The fur union went to hell in a basket a few years ago, and ever since there has been such deregulation—much like in the airline industry—that anything goes. You must be on your toes. The only way to make sure you are getting the kind of quality you deserve is to buy from a reputable furrier. And believe me, a fine mink coat costs more than $995, and while it can cost $3,000 to $5,000, the difference between the coat you get for $5,000 from a department store and the coat you get from a private furrier for the same price is monumental.

The markup in the fur business is in less-expensive coats. The markup on fine skins from a superior wholesale furrier is less than 10%. The real savings in a New York fur-buying spree comes in buying a top-of-the-line coat for $5,500 to $7,500 at wholesale. See **Leonard Kahn** at **Corniche Furs** or **Leslie Goldin** at **Goldin-Feldman.** More about them below.

In terms of what kind of fur to pick, you do have choices and the choices change every few years because of the demands of fashion as well as what the breeders have in stock. Mink is the most practical fur—it goes everywhere in style and wears the longest. It's also very lightweight.

Longhair furs do not wear nearly so well and certainly are not meant for rugged, everyday wear over a prolonged number of years. They are also decidedly passè, although there is a slow growing trend to bring back fox.

Sheared beaver is a good choice if you aren't buying mink. Shearling coats are big for casual wear and weekends. The real sensation is plucked mink. Honest. Could I make this up? And I am talking plucked, not shaved!

People thinking of traditional mink coats think of black and brown shades. Here's the big news: Dark is out, light is in. Honey tones are the must-have of the future.

If your education in mink goes back many years, you may be in for a shock. Most of what you know or thought was important is outdated. The new realities:

- Do not confuse the names of colors with trade names such as Blackglama. Some people will try to tell you that a similar name means the same thing. Blackglama also happens to be very out at the moment, but that's another story.
- Don't get hung up on male-versus-female skins. All new coats are made from female skins; male would be too heavy, and light is what people want, especially in a mink coat.
- Forget all that stuff you learned about "fully let out skins"— the new trend is called "skin on skin"; it looks more like a patchwork.
- If you are looking at fully let out coats, ask how old they are. The value of a fur coat is directly related to how old it is because the skins dry out each year.
- Dyed fur used to be considered a bad thing—one you bounced upon as a reason not to buy a specific coat. Now it's common, even in natural tones, and is not considered a reason to avoid a sale. Often chemicals (if not dyes) are used to enhance or enrich the color and tone of the natural fur. It's the same thing you do to your hair every 6 weeks.
- Italian hippie looks, inspired years ago by the work of the Fendi sisters, are out—don't invest in them now. Coats are more classic, are slimmer and closer to the body. Swing lengths are on the way out. Fringes, studs, flapping tails, and doodads are definitely not worth investing in.

The real news in mink, especially in plucked mink, is color. Bright color. Rich dark color. It's absolutely fabulous. Please note that semantics are everything in this business; furriers who sell "sheared" mink sell a product that is inferior to "plucked" mink—and don't let anyone tell you it's the same process.

Shearing is bad for the remaining fur and breaks down the hide in a way that plucking doesn't. You don't ask, you don't get.

If you are buying traditional mink (not plucked), examine it carefully. Silkiness counts in mink; if the hairs are spiky, long, or coarse, they will wear out. Look at the underfur, which should be dense and thick.

A good mink coat should be practically indestructible. Roll it in a ball and watch the hairs jump back. If the coat doesn't perform, jump away from the sale.

Aside from mink, beaver, and shearling, there is renewed interest in broadtail. Also broadtail with sable trim, especially brown broadtail, which is much harder to find than black. Also cashmere coats trimmed with mink or sable are very big now.

Don't forget fur-lined raincoats or the possibility of having your old mink coat made into a fur-lined raincoat, which is what I did. It costs about $3,000: Your old coat is dressed and plucked and pieced together with quilted parts to keep the coat warm but lightweight. Fur collar and cuffs show, the rest of the fur is inside. You choose whatever shell you want; I picked an Italian microfiber.

Last, but not least, is the category of knitted fur—an invention that came out of Canada and is done with beaver. This is extremely chic, especially in a short length coat in a fabulous fashion color. A car-coat in knitted beaver costs about $3,000 wholesale.

Do not ask a furrier to send an empty box to the home of an out-of-state relative so you can avoid paying New York State sales tax. Tacky, tacky.

There are sources that sell used furs in Manhattan; used furs are also sold at upscale charity shops. The problem with a used fur is that you have no idea just how old it is and how it's been cared for. Buy with care.

A fur coat loses most of its value in its first few years of life because the skins dry out. Don't buy a coat that you think has low mileage only to have thrown out your money 2 years later when you discover the cruel truth. The only way to tell is to open the seams and have a furrier evaluate the pelts.

Superior Furs

Cheap fur looks great until you put it next to quality fur; then you get the idea that quality pays. If you can afford a quality fur, you will never be sorry. A superior mink coat will give you 10 to 20 years of superior wear, looking just about as good as new for the first 10 years. A quality mink coat should be female skins, which are lighter than male skins and wear better. Most mass-produced coats are made of male skins. A quality fur should be ranched in the United States and made in the United States—by someone you trust.

Although there are a half dozen famous furriers in the fur district, most of whom take customers with references, I am only going to give you the names of the two. Both these makers are top of the line. They have private showrooms and are not open for browsers; you go to buy, not to waste their time. You don't have to buy, but the idea is that you don't wander in, touch the furs, and leave. If you want a $2,500 mink coat, they are not for you. If you want a $12,000 mink coat for $5,500 to $7,500, these are your new best friends.

CORNICHE FURS
345 Seventh Ave. at 30th St., 20th floor, ☎ *212/564-1735*

This business is technically named Corniche, but I always call it "Leonard Kahn," after the man who runs it, who has been my furrier for 30 years. If the name sounds slightly familiar, it could be because Ben Kahn is one of the world's most famous furriers. Leonard Kahn is his nephew.

While Leonard has been in the fur business for decades, the business he is in now is relatively new and their product is very new and hot; in fact, they are always bragging that they have the youngest team in the business. Their business, of course, is mostly wholesale—they make coats for big-name designer labels like Bob Mackie, they make coats for department stores (no names, please), and then they sell to some private customers, like me and you.

Yes, Leonard will sell you a traditional mink coat or a not-so-traditional mink coat in honey tones that reverses to suede. Yes, Leonard will take your old out-of-fashion mink and turn it into a raincoat or better yet, pluck it and make it something fabulous.

One word of warning: I heard from some readers who rushed out to see the new plucked minks and their reaction was swift: Yuck. So plucked might not be for you.

Your options here are to buy an already made-up coat, design your own coat, or work with Leonard's designers to get a custom coat.

If you are a special size, this is especially convenient. Leonard has made coats for me, my mother, and my sister for decades; I have actually known Leonard longer than I've known my husband. A custom mink coat will be about $8,000 to $10,000, yet the one I have just fallen in love with—a skin-on-skin, light-as-a-feather, honey-colored reversible job that goes to suede on the other side—is a mere $6,500. I'm saving up.

Coats off the rack are less expensive than custom made and there are sales. A jacket is less than a coat, of course. A cashmere trench coat–style coat with plucked mink collar and cuffs and nutria lining costs about $3,500; a shearling coat ranges from $1,450 on up, depending on quality—the reversible ones cost about $2,250.

I trust Leonard Kahn 100% and I send you there knowing you will get the best deal in New York. Call for an appointment; serious shoppers only.

GOLDIN-FELDMAN
345 Seventh Ave. at 29th St., 12th floor

A solid source for fashion furs. Goldin-Feldman makes coats for many big-name designers. You can get on the mailing list if you are a sale customer, or go in for an appointment. Leslie Goldin is so knowledgeable about furs that she wrote a book on the subject. You may buy off the rack or have a custom order made. You don't have to buy, but only serious shoppers should venture forth.

HANDBAGS

....

If you're looking for a moderately priced handbag, one of the department stores is your best bet. Also note that all the big-name European leather goods stores that carry shoes also sell handbags, such as **Bottega Veneta, Fendi, Prada, Ferragamo,** and **Gucci.** I must say that sale times in these big-name shops may make the goods seem fairly priced.

I went to the **Hermès** sale with my friend Polly—we giggled our way through the upstairs sale section. Some items were fairly priced but the only handbag bargain was a $15,000 bag marked down to a mere $10,000. **Chanel** bags are carried in the Chanel boutique and in Bloomie's and Saks and Bergdorf's and, yes, they do go on sale.

Then there's a whole category of suppliers that I call American Classics such as **Coach** (595 Madison Ave. at 57th St. and 710 Madison Ave. at 63rd St.) or **Dooney & Bourke** (759 Madison Ave. at 65th St.). If you haven't been paying attention to Coach, they have changed their look a lot lately.

For a price break on a handbag, try **Daffy's**—especially their East 57th St. store—which usually has a good selection of leather goods.

There are a few sources on the Lower East Side that will sell or even order big-name handbags at a 20% discount. I really haven't found it worth the trouble, but many do it. I'm more likely to wait for a sale and shop uptown.

J. S. SUAREZ
450 Park Ave. at 56th St.

The most famous discount source in New York for shoes, bags, and small leather goods uses factories in Italy to ship designer-like goods that aren't copies but don't have designer labels. Prices are not low but they are less than in the big-name stores.

I was once in need of a status handbag and was shocked that the average such animal now sells for $500 and up. I was further shocked to realize I hadn't stocked up at any sale and would be forced to buy regular retail. A day-long search of every handbag possibility in Manhattan ensued, and I am pleased to announce J. S. Suarez the winner: They have the large Kelly-style bag (Hermès look-alike) for $375 in a stressed leather that is just beautiful.

They also carry a few brands factory direct, such as **Desmo**—which I buy in Italy.

There are also Judith Leiber–style and rare skin bags as well as Hermès and Fendi and Bottega Veneta look-alikes.

LANA MARKS
645 Madison Ave. at 60th St.

I'm not sure how to categorize this store, with a straight face or with a Disney attitude. The bags here begin around $1,000. They go way up from there, so that $4,000 is not out of bounds. Still, the colors of leather are remarkable and you should go just to stare.

LEDERER
613 Madison Ave. at 58th St.

I don't like this store with nearly the passion that I reserve for Suarez, but when you are shopping Madison Avenue you may notice it and wonder. The store sells Italian-made copies of the big-name handbags. It also has a British cashmere and shooting gear, country-weekend Barbour waxed coat and Wellies business. The two don't seem to mix, but go figure. The cashmeres are pricey, even on sale; see page 139 for other cashmere sources.

TIFFANY & CO.
727 Fifth Ave. at 57th St.

Yes, this is the same Tiffany & Co. you've come to count on for diamonds by the yard. But perhaps you don't know that Tiffany has changed dramatically in the last few years. It now sells leather goods (and scarves) and all sorts of high-quality knickknacks that you can possibly afford and that have nothing to do with registry for your wedding. The really ritzy evening bags do cost thousands of dollars, but you can buy a bag for $200 to $400.

JEANS

All department stores carry a bevy of choices. But specialty stores are holding their own for both new jeans as well as used jeans, and jeans purists are quick to point out that designer jeans pale when compared to Levi's. About 50% of the shoppers who are looking for jeans want to buy Levi's brand; many Europeans come to the United States with a list of Levi's style numbers and sizes for friends and family members.

CANAL JEAN COMPANY
504 Broadway, SoHo

One of the most famous stores in Manhattan and SoHo simply because it's a fine store that understands the basics of retail and theater. The store is a set for mostly new jeans and casual clothes; there is a small vintage department. The store is large, always crowded, and fun to shop with energy gathered from not only the music but the lively crowd. You're never too old for this store, even if you don't wear jeans.

DIESEL SUPER STORE
770 Lexington Ave. at 59th St.; Diesel Style Lab, 416 W. Broadway, SoHo

Italian jeans known to fit the butt. Other fashions and trends as well.

LUCKY BRAND JEANS
38 Green St., SoHo

Wall-to-wall jeans from a relative newcomer in the denim branding biz.

OMG
548 Broadway, SoHo

This is more like a jeans warehouse for new merchandise. They have a few other downtown stores.

ORIGINAL LEVI'S STORE
750 Lexington Ave. at 60th St.; 3 E. 57th St.

Don't get confused; they are all called the "original" store. Levi's opened its first New York store across the street from Bloomingdale's on Lexington Avenue and it is a large and excellent store. The new store, on East 57th Street, has the town talking, but is narrow and deep, which may feel a tad confining, but the videos are cool.

REMINISCENSE
74 Fifth Ave. at 13th St.

The granddaddy of vintage jeans stores, this firm has been a staple in the boutique business since the 1960s (I think I date myself here). Meanwhile, there's the price consideration—the best prices on Levi's in town.

SOHO JEANS
767 Lexington Ave. at 60th St.; 69 W. Houston St., SoHo; 254 Columbus Ave. at 71st St.

Don't let the name of the store throw you off the trail. The store has three branches and one of them is next to Bloomie's and across from Levi's. The stores are small, but they specialize in prime used jeans; all Levi's 501s. They are about $50 if perfect; $40 with holes.

JEWELRY

Jewelry shopping in New York, as in any other place in the world—big city or small—is a matter of trust. The big, fancy jewelers exist not because their designs are so irresistible but because the house has provided years (maybe centuries) of trust. True, every now and then you hear about a trusted jeweler of 50 years going to the slammer for passing off bottoms of Coke bottles as emeralds. But it's rare.

The big-name New York jewelers, whether they are American, South American, or European, have no such scandals attached to them. We're ready to stake our reputations on the big reputations. And that is why we recommend the big stores. Yes, you pay top-of-the-line prices, but you get something very worthwhile: reliability.

Trust is also related to resale. You can always sell a piece of jewelry made by a status firm, such as **Tiffany, Cartier,** and **Harry Winston.** No matter how old it is, a genuinely fine piece of jewelry from a trusted house is a good investment. It may even appreciate over the years. It will hold value for auction or resale and be the kind of thing your heirs fight to inherit.

As my old friend Hans Stern, who is an internationally famous jeweler, explained to me: "Buying from a well-known jeweler is like buying a painting. You are paying for the quality of the art as well as the quality and the reputation of the signature." Some people buy paintings because they like the picture and don't care if it has value; other people have to go to the big dealers and buy signed works by renowned artists so they can trust their purchase. This is a personal choice.

There is a jewelry district on 47th St. between Fifth and Sixth avenues, and you are welcome to shop there. You may find many wonderful things. The prices will be better than at Van Cleef, for sure. It's unlikely that you will be totally "taken." On the other hand, you will never know if you could have done better.

Tip: It pays to know something about what you are doing, but you can have a perfectly good time and walk away satisfied even if you don't know what you are doing. Remember that fun and big-time investments are two different things.

Like all other businesses, the jewelry business is run by insiders. Strangers off the street can, and do, get taken. Industrial-grade diamonds may be sold to you; color-enhanced stones may be touted as the best money can buy; irradiated stones will not give you cancer, but they may not be what you had in mind. Dealers know what they are doing; I do not. Consider yourself warned. If you want fun, go to the district. If you want safe, go to a trusted jeweler.

Never be afraid to walk into a big-name jeweler. You needn't be in the market for a $106,000 bracelet to be a customer at a fancy jeweler. You may find something for as little as $50; surely you will find many choices at $500. How you are treated is a function of how well dressed you are and how you demand to be treated. Some places pride themselves on having a fancy name but being accessible to regular people like us; Tiffany & Co. is one of those places. They don't want you to come for breakfast; they want you to buy something as a souvenir of your trip to New York.

Faux jewelry is, of course, socially acceptable. It's always been worn, but fewer people talked about it, that's all. Almost all important jewels are copied in paste—to fool the burglar. Even Elizabeth Taylor has admitted that there are paste copies of her gem collection.

Cheap faux often looks blatantly fake—the gold is too brassy; the gems are lackluster; the fixings are not fine. If you are planning on passing off your collection as something related to the crown jewels, choose carefully and pay the extra money. A good fake necklace will probably cost $300; good fake earrings may be $50 to $100.

If you want a bad copy of a good watch, they are currently sold on every street corner for about $25. A good eye can see that the watches are too thick to be real. These same watches, by the way, cost $10 on Canal St. I bought one for a friend (a Rolex), who reports that the crystal fell off on the first day.

Used and antique jewelry can be bought at auction, in certain jewelry shops, and in antique shops and country shops. But even earrings from the 1950s are pricey these days, so have a good eye and know what you are buying. For old and used watches, check out **Aaron Faber,** 666 Fifth Avenue, and **Tourneau,** which has a retro department.

Sterling silver with semiprecious gemstones is a great look; it's also immensely affordable. While Tiffany does sell this look, many smaller boutiques have come to specialize in it. David Yurman has become famous for his combinations of silver and gold.

A few wholesale resources also sell retail. The wholesale price is in code; you must show your business card and be legit to get wholesale, but at retail you still get a discount.

The Big Names

Of course New York is famous for the big-name jewelers; Americans as well as international comers from around the world. While luxury is more in style than ever before (at least since the Depression), one of the most interesting trends with these big names is that they are cultivating a younger image and offering affordable items to bring you into the family. Bulgari has recently added silks, handbags, and sunglasses to its range and opened a store on Madison Avenue meant to be less intimidating than its spiffed up and really drop dead Fifth Avenue rehab; Hans Stern, my Brazilian buddy, has turned most of his business to his sons who have retooled the Fifth Avenue store and come up with a very kicky gimmick—the rings have stars cut into the undersides of the gold. A dazzling notion! All of New York sparkles a little bit more now that we have more options.

BULGARI
730 Fifth Ave. at 57th St.; 783 Madison Ave. at 67th St.

CARTIER
653 Fifth Ave. at 53rd St.; 828 Madison Ave. at 69th St.

DAVID YURMAN
729 Madison Ave. at 64th St.

H. STERN
645 Fifth Ave. at 52nd St.

HARRY WINSTON
718 Fifth Ave. at 56th St.

TIFFANY & CO.
727 Fifth Ave. at 57th St.

VAN CLEEF & ARPELS
744 Fifth Ave. at 57th St.

Discounters

FORTUNOFF
681 Fifth Ave. at 54th St.

You name it, they've got it—from pearls to diamonds to gold to precious and semiprecious; sterling to wear and sterling to eat with; and even some modern high-fashion pieces. To be frank, there's something lacking in these styles. Maybe the designs are just too ordinary. Lots of people shop here for a bargain and like it.

This is not as sophisticated as I would like, but it is a good source for discounted basics such as pearls, mabe earrings, simple contemporary gold earrings, chains, silverware, and the like. Don't forget to go upstairs.

For watchaholics, there is a Swatch collection.

For antique jewelry buffs, look left when you walk in the door for the estate department.

For those who have been working the diamond district, come with your pen and paper and don't be shy. I was set to buy a pair of seashell earrings (don't ask) at a discount source in the district for $750, which I considered quite good. Then I found a similar pair at Fortunoff, for $550. The pair at Fortunoff were not as well made as the pair I wanted, but they made me lose faith in my original jeweler.

Don't buy from any no-name jewelry source until you have at least educated your eye and your budget to Fortunoff.

Fancy Fauxs

ERWIN PEARL
677 Fifth Ave. at 53rd St.

Erwin Pearl is a mass manufacturer of costume jewelry, and everything here is fake. Even their pearls. The good news is that there sure is a whole lot of selection in that line. The bad news is that it's a little confusing for real costume jewelry aficionados. Erwin's specialty is fake pearls and they excel at it; this is the place to find dozens of different styles of chokers, multiple-strand ropes, and kinds or colors of pearls in classical or trendy styles.

However, much of their other work, be it in silver, dress-up fancies with cubic zirconia, enamel, or beads is derivative. Because there are so many different styles to choose from, it's almost overwhelming.

Prices begin around $25 but can escalate to several hundred.

GALE GRANT
485 Madison Ave. at 52nd St.

Avoid this place at lunch hour, when every other chic woman in New York is trying to buy her fakes. Some of it sparkles a bit too much, but you can get great costume jewelry and some fabulous imitations here. King Tut's tomb wasn't this much fun.

JADED
1048 Madison Ave. at 80th St.

Awash in a sea of jewels, Manhattan also has an ocean of imitations out there. For the rare piece that is part faux and part art (an original creation that is not made with precious stones), stop by Jaded, where the designs are private label and the action is uptown. This is the classiest faux in town.

Prices range from $60 to $100 for earrings, but the workmanship is excellent and the pieces are unique. This is the "in" place for the Ladies Who Lunch who want to look fashionable and yet different. If you are looking to make just one Manhattan splurge that defines the essence of New York, this could be the place.

MARIKO OF PALM BEACH
998 Madison Ave. at 77th St.

When I look in the windows at this store and begin to covet the costume jewelry, I become certain that I am either getting old or simply cracking up. This is major glitz; this is where there are copies of major Tiffany & Co. pieces of jewelry but also copies of the hipper Elizabeth Gage pieces. These pins are for women who wear fake copies of $37,000 brooches and get away with it. In fact, any time I come here I wonder why anyone would invest in real jewelry when you can shop at a place like this. Earrings begin at $50.

RENE
1007 Madison Ave. at 77th St.

This store sells belts, handbags and costume jewelry of such quality that you cannot tell it's not the real thing. Expect to pay for it, but there are inspirations from *everyone*—including Elizabeth Gage, Bulgari, and Van Cleef.

Watches

AARON FABER
666 Fifth Ave. at 53rd St.

This famous store for retro watches of all kinds has plenty of Swatches and should be your first stop for getting a grip on the trend and for seeing models you might not see anywhere else. Prices are top of the market, but their reputation is impeccable.

MACY'S
Broadway at 34th St. (Herald Square)

Macy's is famous for its Swatch collection. Honest.

SWATCH
500 Fifth Ave. at 42nd St.; 7 E. 57th St.; W. Broadway at Prince, SoHo

Yep, the guys from Switzerland have opened their own little store on Fifth Avenue, although why they chose this space is beyond us. The store is no bigger than a cubbyhole. But the staff is knowledgeable; you won't be cheated on new models but may have to buy watches in packages. They do not specialize in old models, although they sometimes have a few on hand.

TOURNEAU
26 E. 57th St.

You don't remember this, but early in this book I mentioned "concept stores"; I've also talked about retail entertainment. Well, I don't know how to break it to you, but there's a terrifying example of both "concept stores" and retail entertainment right in the middle of your shopping day: the Tourneau store, which seems to be taking its cues from the NikeTown School of Retailing.

Certainly Tourneau has a good reputation and I'd trust them with my Rolex (if I owned a Rolex); surely they have flexible hours (open 7 days a week) and more than a good selection of watches, with every major brand exhibited in its own boutique space in this enormous store. They just frighten me because I'm interested in keeping time, not making time, and whoever designed this store doesn't seem to know the difference. You just have to see it to believe it. Shop at home by calling ☎ 800/348-3332.

MAKE-IT-YOURSELF MARKETS

Make mine a picnic, of course. Save money and celebrate life and food and big-city riches by shopping at any of Manhattan's green markets (farmer's markets) or fabulous specialty food markets. There are zillions of other ethnic markets and goody stores—entire books have been written on the subject. Also note: The green market at Union Square is one of the most special things about Manhattan; I'd put it on my top-10 to-do list.

Food Neighborhoods

If you are a foodie looking for some ethnic markets, perhaps you want to hop on the E or F train and jump off at Roosevelt Avenue in Jackson Heights, Queens, where you are looking at about a 1-mile stretch of the new offices of the United Nations of grocery stores. Just prowl Roosevelt Avenue; it'll change from Irish to Filipino to Colombian to Korean.

If you want to stick to Manhattan, an old standby is what I call **The Spice Neighborhood,** which also includes many Italian markets as well as specialty food shops—browse on Ninth Avenue in the high 40s. Don't overdress. Here you'll find burlap bags laden with spices and/or coffee beans. And I'm not talking Starbucks, my dears.

Green Markets

The best of them all is at **Union Square,** Broadway between 14th St. and 17th St., Mondays, Wednesdays, Fridays, and Saturdays— Saturday is the best day. Others worth exploring includ e:

PS NO. 41
Greenwich Ave. at Charles St., Saturdays and Sundays

A flea market with green market; nice, but not extraordinary.

PS NO. 44
Columbus Ave. at 77th St., Sundays

Just a small area for fruits, pies, pretzels, honey—nice, but not anything to write home about.

Specialty Markets

New York's middle name is "Melting Pot," hence a plethora of ethnic and exotic markets. There are so many that you can actually buy an entire book just devoted to the foods and markets around the five boroughs. These are just a few of my regular haunts; I do not include any of the fabulous ethnic neighborhoods in the outlying areas.

BALDUCCI'S
155 W. 66th St. between Broadway & Amsterdam.

A foodie's dream come true!

BROADWAY FARM
2335 Broadway at 85th St.

Uptown a few blocks, this is another version of Fairway, although not owned by Fairway. It's hard to tell the difference, except the Farm is clean and neat and brand-new.

DEAN & DELUCA
1 Rockefeller Plaza; 560 Broadway; 1 Wall St. Court; 121 Prince St.; and 235 W. 46th St.

For the uninitiated, Dean & Deluca is the dean of fancy food markets, the fanciest of the chic, the chicer than Armani purveyor of things imported and sublime and did I need to say expensive? Also some cookware, a few cookbooks, and a well-rounded selection of everything to eat to cook or to go. My problem with them is that I've seen the same foodstuffs in other markets for a lot less money and I won't pay outrageous prices for the privilege of being chic. Nonetheless, a landmark, an icon, a statement in food and fashion.

FAIRWAY
2127 Broadway at 74th St.

Best for exotic mushrooms, dried fruits, and cheeses. It's a grocery store with so-so regular produce but great exotics, many imported foodstuffs, and then the usual things you may need for one-stop neighborhood shopping. Upstairs is an enormous health food department. Great fun. Prices range from extravagant to very fair.

FAUCHON
Swissôtel, Park Ave. at 56th St.

Retail shop selling products from France; tea salon and latest member of the croissant team to take New York.

TUSCAN SQUARE
630 Fifth Ave., entrance on W. 51st St.

Nestled directly behind the new Sephora store in Rockefeller Center, this is the store that started the makeover of the area. This store pulls together concept, attitude, and yes, food. This is a restaurant, a store, a market, a take-out place, a video center, a wine institute, a piece of entertainment, and a work of genius. The market, downstairs, opens at 8am and sells many foodstuffs that grew from the brains behind Dean & Delucca.

ZABAR'S
2245 Broadway at 80th St.

I used to hand-carry the garlic lemon chicken back to Los Angeles with me. What becomes a legend most? The home of every take-out and specialty food for New York mavens for decades. It has changed over the years (or have I?) and I haven't found that type of chicken for ages. Ah, what we used to be.

MENSWEAR

There's no question that Manhattan is the men's shopping capital of America. Furthermore, it's one of the few cities where there is so much bargain merchandise that even a man who hates to shop will be astonished by the opportunities to save. Foreign businessmen and dignitaries, step this way. Large-size men, turn to page 189; New York is your place, too.

Almost every man to live in, or even to visit, New York has been to Barney's and has an opinion about it. Barney's is surely the most famous men's store in New York. Now that there's uptown and downtown Barney's, men have even more to explore and can exclaim that perhaps they need no other store in Manhattan.

If you still want more, stroll the area I call Men's Mad—Madison Avenue in the mid-40s—where there is a cluster of men's shops (most of them famous names), most of them specializing in conservative business attire. This is where you find your Brooks Brothers, Paul Stuart, Joseph A. Banks, and more.

For those willing to go for the gusto and get in some discount, see page 263.

ALAN FLUSSER
16 E. 52nd St., penthouse; 50 Trinity Place, upstairs

The most secret and sophisticated shop in New York, for those gentlemen who think Polo is a clichè. The look is very traditional, expensive, and elegant in a European American mixture, but the body is strictly American. Flusser himself is the leading authority on the subject of men's fashion in New York, and is expert on what goes with what. Pink socks are his trademark.

ALFRED DUNHILL
450 Park Ave. at 57th St.; 846 Madison Ave. at 69th St.

The shop for the man who has everything, can't stand to shop, and wants to drop in at "his" store to fulfill his needs for suits, accessories, and smokes. Very much a private club. New store in the Vendome stretch beneath what was once the Westbury Hotel.

ASCOT CHANG
7 W. 57th St.

Ascot Chang is a famous institution in Hong Kong and, indeed, around the world. He is one of the world's best-known and best-loved shirt-makers. Now he's come to New York (well, his son has) to open a more conveniently located shop for those who know how comfortable a custom shirt can be. Prices are higher than in Hong Kong, but not unreasonable—you'll pay about $50 for a custom shirt. (It's $30 in Hong Kong.) The shop has ready-made shirts, as well as made-to-measure; you can choose from about 2,000 fabrics. Women's shirts are not available ready made as in Hong Kong, but can be custom ordered. There are also suits, suspenders, ties, tennis togs, and the usual needs of a well-dressed gent.

BARNEY'S
660 Madison Ave. at 60th St.

The main store on Seventh Avenue is a virtual department store of men's clothing, with everything in every price range. It's absolutely mind-boggling. Word has it that you should have your own tailor do your alterations.

Open every day of the week and until 9pm except Sunday evening, when it closes at 5pm.

The Madison Avenue store connects to the main store on the first floor only (look behind the fragrance counter, see that doorway?). You then go up escalator after escalator to layers of men's tailoring paired with a boxing ring, various health and beauty services, and furnishings.

A small but extremely elegant shop is in the World Financial Center—this store has suits and everything the businessman who has to dash out of town for a few days needs.

BEAU BRUMMEL
1113 Madison Ave. at 83rd St.

Begun in Queens and now branching out to dress chic men everywhere, Beau Brummel specializes in European clothes that look good on skinny men. Hugo Boss, the German line, is a big seller, but there's also Gianfranco Ferrè and other big names. There are on-premises tailors for instant fixes; and best of all, businessmen can make a private appointment for a room upstairs where—should they care to—they may eat and shop at the same time. It's not cheap, but it is exclusive. There are a few stores dotted around town.

BERGDORF GOODMAN MAN
745 Fifth Ave. at 58th St.

I don't know how this store has stayed in business, but it is gorgeous and wonderful and special and filled with designer names but, alas, few customers. I think they should just call it a museum and charge admission. The ultimate in power dressing for meetings, weekends, bedroom, boardroom, and even bathroom. This is where the Masters of the Universe shop. Check out the cafe upstairs for a quick bite.

BROOKS BROTHERS
346 Madison Ave. at 44th St.; 666 Fifth Ave. at 54th St.;
1 Liberty Plaza

It's not that I am a traditionalist or conservative dresser or anything old-fashioned or uptight, but, I'm sorry to say, I don't get it when it comes to the new Brooks Brothers on Fifth Avenue. I mean, I understand it conceptually—young, modern, hip store to lure in young customers, convert them to the brand that has a reputation for being old-fashioned. Great. It's just that the new store leaves me more bored than the old one.

You go see for yourself; please report back. They do carry men's and women's clothing, mostly for the workplace. Note that the clothes and the look are not the same as in the regular store on Madison Avenue, where, thankfully, little has changed.

You can tell a proper Brooks Brothers suit by the square boxy cut, which is why it's a uniform for a certain kind of businessman. Brooks Brothers does a steady business in ultraconservative, always correct uniforms. This is actually a better store for sportswear and casual clothes, and it does have women's and boys' departments. In fact, they've beefed up the women's department and hope to make a major statement in career clothing. Sales are good; there's a factory outlet in Woodbury Common.

JOSEPH A. BANKS
366 Madison Ave. at 46th St.

A Boston retailer that is just trying out the tempo of New York, Banks has an interesting story. Its look is very similar to Brooks Brothers, but its prices are lower. The business includes a women's division, but women's clothing is not sold out of the Manhattan store; they will give you a catalog for women and petites. The store isn't very big or splashy, but for conservative dressers looking for traditional clothing, this is almost a price war.

SULKA
430 Park Ave. at 55th St.; 840 Madison Ave. at 70th St.

European flair and tradition with enough edge and humor to convey that you are rich enough to be laughing all the way to the bank, but always impeccably assured and properly attired.

SHOPPING CENTERS

The big malls are in the metropolitan areas outside of Manhattan. In New York City, all you get in terms of a mall is several floors of retail space in an office complex—such as "The Market" at Citicorp or "The Atrium" at Trump Tower. Both are boring. Don't laugh, but the best of the mall-like spaces in Manhattan has become Rockefeller Plaza.

575
575 Fifth Ave. at 47th St.

The poor person's Trump Tower in the not-so-shabby neighborhood of Fifth Avenue and 47th St. This shopping plaza is anchored by a small branch of **Ann Taylor.** There's a New York Yankees team merchandise store here as well.

PIER 17 PAVILION
South St. Seaport

This is actually part of the South Street Seaport complex, and if you are just wandering around happily you will probably discover it for yourself. But if you aren't paying much attention, or the crowds are too dense, you might not realize that besides the Faneuil Hall–like South Street Seaport complex, and the short stretch of street-level shops on Fulton Street, there is an additional building along the water next to the lightship Ambrose that is really a mall on its own, complete with escalators and a branch store of many of the major chains in America. There's **Banana Republic, The Sharper Image, The Limited, The Limited Express, Foot Locker,** and others.

ROCKEFELLER CENTER/ROCKEFELLER PLAZA
30 Rockefeller Plaza, off Fifth Ave. at 50th St.

On rainy days you can make your way across midtown underground if you know how to work the city of halls and shops that lie beneath Rockefeller Center. This is more than a mall, it's a village.

Besides fast-food restaurants and a few nice ones (**American Festival Cafe** and the **Sea Grill**), there are food markets, party stores, demidepartment stores, candy shops, newsstands (with great magazine selections), and many service-related businesses—banks, a post office, travel agencies, Federal Express, and men who shine your shoes—all underground. Most of the stores are not anything you haven't seen before.

Aboveground is quite another story—one of New York's revolutions in retail happened right here. There's a tiny avenue of storefronts that leads to the Christmas tree and the ice-skating rink (in season) at Rockefeller Plaza; there's a spacious branch of **The Metropolitan Museum of Art** gift shop.

Around the corner, on a tiny street called Rockefeller Plaza, there's a small branch of gourmet food purveyor **Dean & Deluca,** which has a coffee bar and snacks to eat or take out. This place is especially hot since hanging out in front of the studio for the *Today* show at NBC has become such a tourist thing.

Along with **NBC Experience**—the network's retail store—there's a new branch of **J. Crew** in the same building; there's also the **Banana Republic** (which opens at 9am) and **Sephora** as well as **Tuscan Square**.

THE TRUMP TOWER ATRIUM
725 Fifth Ave. at 56th St.

The problem with the Trump Tower is that everybody wants to see it but nobody thinks he or she can afford anything there—so little actual shopping is going on while the mobs come and go. Donald Trump has gone on to other adventures, but still gets a lot of mileage out of his luxury tower where you can live or shop. The atrium space is Glitz City, with tiers of space (and lots of marble and brass) on five levels devoted to stores. Many are branches of famous names, such as **Asprey,** the London purveyor of fine goods. An escalator connects the floors, but you can also come up to each level in an elevator. Every visitor to New York should see this place.

With the downsizing of the mean income of the neighborhood, many affordable stores have come to roost—including **NikeTown.**

YAOHAN PLAZA
595 River Rd., Edgewater, New Jersey

OK, I admit it—this is a ringer. But it's so much fun you must give it a little consideration. Yaohan Plaza is in New Jersey, home of the Manhattan shopping centers and where everyone who craves a mall should be going. But wait, this is no mall or ordinary shopping center. It's a small strip village that is totally Japanese! The largest store is a supermarket that includes eateries; there's a row of stores selling cosmetics and gift items as well as clothes. The supermarket has a cozy combination of Japanese goods that you can't get in too many other places, as well as American goods, and then a Japanese dry-goods selection (you know, rice steamers, teapots). The packaging alone will make you nuts with glee. This is a shopping and artistic adventure if ever there were one. You can drive from Manhattan (the complex is just about under the George Washington Bridge), you can take a ferry from Eleventh Avenue and 34th St. in Manhattan to the Port Imperial ferry terminal and get a taxi there, or you can take the Yaohan shuttle bus across the street from the north exit of the Port Authority Terminal on West 42nd St.

SPECIAL SIZES FOR MEN

BARNEY'S
660 Madison Ave. at 60th St.

Barney's has one of the most complete ranges of sizes in stock in New York; you just may want to give it a shot. They also do alterations on premises. The famous warehouse sale has plenty of selection in all size ranges.

ROCHESTER BIG & TALL
1301 Ave. of Americas at 52nd St.

Big-name brand names are carried in large and tall sizes here; I must say that the prices make me shiver and I find it better value to have my husband's clothes made to order by our tailor in Hong Kong. But if you like to buy ready-made, there is a very good selection of quality looks and makes.

SPECIAL SIZES FOR WOMEN

New York is one of the best cities in the world for specialty sizes; most of the department stores have made it their business to stock well-developed petite and plus-size women's wear. Even the store catalogs now feature garments available in a range of sizes, including "Misses," which is their term for plus sizes. Many designers, retailers, and boutiques are willing to help you look as elegant as possible, no matter how big or how small you may be.

If you can get in over a weekend, or can buy wholesale, try 498 Seventh Avenue for its large-size showrooms. Many established names also have petite or plus sizes, such as Anne Klein and Liz Claiborne (petites), which are sold at their outlet stores. Don't forget that Bill Blass cuts up to size 16 (he's the only big name that does) and that any couture garment can be made to measure.

ASHANTI
872 Lexington Ave. at 65th St., ☎ *212/535-0740*

Sizes 14 to 28 in everyday, business, casual, and dress-up styles. They also host specialty 1-day events that highlight a specific look and show you how to put it together. Clothes tend to be colorful, exciting, sometimes ethnic, and never boring.

AVENUE
711 Third Ave. at 46th St.

From those friendly folks who brought you **The Limited** and **Express,** now we have Avenue, the same inexpensive and hot fashions in plus sizes only. There are jeans, weekend clothes, and career clothes as well as accessories and hosiery. Worth a trip to New York.

FORMAN'S COATS/PLUS SIZES
78 Orchard St.

PLUS NINE
11 E. 57th St.

The store is upstairs, above Hermès, thank you very much. You buzz to be let in. There is a large selection of shoes, all high quality and from big-name firms—prices to match. I prefer to buy cheap shoes, but when I want true quality, I shop here.

They do have seasonal sales as well as a standing selection of dressy shoes and shoes that can be specialty dyed to match. Sizes begin at $9^1/_2$ and go to 12.

TEENS

The teens mostly just hang; few shop with grown-ups. I think the West Village, particularly West 8th St., is just a beginner's phase that all teens must go through. SoHo is far more sophisticated. Lower Fifth Avenue has become a mall of sorts.

Teen buys include vintage clothing and jeans, cutting-edge street fashion that must be cheap, and lots of accessories, including shoes of the moment.

With H&M and Sephora next door to each other on Fifth Avenue (near 51st St.), the whole teen geography of Manhattan is shifting.

VINTAGE

With slips from the 1940s the rage in fashion, vintage is once again acceptable for alternative dressing. But then, was it ever unacceptable? The teens wear vintage jeans, the models wear vintage slips, the fashion editors wear vintage Pucci. Also remember that vintage is so chic it's become an auction staple. William Doyle Auction House has tried to corner the market, but the bigger-name auction people are moving on in. See page 278 for more resale shops.

DARROW VINTAGE CLOTHING
7 W. 19th St.

KENI VALETNI RETRO-COUTURE
247 W. 30th St., 5th floor, ☎ *212/967-7147*

Knock three times and whisper low, or call for an appointment. This is a secret celebrity resource; serious collectors only.

STELLA DALLAS
218 Thompson St. (Bleecker and W. 3rd St.)

Couture and name clothes especially from the 1930s and '40s—big celebrity source.

WHAT GOES AROUND COMES AROUND
351 W. Broadway, SoHo, ☎ *212/274-8340*

Not only is this source in the heart of SoHo, but it's a great place for spotting celebs who like to wear vintage clothes. The store has been so successful that it now has a wholesale showroom and regular retail customers can also make an appointment to shop there; call for an appointment—the showroom is in TriBeCa.

Expensive: Men's & Women's

ROSE IS VINTAGE
96 E. 7th St.

Much Pucci.

RESURRECTION
123 E. 7th St.

More Pucci.

WOMEN'S SHOES

Shoe stores come in all flavors in Manhattan: Department stores usually have two different shoe departments; there's teenage cheapie shoe stores (just take a look at West 8th St. next time you are in the Village) and, of course, there are now temples to the running shoe or any kind of athletic shoe. Entire clothing empires and fashion statements have grown from houses that originally manufactured just shoes and small leather goods (Ferragamo, Gucci, Prada, even

Bally). Also note that Nordstrom's, the Seattle-based department store, is famous for its shoes; there are Nordstrom's
stores in the suburbs and rumors of Nordstrom's coming to
the East Side. But then, Nordstrom's also has a shoe shop
on-line.

Big Names in Shoes & Leather Goods

BALLY
628 Madison Ave. at 59th St.

BOTTEGA VENETA
635 Madison Ave. at 59th St.

BRUNO MAGLI
543 Madison Ave. at 54th St.

FENDI
720 Fifth Ave. at 56th St.

FERRAGAMO
663 Fifth Ave. at 53rd St.

GUCCI
685 Fifth Ave. at 54th St.

HERMÈS
11 E. 57th St.

LONGCHAMP
713 Madison Ave. at 62nd St.

LOUIS VUITTON
21 E. 57th St.; 116 Greene St., SoHo

MANOLO BLAHNIK
31 W. 54th St.

PATRICK COX
702 Madison Ave. at 61st St.

PRADA
45 E. 57th St.; 28 E. 70th St.; 724 Fifth Ave.

STEPHANE KELIAN
158 Mercer St., SoHo

STUART WEITZMAN
625 Madison Ave. at 60th St.

WALTER STEIGER
739 Madison Ave. at 64th St.

Specialty Shoes

ANDREA CARRANO
955 Madison Ave. at 75th St.

Italian shoemaker now known for doing the ballet flat in tons of hides and shades.

BELGIAN SHOES
60 E. 56th St.

Belgian Shoes are handmade moccasins with a distinctive look that has made them a status symbol. They either fit you or they don't—mine bit me—and the store will not take returns. Still, many swear by them.

CHRISTIAN LABOUTIN
941 Madison Ave. at 75th St.

The darling of Paris tootsies has opened a teeny space in Manhattan where his wild and witty work is showcased—don't panic if the shoes in one pair don't match—they aren't supposed to. The red sole is his trademark.

JPTOD'S
650 Madison Ave. at 61st St.

I'm not sure what was better, finding that Tod's fit me in America (in Italy I have to buy men's sizes) or finding the factory outlet store in Woodbury Common where the shoes I paid $278 a pair for are marked down to $150 a pair. Oh well, when the shoe fits and all that.

Tod's are stylish flat and driving shoes; they are handmade and last forever. I would pay anything for mine because they are the only shoes I can walk all day in. Now they have many styles, have their first pair of high heels, do handbags, have a line of sport shoes called Hogans and will even custom engrave your own initials into the shoe. Hot damn.

SIGERSON MORRISON
242 Mott St., NoLita

For the Manolo crowd.

Moderate to Mass Retail Big Names

GALO
504 Madison Ave. at 54th St.

NINE WEST
711 Madison Ave. at 62nd St.

SACHA OF LONDON
294 Columbus Ave. at 75th St.

UNISA
701 Madison Ave. at 61st St.

VIA SPIGA
765 Madison Ave. at 65th St.

Chapter Eight

....

NEW YORK BEAUTY & BEYOND

Beauty may be only skin deep, but it's a huge business in New York, as elsewhere. Day spas are everywhere, French hairdressers are celebrities—hell, all hairdressers are celebrities. There's many a Manhattan socialite or heiress or Fortune 500 type who has been seen on the arm of her hairdresser, in the arms of her hairdresser, or even walking down the aisle with her hairdresser.

There's so much going on that I felt we needed a whole new chapter, just to deal. I also thought information on a few beauty services could be helpful, particularly for visitors who may need (or just want) to have their hair done or to be made-over in the most chic city in America. Other cities in America, and the world, have department stores filled with beauty aids, but no city has the beauty energy that Manhattan now has, with thanks to everyone from Avon to Sephora, Bergdorf's to Bliss.

This chapter incorporates such diverse subjects as cosmetics, hairdressers, bath specialists, perfumers, and even spa listings. If you're into the sociology of it, you will want to know that many of the most recent changes in New York revolve around the beauty business—a spiral effect followed the announcement (and subsequent opening) that **Sephora** would have a huge U.S. flagship store at Rockefeller Center. Even before that, the beauty world was shaken up when **Avon** came calling at Trump Tower. Just about all we lack now is a branch of

London's Lush, but you won't miss it when you see what else is going on.

So light up a Diptygue candle, rub a little Origins energizing oil on your brow, and hold the hair out of your eyes with a Frederic Fekkai elastic band. Preferably one that says *Adorable, ma chère*. Take this book and head over to one of those upstairs manicure salons where you can get your nails done for $10 (add $2 tip, please) and read while your nails dry.

THE GEOGRAPHY OF BEAUTY

There are beauty businesses in just about every block of Manhattan, certainly every neighborhood has its own mom-and-pop shops, so to speak. The largest concentration of hip and hot sources is now in SoHo, which many people in the industry have nicknamed the Lipstick District. The latest trend is for downtown stores to open an uptown branch.

Upper Madison Avenue has several sources, but is best known for its string of very fancy pharmacies, which carry European brands. Midtown is dotted with the major department stores as well as flagships of many specialty stores that have makeup brands, including everyone from Banana Republic to Gap to Sephora and Benetton. Midtown also has some of the small specialty multiples such as Mary Quant, Crabtree & Evelyn, L'Occitane, and even Cosmetics Plus.

BIG NAMES IN BEAUTY

AVEDA
509 Madison Ave. at 53rd St.; 456 W. Broadway, SoHo

AVEDA INSTITUTE
233 Spring St.

Aveda is one of the leaders in aromatherapy in the United States; their various hair cocktails are tailor made for colored and problem hair. They have products for men and women as well as aromatherapy treatments. Some of the best gifts in Manhattan ($10 to $12) come from this tiny shop. There is a spa in SoHo and there are some small retail shops around town— the line is also used and sold in hair salons around the country. Sometimes you find a few items from the hair care line in the grocery store or drugstore, but never the full range, never the candles or aromatherapy, and never the makeup.

The institute is on the edge of SoHo and offers treatments as well as products and even clothes.

AVON
Trump Tower, 725 Fifth Ave. at 56th St.

Avon Centre Spa & Salon is an important piece of the puzzle that makes up the New York beauty scene. This world-famous brand, which heretofore was only sold door to door and had no stores, suddenly opened a glamorous New York spa and beauty center and introduced new products sold just here. It's been so successful that more freestanding stores and spas will be opening around America. The Aromatherapy Salt Glow is fab. Prices are not the highest in the city, but they aren't down home either.

THE BODY SHOP
485 Madison Ave. at 51st St.; and many locations around town

Despite some financial woes, there are still plenty of branches of this popular English brand. Note that there's a trend in the United Kingdom now for The Body Shop to offer spa services in some of their stores; this will eventually come over to the United States and will broaden the world of Body Shoppers. Now I find I'm tired of the line, but I still live for my Nut Body Butter. (Yes, I gave up mango for nut!)

H20 PLUS
650 Madison Ave. at 60th St.

This is a Chicago firm that has taken the malls of America by storm; it's now so big that it has its own glitzy shop on Madison Avenue. Not at all similar to the Body Shop, H2O is more bath, spa, and water oriented—they even sell great toys for the tub (for children, please!). They've got this bath glove thing that works on the same principle as a loofah (but it actually fits on your fingers) and it's truly wonderful. And not much money. Great gift for teens, kids' products, a men's line, even a line for babies. Refreshingly new if you aren't familiar with the line and well priced, with many items in the $10 to $15 range.

ORIGINS NATURAL RESOURCES
402 W. Broadway, SoHo

A division of Estée Lauder, Origins began opening its own retail stores in Cambridge, Massachusetts, and then moved into SoHo with a small store offering merchandise and treatment. Other shops are slowly opening around town and in other U.S. cities; they now have their own spa at Chelsea Pier!

While the line of natural-ingredient beauty aids, shampoos, aromatherapy treatments, and cosmetics is also sold in traditional department stores, this store has a wider selection and some products not available elsewhere.

I love this line; I often send out gifts from here—"Stress Buffer" is my fave, but I use "Jump Start" in my bath when I can afford it. At $25 for a bottle, it's a rather big splurge. I tried an eye shadow once but wasn't impressed; I'll stick to the aromatherapy. Also available in limited range at the Lauder outlet store in Woodbury Common.

SEPHORA
636 Fifth Ave. at 51st St.

While Sephora has several other shops in Manhattan (SoHo, Times Square, World Financial Center) and may have 20 more by the next edition of this book, the Rockefeller Center shop is the flagship. This one is making a huge impact on the tourist sights in New York, not just the world of beauty. Indeed, Sephora is a sightseeing destination; some people just go to gawk, whether they buy anything or not.

Let's start with a short history of this French firm, which was getting innovative on its own and was then bought by LVMH, which turned it into a global power. The store in New York is 7,000 square feet larger than the flagship store in Paris, so New York is as good a place as any to learn how they play in the big leagues. The concept is open racks of products organized by brand and by style so items are somewhat cross-merchandised.

Now then, aside from being a great resource for an amazing number of beauty brands, Sephora is actually more important as the most exciting piece of retail-cum-theater to hit the streets in years. This makes NikeTown and the NBA store look like the minor leagues.

When you walk into the store you are confronted with a barrier of black scrim that sets the tone—this ain't like no other store you've seen before. Then you find your way up, down, and around on escalators that give you three floors of beauty products—fragrance in the basement, well-being upstairs, and makeup on the ground floor.

Because Sephora is located directly across the street from Saks Fifth Avenue, some major cosmetics brands would not sell to it, or others would sell only in limited lines. So I can't tell you this is a one-stop, nor can I tell you that Saks has packed its bags and gone home or tell you that Sephora has made all other stores obsolete. You really need both Sephora and Saks before you die, or put your face in a jar by the bedside.

I can tell you that Sephora carries many lines you've never heard of, has brands for women of color, and even has its own house brand that looks like Makeup Forever to me. This line was also bought by LVMH, so I'm pretty sure the house brand is made by Makeup Forever.

Here's one of my favorite things about the store. They do not have samples, but if you want to try something, you go to the desk and a salesperson gets a small container and makes up a custom sample of anything and everything you want to test. However, there are often private parties and promotional events in the store when samples are given out.

There is a no-gift-with-purchase policy at this store; gift with purchase is reserved for U.S. department stores only.

How to properly pronounce the name of the stores? Well, if you are American, you say Se-phor-*ah*; if you are French, it's *Seph*-or-ah. Go figure.

DEPARTMENT STORES

All department stores have enormous makeup and perfume departments, usually on the street floor. **Macy's** has recently expanded its—still on the ground floor—while **Bergdorf's** has taken the dramatic step of creating a totally new department not on the ground floor but one floor below. **Saks** prides itself on the largest selection of perfume brands in the city, and carries many brands of perfume and makeup not found across the street at Sephora. **Bloomingdale's** has one of the best makeup departments in the city and often has unusual or creative promotional events. They also strive to get some of the unknown or little-known brands, such as Isabella Rosselini's Manifesto line of makeup.

It is the specialty stores that go for the gusto—**Takashimaya, Henri Bendel,** and **Barney's** all carry brands that might not be found elsewhere in the city, even at Sephora.

MAKEUP BRANDS

I guess makeup must be almost as lucrative as perfume; many stores have launched their own makeup brands in the last year or so. Monica Lewinsky even gave Club Monaco a huge boost when she wore its lipstick for her Barbara Walters interview ("Glaze" is the answer) and the country went nuts wanting to buy that shade. The Gap started with bath and aromatherapy and is going into color cosmetics; so is Banana Republic. Tommy Hilfiger has a whole Tommy Girl line of makeup now, sold in his stores and department stores such as Macy's.

At the other end of the, uh, spectrum, Versace went into color cosmetics before he died—that line is now carried in department stores and in Sephora. Many other big-name designers have color lines (Yves Saint Laurent, for one) or are about to launch them.

The names on the list below are specialists in the field. Many of them were created by makeup artists or models.

FACE STOCKHOLM
687 Madison Ave. at 62nd St.; 110 Prince St. (corner of Greene), SoHo

One of those rare SoHo stores that moved uptown; Face comes from Sweden, and began life as a model's choice in 1980. There are more than 100 shades of nail polish; almost 200 shades of lipstick. Everything is out so you can test it.

HELENA RUBINSTEIN
135 Spring St., SoHo

Well, Madame Rubinstein is quite dead but her line—which has flourished in Europe—has just been brought back to the United States and her small shop in SoHo helps spread the word through makeup and spa facilities. They do a rush hour program for those in a hurry. For an appointment, call ☎ 212/343-9966. Famous for the vitamin C face-care cures, but the lipsticks happen to be glorious.

MAC
14 Christopher St.; 131 Spring St., SoHo

This is a Canadian brand of makeup that is worn by models and became enormously chic with such a devoted following that it was snapped up by Estée Lauder. The line is sold at Bendel's on Fifth Avenue and a few other specialty department stores as well as from their own store in SoHo.

The reason the line is so popular is that it supposedly lasts longer than other brands. I think the reason it's so popular is that the prices are rather low and the image is very high. The colors are sublime; I buy a new eye shadow ($14) any time I'm down and out. This brand is muuuch cheaper than major U.S. or European brands.

MARY QUANT
520 Madison Ave. at 53rd St.

If you're old enough to remember Mary Quant as the queen of Carnaby Street in the Swinging Sixties, you already know who she is and about her makeup. She's come back into style and has opened several makeup shops around the world, a few in London, one in Paris. The stores also sell some accessories. While I am big on nostalgia, I tested a few items and wasn't that impressed. They say her forte is color concepts.

NAOMI SIMS
25 E. 17th St.

For those of you too old to know, Sims was the first black model to break the white barriers and is a legend in her own time. Beautiful Sienna is her best-selling shade; the line is for women of color.

S5
98 Prince St., SoHo

The S stands for Shiseido, the Japanese firm that owns this line. This is a concept line with skin care, aromatherapy/bath products, and color cosmetics. Prices are moderate and the store is large, well organized, and fun to shop. Shiseido will also be opening an information and product testing center—that sells no product, but gives out samples—at Shiseido Studio, 155 Spring St. Stay tuned.

SHU UEMURA
121 Greene St. between Houston and Prince, SoHo

This Japanese line is carried in some department and specialty stores (Takashimaya, Sephora), so you needn't make the pilgrimage to the one store—but it is great fun. There are more shades in this line than just about any other line in the world and many pieces of equipment as well; also a skin-care range.

CULT FAVES

FRESH
1061 Madison Ave. at 80th St.; 57 Spring St., SoHo

This Boston business invaded New York and just may go global. The products are somewhat farm or health inspired, made with milk, eggs, honey, and so on. There are these sugar cube fizz balls for the bath that are a bit pricey, but heavenly.

L'OCCITANE
1046 Madison Ave. at 80th St.; 510 Madison Ave. at 52nd St.; 146 Spring St. at Wooster, SoHo

I'm not certain how to classify this one; they do it all. This is one of my favorite French brands in America with their perfumes, aromatherapy, soaps, candles, incense sticks, color makeup, treatments, and products from the south of France as well as a mail and phone catalog. If you don't know this brand, please sniff your way over and inhale deeply. Also room sprays, home scents, and travel kits.

PHARMACIES WITH A TWIST

CASWELL-MASSEY
518 Lexington Ave. at 48th St.

Very similar to an old-fashioned British chemist shop (pharmacy), Caswell-Massey is best known for its private-label products, which have been going strong for hundreds of years now. George Washington didn't sleep here, but he shaved here.

Sort of. He used their cologne, to be exact (it's No. 6). A zillion different products; mail order possible. Branches around town.

CRABTREE & EVELYN
Rockefeller Center, Fifth Ave. at 50th St.; 1310 Madison Ave. at 87th St.; 520 Madison Ave. at 53rd St.

I know this will come as a shock, but here goes: Crabtree & Evelyn is not a British firm, nor is it 100 years old. In fact, it was born in the era of the natural 1970s in New England and has become an international soap-and-jam empire based on the old English look. They have stores in Manhattan as well as in suburban malls everywhere. There is a factory outlet store in Freeport, Maine and Manchester, Vermont.

KIEHL'S
109 Third Ave. at 13th St.

This pharmacy is old-fashioned in the most yummy sense of the word; you can actually feel the tradition in this store. Kiehl's offers the kind of ambience other stores ape. Their specialty is their own products, created from knowledge based on hundreds of years of customer feedback and satisfaction. OK, so it's only 150 years old. You get the point.

Their goods have become the rage in Europe, so they make excellent gifts for foreign visitors to take home or for travelers to bring overseas. Some of the uptown department stores and European-style drugstores in Manhattan also sell this line. A very "in" kind of product that shows you know the very best.

DISCOUNTERS & OFF-PRICERS

COSMETICS PLUS
515 Madison Ave. at 53rd St.; 666 Fifth Ave. at 53rd St.; 1320 Ave. of the Americas at 53rd St.; 1201 Third Ave. at 70th St.; 175 W. 57th St.

This small chain of stores has branches in many Manhattan business areas; it caters to women who work in the office buildings who may need mascara or a pair of panty hose, a new lipstick, a fancy brand of French shampoo, or the latest scent. Or maybe a bottle of Skin So Soft.

It offers a 10% to 15% discount on many major American and European brands of perfume, and sells fragrance as well as health and beauty aids. Always a great place to roam and explore. If you are visiting from a foreign country, you might want to cross-reference these prices against those at the airport duty free—they are competitive. No Lauder products.

Now for the confusing part. I like this store and I'm a big fan, and I used to think it was the best thing since sliced bread. Until I actually needed something (a simple Chanel No. 5 refill) and they didn't have it. On further examination, I found that the line seems deep in brands until you want something specific, and then you find they are nowhere near as fully stocked as a department store. So for the small discount of 10% to 12%, you may be getting more aggravation than you planned on. I end up buying what I need at Saks—it can be easier if you have a specific need. If you're just fooling around, the store will surely meet your needs.

On the other hand, the selection of professional brands of hair care items is astonishing and prices are fair enough.

JR TOBACCO COMPANY
562 Fifth Ave. at 46th St., ☎ *800/JR-CIGAR or fax 800/ 4-JR-FAXX*

Yes, it is a tobacco company, but in one corner of the store they sell discounted perfume and they have a big mail-order business. This store is not far from Perfumania, so you may want to shop for comparisons and contrasts. They are very different kinds of places. JR also sells men's fragrances and has a bigger selection of better name fragrances than Perfumania. (But it's not as much fun to shop at JR.)

On the few price checks I ran between the two stores (there wasn't a lot of identical merchandise to match up), JR ran about

Skin So Soft

I also feel compelled to tell foreign visitors about Skin So Soft. Skin So Soft is an Avon bath oil not usually even sold in retail stores but through private Avon distribution. Years ago it was secretly discovered that Skin So Soft prevents bug bites, although the U.S. Food and Drug Administration won't touch this one with a 10-foot mosquito net. The demand for Skin So Soft in the United States is not as a bath or beauty product, but as a protection from mosquitoes, black flies, and other annoying bugs. Anglers love it. A small bottle costs $4.

$5 per item cheaper. You can phone or fax your order; they will mail all over the world. No Lalique.

PERFUMANIA
342 Madison Ave. at 43rd St., ☎ *800/927-1777*

There are several branches of this discounter around town (also at nearby outlet malls including Woodbury Common). The stores operate on a very interesting discount plan—the tags are color coded; each color represents the amount of the discount. Your saleswoman will actually try to dissuade you from buying an item that is minimally discounted.

Hot new or breaking scents are not carried, but after 3 or 4 years in the mainstream, a big-name fragrance will make it here. I wore Dune for years, which I bought at duty-free stores; the Perfumania price was always competitive. Chanel is sold here at a price almost as low as the duty free on the airplane.

The range is a mixture of American and European names; for some reason they do have Shalimar although not the total Guerlain collection. As you know, Guerlain fragrances are very difficult to find discounted anywhere. I think this is a special North American blend of Shalimar.

One of the specialties of the store is packaged kits with several items included in a box or basket; the savings are far greater on the total than if you bought just one of the items on a unit basis. They also buy up lots of discontinued scents, so if your favorite is no longer in stores, try this source. I'm mad for Fendi's Asja, which is only sold here because it has been discontinued. I think that sums up the entire place. Men's fragrances too.

Perfumania has stores all over the United States; it publishes a price list so that you can travel with the list and compare prices at duty-free stores. You can call the number above for a catalog or for mail order.

THE BEAUTY PHARMACIES

BOYD'S
655 Madison Ave. at 60th St.

You go to Cosmetics Plus for the discount; you go to Boyd's for the selection. The prices are high, but boy is it fun to browse here. This place is almost a department store jammed with health and beauty aids, hair gizmos, headbands, accessories, and every imaginable beauty product—which you can play with and test to your heart's content. Perfumes, too. Many European brands not commonly found in the United States. A cornucopia of delight.

CLYDE'S
926 Madison Ave., ☎ *212/288-6966*

See page 14. Uptown and slightly more posh version of Boyd's, but more low key and elegant.

ZITOMER
969 Madison Ave. at 76th St.

Larger and more extensively packed than Boyd's, also carries some clothing—a virtual department store of great stuff.

BEAUTY SUPPLY

ALCONE
235 W. 19th St.

This is a professional and theatrical makeup supply store; since I come from Los Angeles I am addicted to Tuttle for not only professional appearances and on-camera work, but also for those days when I need real help with the skin texture. Various other professional brands as well as supplies, brushes, cases. These are products you can't find in department stores anywhere in the world; when you're doing Chelsea or lower Fifth Avenue, make it a point to head over to this solid source. Your life will change forever. They carry the Trish McEvoy line as well as Il-Makiage, an Israeli brand that has a sort of cult status in some circles—known for great color.

RICKY'S
590 Columbus Ave. at 89th St.; 718 Broadway, SoHo; 44 E. 8th St., and more

A small chain of beauty supply stores that have reached cult status with many in the beauty biz. Also known as beauty supply to the stars, the models, the rich and famous—this is the store where the makers and the shakers hang out because it's a semiprofessional source of supplies and goods. It's so much fun they should offer sleepovers, like they do at FAO Schwarz.

Ricky's does sell what the business calls "diverted goods," which some others call gray goods (when they are from foreign markets). It means they are legally made name-brand products, but the source did not want them sold at discount yet could not prevent them from being released through a middleman. (Well, that's an oversimplification, but you get the idea.)

Ricky's has been expanding like crazy and now has branch stores in most major trading areas of Manhattan, including SoHo.

PERFUMERS

....

Of course all department stores, many discounters, and specialty stores sell perfumes. The listings below are specialty houses known for their own line of scents.

CARON
675 Madison Ave. at 60th St.

Although nothing will ever be as *charmant* as Caron's store on the avenue Montaigne in Paris, this new store is great fun, as are the Caron scents that are largely unknown in America. I wear the one that was created for the first air hostesses (in 1947); I used to wear Fleur de Rocaille in the old version. The fragrances all come with a lot of history; many are attached to celebrity names. They will refill your bottle.

CHANEL
15 E. 57th St.

Yeah, yeah I know all about it: Of course Chanel is sold in every department store in America. But there is a tiny line of fragrances, created by Coco Chanel herself, which are only sold in Chanel boutiques the world over. There's about five of them; I know this because I wear one of them, Cuir de la Russie (Russian Leather).

CREED
9 Bond St., East Village

This was an English perfumer in Victorian times, which then relocated to Paris and is therefore a French perfume house. They are extremely exclusive; few department stores carry the line, although Barney's has some of the scents. There are fragrances for men and woman; many were created for royalty or celebrities. The store alone is worth the trip.

DEMETER
83 Second Ave. between E. 4th and 5th sts., East Village

This line began as a curiosity aimed at the teenage market, with unisex fragrances that were, shall I say, in the "alternative" category—scents such as Dirt, Grass, Sushi, Mud, or Tomato— even though tomato happens to be in many French designer scents. The business went nuts and voilà, a freestanding store in the downtown area to better serve the hip people (and students) of New York. The line is also carried in some department stores but the store has all 140 scents and many line extensions.

PENHALIGON
870 Madison Ave. at 70th St.

English brand, now expanding around the world and going global. One of those brands that is old-fashioned yet classical with scents for men and for women; almost a cult unto itself.

HAIRSTYLISTS

Note: For bargains on haircuts and color, see "Hair Deals" on page 289.

ELIZABETH ARDEN
691 Fifth Ave. at 54th St., ☎ 212/546-0200

I guess every woman who needs beauty services and doesn't know where to go or whom to trust turns to the famous Red Door of Elizabeth Arden. I never imagined sophisticated people went there until my chum Ellen, who lives in Houston but comes to New York on business frequently, took me to meet Gregory, who does her hair at Arden. I have known Ellen since we were 15 and seen her through many a hairstyle and Gregory is good. Seriously good.

Ellen also has her nails done here as well as any other beauty services she needs, since everything is offered under one roof (try Alla for waxing) and it's all convenient to her hotel.

FREDERIC FEKKAI
15 E. 57th St., upstairs, ☎ *212/753-9500*

OK, read my lips: Fred-er-reeeek, that's how we say it.

If you say Frederick, you obviously know nothing. This multifloor salon offers the works, hair, beauty, spa, cafe, and products. I don't find it very calming but it sure is fascinating. Painted the colors of the south of France, complete with fountain. It's the beautiful women and the models and the photographers that I find so distracting. Still, a real trip. Lip pencils are sensational. Call ahead for an appointment. It takes about 3 months to get the master himself, and many, many francs.

Fekkai has expanded into accessories such as headbands (adorable), handbags (very chic), and has even written a book. He has a freestanding accessories store on Madison Avenue.

JEAN-CLAUDE BIGUINE
1177 Ave. of the Americas at 45th St.; 450 Park Ave. South; 61 E. 45th St.; 925 Lexington Ave.

The theory here is French class to appeal to the American masses. This is a French chain of hair salons; just walk in for a *coupe, le brushing*, or whatever Madame needs; appointments are optional. Certainly more fun than Jean Louis David!

Biguine is a bigwig (yuck yuck) in France, but only has a few salons here in America; he also has a new cosmetics line in France that I hope will come to the United States soon. He is known to be more with-it than Jean Louis David; prices are also lower with a wash and dry at a mere $15! Note, the stores sell hair care products but not yet the makeup line.

OSCAR BLANDI
Plaza Hotel at Fifth Ave. and 59th St., ☎ *212/593-7930*

If you thought no one important ever went to a hairstylist in a hotel, then you haven't met Oscar Blandi or seen his fancy new digs, just installed in the landmark Plaza Hotel. Nor have you read his client roster, a virtual who's who from *In Style* magazine. And yes, he did the fancy yet chic and simple do that Jessica Sklar wore on her wedding to Jerry Seinfeld. Forget about tea at The Plaza, come for cut and color instead.

SPAS

The day spa business has become so huge that it's hard to know a department store from a spa from a beauty parlor any more. Frederic Fekkai actually has full spa services; I went for the fake tan once. Macy's has opened a spa area; hotels have long had spas, some even offer special jet lag or shopping treatments to rejuvenate you. Certainly Avon Centre is a full service spa. Those listed below began life as spas but may have expanded into products and other items.

AVEDA INSTITUTE
233 Spring St., SoHo, ☎ *212/807-1492*

See page 194 for more.

AVON CENTRE SPA
Trump Tower, 725 Fifth Ave. at 56th St., ☎ *212/755-AVON*

See page 195 for more about the center, uh, centre.

BLISS
568 Broadway, SoHo, ☎ *212/219-8970; 19 E. 57th St. upstairs,* ☎ *212/219-8970*

Bliss may be responsible for starting the day spa craze in New York. The firm became so hot that it was gobbled up by

LVMH, which is why they are located in the Louis Vuitton building on East 57th Street, almost next door to Chanel and Frederic Fekkai. The business also morphed itself into a catalog of products.

ORIGINS SPA
The Sports Center, Chelsea Piers, Pier 60, ☎ *212/336-6780*

I don't know that I'd go all the way over here just for a rub-down, but it's a great place to know about if you're in this neck of the woods and love Origins as much as I do. Actually created more to serve the local community that uses the gyms here. Call for an appointment.

Chapter Nine

....

NEW YORK HOME

HOME SWEET APARTMENT

....

Most New Yorkers come to think of a whole house as a luxury or a dream; those of us who have already fled to the suburbs (with houses and yards) shake our heads and wonder if we could ever live in an apartment again. Yet New York keeps attracting a portion of the workforce that must reside in the city, so building a comfortable nest becomes imperative. Besides, didn't Faith Popcorn predict that in this century we would all be cocooning?

For those with gobs of money, it's not hard to get in touch with the great names in interior design, to soon have digs that will be featured in *Architectural Digest*. Big spenders talk about designers on a first-name basis (Rose, Charlotte, John) as if these people had no last names and were celebrities of the same caliber as Liza, Goldie, and Cher. Some of them even have nicknames; Mario Buatta is known as the "Prince of Chintz."

You may want to call me the Princess of Chintz from the kingdom of chintzy. I'm always on a budget! My home is furnished from tag sales. I did my first apartment in New York with castoffs found at curbside. I still hate to pay full retail price—especially when it comes to home furnishings and decorative items.

If you're going high end, toss this book aside and ask your social secretary to dial a designer. Or ask one of your friends as you lunch at Swifty's to pass on a recommendation to you, dahling.

If you do your own decor, are always looking for a deal, and need a few pointers—did you call me? Better yet, would you like to pick the brain of a real live Manhattan interior designer? Paul Baumrind, New York correspondent, is passing on some of his sources, too. And he does not send people to Ikea. Read on, read on.

TO THE TRADE

If you are seriously planning a renovation or refurbishment, you know the three little words most important to you are no longer, "I love you" (or, "You look younger"), but, "To the trade."

Such a slogan signifies that the business will deal only with the design trade; those designers who wish to work with such firms must register and fill in papers with their financial and credit history, thus opening an account.

In short, you can print up business cards that infer you are a designer and may get you into a showroom, but chances are you cannot do business with the house until you open an account and establish credit. This can be very tricky, moderately tricky, or easy as pie; it varies from house to house.

Since business is worse than crummy these days, there is frequently more latitude. Except with the biggest, most snobby houses.

Once you are able to buy direct, as they say on the street, you will learn two new favorite words: *net* and *gross.*

Net is the wholesale price. Gross is what the designer will charge the customer in order to eat dinner or buy new needlepoint pillows for the dog. If you are your own only client, your savings are the difference between net and gross. If you get these two mixed up (I do), you will never pass yourself off as a pro when you work the showrooms.

SHOWROOM ETIQUETTE

Assuming you are faking your way through this, we have some step-by-step instructions. First of all, if you do have a friend who is legit or at least knows the ropes better than you do, it's nice to make a run with her so you know how to behave and aren't a nervous Nellie when it comes time for you to go it alone.

In order to make a go of it on your own, please remember:

- No showroom in the world wants to do business with tourists just in for the day. Wear proper business clothing; have well-made business cards; carry a shopping bag or tote or attaché case for samples and do not carry a diaper bag. A Polaroid camera is actually OK, although design showrooms will not let you take pictures. Antique showrooms will. Do not have your Canon Sureshot draped around your neck.
- Be warm, friendly, confident, and above all, professional. The regulars are well known. You are a newcomer. Walk to the desk, introduce yourself, offer a business card and a handshake (when appropriate), and sign in (if indicated). Explain your needs: "I have a client who asked me to take a look at your line. She's just wild about—."
- Take the provided paper and pencil and write down style names and numbers as you work the boards of samples. When you go to the desk (this is just like the library) ask about the policy on taking out samples. You will most likely have to register and establish credit to take out a sample. Find out when the sample is due back. Return it on time.

Ask about delivery dates. Contrary to popular belief, a showroom is not a warehouse. The fabric or wallpaper you want is not on a shelf in the back somewhere. It may not even exist. Standard delivery is 6 weeks. Some take less, some take more, much more. Some take months or years. You never know. You are expected to pay for half of the order when you "write paper" (place the order) and the remaining portion upon delivery.

• Be kind, gentle, and low key. Let someone else have the hissy fit.

SPECIAL PROMOTIONS & EVENTS

Aside from the goings-on in the D&D industry, there are a lot of tabletop people who are actually in the gift industry or other aspects of design. Many of them hold sample sales that are announced in the *S&B Report* (see page 276), the *New York Times,* or wherever. In the 6 weekends before Christmas, a large number of warehouses open to the public.

There are also special events and charity galas at which designer tabletop and home furnishings are sold for cost or less. *Metropolitan Home,* the magazine, sponsors an event each year. **DIFFA,** the AIDS charity for the design community, has various events and fund-raisers. You can save money and do good works at the same time. **Elle Decor,** another design magazine, is also a good source for learning about trade-related events.

BEHIND CLOSED DOORS

There is an enormous business being done privately in Manhattan, and in other cosmopolitan cities in the world. People with taste, a little money, and a few friends are pursuing their personal interests and sell from their collections on a private basis. They usually sell out of their homes, which is why their numbers and addresses are kept quiet.

While there are a few clothing and accessories people who operate this way, the bulk of the business is in antiques and collectibles—especially items picked up at markets around the world and brought in on an individual basis. If you have an area of interest, ask dealers if they can recommend any private resources who might help out. You'll need an appointment after that, and usually the name of your connection before you'll get the address.

REGULAR RETAIL

There's hardly such a thing as regular retail anymore, and the days when a family walked into B. Altman and chose a living-room suite are as dead as B. Altman himself. Nowadays, most department stores do not even have furniture departments.

The "regular retail" home-furnishings business has been inherited by the mass merchants who offer style and value: **Ikea, Pottery Barn, Crate & Barrel.** Terrence Conran is back and wow—look out New York and welcome back Sir Terry; due to legalities I won't bore you with, remember that the name of the new store is **The Terrence Conran Shop,** not Conran's! Many Manhattanites are willing to drive to the suburbs to get even better buys; Ikea (in Elizabeth, New Jersey) has thrived.

ABC Carpet & Home has become one of the few full-service home-furnishings stores in the city. It's actually one of Manhattan's showplace circus stores; it's like shopping in Never Never Land. They have created an entire renaissance in the neighborhood around them, so that the concept of full service has actually spread to neighborhoods of New York.

Most of the big-name American designers—and many European ones—have gone into the lifestyle business as have some of the chains. Thus **Banana Republic** has a home decor department downstairs in its Rockefeller Center store; **Donna Karan** sells home style on Madison Avenue as does **Calvin Klein.** The **Versace** people and the **Dolce & Gabbana** boys have been doing decorative arts for several years now.

There are also a large number of big-name boutiques specializing in table arts and home needs; God only knows how these people stay in business.

There are design concepts that come from Europe and find a place in America; there are copycat firms that charge a lot of money for newly made antiques; there's style, there's wit, there's bad taste—all easily accessible, some easily affordable. But more important, now there's good taste that's affordable. And New York will never be the same.

TRENDSETTERS IN HOME STYLE

···

FELISSIMO
10 W. 56th St.

Now that Manhattan also has Takashimaya, Felissimo has lost a touch of its *bellissimo*—or, to be more exact, the two stores are so similar that Felissimo doesn't seem as fresh as it once did, which isn't very fair since it came to New York before Takashimaya.

Felissimo takes up an entire town house, just west of Fifth Avenue, and sells artsy-fartsy gifts and tabletop in the most sumptuous, gorgeous, elegant surroundings in town. It was here that I first discovered the wooden postcard for $5, which I think is one of the best souvenirs of New York—although they do sell them at Barney's also.

Felissimo does sell more than tabletop; it is simply a gallery of good taste. It's a pleasure to submerge your senses in the tranquillity of the space and to get lost in the true joy of shopping. Try their new scent as well.

PIERRE DEUX
870 Madison Ave. at 71st St.

There are actually *deux* Pierre Deux in New York, because the two Pierres have left the design firm but continue to run their very wonderful antique shop in Greenwich Village—where they began in the first place.

On Madison Avenue we have the design source, no longer owned by the Pierres and much smaller than it was in its heyday. Still, this is the source for the French country look. Truly, I have fantasies about French provincial fabrics. They carry Souleiado and Les Olivades brands. Some pieces are exclusive to the United States. They do have sales and, frankly, once you get hooked on this kind of color and style, nothing else will make you smile in just the same way. Of course, I'm partial. My house is covered with this stuff.

RALPH LAUREN
867 Madison Ave. at 72nd St.

There isn't a bigger influence on modern mass design in America than Ralph Lauren and his English old-world, old-style country looks. While much of what Ralph does is actually derivative, when he executes a design he sets trends that the rest of America wants to follow. If you were to take a look around my house, you'd see the Lauren influence. Even the bathroom is stacked with old luggage and vanity kits.

I personally don't know anyone who hasn't craved the look—whether he or she can afford it or not. To see it all in action, stop by the store in the old Rhinelander mansion on Madison Avenue. There are also Ralph Lauren bedroom boutiques in a few department stores and at ABC Carpet & Home. Much of the big-time home-furnishings line is available to the trade; to get the bed linens at discount try any of the Ralph Lauren factory outlet stores outside of the city.

SHABBY CHIC
93 Greene St., SoHo

If you adore the look of comfy, oversized, upholstered furniture that could have come straight from Grandma's (or the attic), then you've come to the right source. This newly made and oversized (even Grandma's stuff wasn't this stuffed) furniture is setting the design industry on its ear. The furniture pieces are not inexpensive, and some of your friends may be amazed that you paid a fortune for mismatched faded chintz or a giant cabbage-rose couch complete with slipcovers and throw pillows. The business has become so successful that there are now showrooms in most major U.S. cities.

TAKASHIMAYA
693 Fifth Ave. at 54th St.

I have raved in other parts of this book about Takashimaya. Even if you don't have time to go upstairs into the body of the store, poke into the atrium; take a look at the French florist booth. Go upstairs (make the time)—the displays are beautiful and the style is far more country French than Japanese. And yes, there are a number of affordable items. Well, a few, anyway.

TIFFANY & CO.
727 Fifth Ave. at 57th St.

If you're thinking breakfast at Tiffany's, then you should be thinking about the trend-setting tabletop designs this store has become famous for. In fact, they have even published a book on their table settings. Furthermore, the store has moderately priced items, so that while the reputation is blue stocking, you will find that just about anyone can afford something or another here. It's not an outlet store, but the visual treat of seeing the creative hand at play and the often fair prices may convince you that it's not so crazy to shop here after all. The trends that Tiffany's continues to set always involve an eclectic view, so that you can learn how to mix your flea market finds with Tiffany delights for the perfectly groomed table.

THE COMPLETE LOOK

HOWARD KAPLAN
35 E. 10th St.

Celebrities shop here; the owner, Howard Kaplan, has become famous as a country-look expert. He's closed on weekends—that's when he goes shopping for more finds. Even if you can't afford to buy big pieces of furniture, if you love country-home decor, please stop by. He even has his own wallpaper and faïence.

JONAL
25 E. 73rd St.

It's very English—Nina Campbell, in fact—and very pulled together in a comfy way, with fabrics, beds, and everything else you need right down to the finishing touches. The whole thing is sumptuous. And expensive.

WILLIAM WAYNE
850 Lexington at 64th St.

Started out downtown as a funky little resource, turned rich and famous (I even saw them on CNN), and now have not one but two stores on Lexington Avenue. One features wonderful accessories and tabletop items; Paul adores this store because he says it reminds him of my living room. That's a polite way of saying this store is crammed with fun junk. Many items with monkey or animal themes. The other shop has more of a country look and features garden and outdoor furniture. This is one of those New York cutie-pie stores that all the magazines feature and that everyone oohs and aahs over and that you just have to see even if you don't buy anything.

MASS PLUS CLASS

Perhaps the biggest change in the social and design scene in New York is that good design at low prices has not only become readily available, but almost de rigueur in every economic bracket. A few years ago, the middle class trekked to New Jersey to save tax and shop Ikea.

ABC CARPET & HOME
888 Broadway at 19th St.

ABC WAREHOUSE OUTLET
1055 Bronx River Ave., the Bronx

If you've ever doubted that retail is theater, you haven't been to ABC Carpet & Home. There are two stores across the street from each other; the main store has been redone into a showpiece that will make your jaw drop open the first time you wander in.

ABC sells a whole lot more than carpet—they sell a lifestyle look. The street floor is almost an emporium of goods with things for the home, for kids, for gifts, and even an Origins boutique. Upstairs there's carpets on one floor, sheets on another, fabrics on another. The thought that this is a discounter pervades, although frankly, I find the prices high. I don't think they know the meaning of the word discount here. They do know the meaning of the words *style, selection,* and *serendipity.* But wait. Paul, my resident interior designer, says he has seen Ralph Lauren fabrics here (current fabrics, no less) for less than in the D&D building. So sue me! There are discounts. Just don't assume there are bargains and then you won't be mad at me.

BED, BATH & BEYOND
620 Ave. of the Americas at 19th St.

Beyond is right—this place is almost beyond comprehension. I've seen stores in my life, but this one is amazing—it takes up the space of almost an entire city block.

This is one of Manhattan's first superstores and it is crammed with stuff, I mean packed, with plastics, with sheets, with bath towels, with everything in the world you can imagine. It's not unlike suburban branches of this national chain except for the size and grandeur of the structure. Still, you've gotta see this to believe it. Yes, they have kitchen items, too.

First-time apartment dwellers: This is a major resource.

CHAMBERS COMPANY STORE
1451 Second Ave. at 76th St.

Markdowns from the lush bed and bath catalog.

CRATE & BARREL
660 Madison Ave. at 60th St.

Chicago is no second city when it comes to exporting its most famous store to Madison Avenue. Although I have trouble telling the difference between merchandise from Pottery Barn and Crate & Barrel, there's no question that Crate & Barrel has taken Madison Avenue by storm and created almost as much excitement as Barney's did when it opened up here a few years back.

In case you are not familiar with this store or the very concept, it's very simple: Crate & Barrel is The Gap for your home.

There are two floors filled with merchandise, gifts, furniture, and a total lifestyle look. More important, the lifestyle seems perfectly fitted to the times and the places New Yorkers inhabit (be it city apartments or country weekend retreats) and the prices are considered bargains. The walls are covered in pine, the displays are great, the salespeople are friendly, you pay with some sort of newfangled electronic device that is a hoot. Most things cost less than $25. You've never had so much fun in your life.

I wanted very much to hate this store. I wanted very much to be bored. I wanted it to be just like its store on Michigan Avenue in Chicago so I could say, "You've seen it already." The truth is, this store is dynamite; this store is the backbone of the new Madison Avenue. Bravo, Mr. Segal, you've created a new landmark for New York.

DOOR STORE
1 Park Ave. at 33rd St.; 123 W. 17th St.

The Door Store sells a whole lot more than doors; in fact, we haven't noticed that they sell doors at all. They should be called the Chair Store because they sell a fabulous unpainted Chinese Chippendale dining chair (with or without arms) for about $169 that is one of the best buys in mass furniture and style. There's more. They also have a store in Secaucus that has a room of discounted leftovers that may appeal. Many branches in Manhattan.

ETHAN ALLEN
1107 Third Ave. at 65th St.; 192 Lexington Ave. at 32nd St.

Reproduction furniture that has been popular in suburban areas for ages is now making a big splash in Manhattan with several large new showrooms. Paul and I are both cringing even as we tell you this. The look is country and/or colonial in various woods and veneers and the specialty is complete suites—bedroom sets and/or dining room sets. But then you can buy a whole living room, too. We'd rather buy from flea markets, but you might like brand-new. Suit yourself.

GRACIOUS HOME
1220 Third Ave. at 71st St.; 1217 Third Ave. at 71st St.

Hardware, bed linens, vacuum cleaners, paint, electrical supplies, wallpaper, and everything else you could possibly need as you renovate, restore, or redo your home or apartment. Prices are in keeping with regular retail in Manhattan, but most people don't mind because of the selection. Two stores across the street from each other. Open 7 days.

IKEA
Exit 13A, New Jersey Turnpike, Elizabeth, New Jersey; Exit 41S, Long Island Expressway (or Exit 35S, Northern State Parkway), Hicksville, New York

Ikea is a Swedish design firm that is famous for its knock-down furniture—that means everything comes in a flat box and you build it. Prices are also knocked down, and while the furniture won't last a lifetime, it's great for a first apartment, a kids' room, or an office. There's bus service from the Port Authority in Manhattan.

RESTORATION HARDWARE
935 Broadway at 22nd St.

I wish I could rave about this store the way many people do. I like the gimmick of the personal descriptions of each item; I find the merchandise very bland and so much like Pottery Barn meets Williams-Sonoma with a dash of Archie McPhee that I just don't even know how these people stay in business, let alone thrive. Still, this is a strong resource for stuff for your home.

SIMON'S HARDWARE
421 Third Ave. at 29th St.

Paul gives us this professional source where anyone can shop; they specialize in doorknobs.

THE TERRENCE CONRAN SHOP
415 E. 59th St.

This store has a saga that is almost as big as the selling space; it took ages to get the approvals needed to build under the 59th Street Bridge (Queensboro Bridge; Feelin' Groovy Bridge) and to open the BridgeMarket and the surrounding Conran celebrations. Never you mind; take the cross-town bus. The point is to be more cutting edge than Crate & Barrel but not too expensive. After all, half the Yuppies in New York live in the surrounding blocks.

The store has an enormous restaurant, Gustavino, and about 25,000 square feet of selling space. Worth the trip—another of the best new stores in New York. Why are the good ones imported?

BIG NAMES IN TABLETOP

BACCARAT
625 Madison Ave. at 58th St.

BERNARDAUD/LIMOGES
499 Park Ave. at 59th St.

BUCCELLATI
46 E. 57th St.

CARTIER
653 Fifth Ave. at 52nd St.

CHRISTOFLE
680 Madison Ave. at 62nd St.

DAUM
694 Madison Ave. at 62nd St.

HOYA
450 Park Ave. at 57th St.

LALIQUE
680 Madison Ave. at 61st St.

ORREFORS
58 E. 57th St.

PUIFORCAT
811 Madison Ave. at 68th St.

ROYAL COPENHAGEN/GEORG JENSEN
683 Madison Ave. at 61st St.

STUEBEN
667 Madison Ave. at 60th St.

TIFFANY & CO.
727 Fifth Ave. at 57th St.

VILLEROY & BOCH
974 Madison Ave. at 68th St.

TRENDSETTERS IN GIFTS & TABLETOP

ADRIEN LINFORD
1320 Madison Ave. at 93rd St.; 927 Madison Ave. at 73rd St.

Paul says that much of the merchandise in gifts, tabletop, and rich-lady necessities he sees here is also at Barney's. They must be doing something right because they've just opened a new shop in the thick of the Euro-shopping on Madison.

AVVENTURA
463 Amsterdam Ave. at 83rd St.

West Side chic in a store specializing in the best of Italian modern design and tabletop. Closed Saturday but open Sunday.

BARNEY'S
660 Madison Ave. at 62nd St.

A marvelous store and a boon to Madison Avenue, but most of all, a fabulous gift and tabletop resource; don't miss Chelsea Passage.

BERGDORF GOODMAN
754 Fifth Ave. at 58th St.

The seventh floor is the only stop you'll need if you want to get a quick survey of elegant choices for your home. This floor has beautiful china, linens, and stationery, but we visit for the nooks and crannies filled with the best-bought wonders of the world—from hand-painted dinner napkins sprinkled with gold dust, to Venetian glass swizzle sticks.

The Christmas goodies are a must-see each year.

Kentshire of London has a shop here for antiques. Some sale products are hidden in small corners; ask. Paul says the new Barney's puts them to shame. I still like it here, but he's yawning.

MacKENZIE & CHILDS
824 Madison Ave. at 69th St.

This is a small design firm from Vermont that has its own very special shop on Madison Avenue selling hand-painted everything. There's more than tabletop, but you get the idea. True innovators and *créateurs*. It's a look, but *ooh la la*.

Anyone who has ever dreamed of coming to New York to see the best and most brilliant of American talent has got to step into this store to soak up the genius and the glory. You probably can't afford to buy more than a doorknob. But what a doorknob.

"REAL PEOPLE" TABLETOP

The only resource you really need for tabletop, whatever your budget, is the new Crate & Barrel. But if you're looking for a few other resources, well, New York's got more. And the more the merrier.

PIER ONE
461 Fifth Ave. at 40th St.

Imports from the world of inexpensive, Indian-made clothing and fashions offer high style at low prices. A one-stop supermarket of wicker for your beach house, furnishings for your first apartment, or your kid's room. The Fifth Avenue store is a little jazzier than many suburban branches and offers a bit more in the way of gift items rather than big pieces. Great gift wraps around holiday season.

POTTERY BARN
100 Seventh Ave. at 16th St.; 250 W. 57th St.; 117 E. 59th St.

Can they stay in business now that Crate & Barrel is in town? Only time will tell. Maybe they'll open up a superstore on 57th St. They've already got space on West 57th St. Hmmm. And they do have an outlet store in New York. So they are contenders. And racing to catch up.

Whenever I need Christmas gifts in the $10 range, this is my first look-see. Aside from their Christmas specialties, there are paint supplies for would-be spongers and a host of coffee mugs, plates and platters, dishes and serving pieces, candlesticks, and giftables. Add to the resource list for beach homes and first apartments. Great stuff.

WILLIAMS-SONOMA
110 Seventh Ave. at 16th St.; 1175 Madison Ave. at 86th St.; 20 E. 60th St.

Since it is more cooking and cookware oriented, this national chain probably will not be as hurt by Crate & Barrel. Housewares, cookware, gourmet foodstuffs, and tabletop are the specialty. It has national bridal registration and a large mail-order business. Located in many suburban malls as well. Note they are moving into the **Grande Cuisine** mode with their stores.

TABLETOP FINDS

FISHS EDDY
889 Broadway at 19th St.; 531 Hudson St.; 2176 Broadway

See page 106 for the dish on all the dishes at Fishs Eddy. Great first stop for dishes for those starting out in their first apartment, if you're into restaurant supply and funky styles.

FORTUNOFF
681 Fifth Ave. at 54th St.

Similar to Fina but not really a discounter. Check out silver, tabletop, china, dishes, and even Swatch watches; a good place to see it all, to register for it all, to drool over it all.

MICHAEL C. FINA
545 Fifth Ave. (on the second floor) at 46th St.

New townhouse–like feel to fancy digs. All major china, crystal, and silver lines are discounted here—Lenox, Val St. Lambert, Wedgwood, Spode, Noritake, Royal Doulton, and more. The jewelry counter is boring, but the gift shopping is tremendous fun. On a price-by-price basis, Fina may not always offer you the best prices in the world. But for $15 to $25 wedding gifts, and for $13 teachers' Christmas presents, look no further. Call ☎ 800/223-6589 to reorder by phone.

FACTORY OUTLETS IN TOWN

···

PORTICO OUTLET STORE
231 Tenth Ave. at 24th St.

Originally the Pottery Barn outlet, this has been taken over by Portico—the upscale sheets, bed, and bath retailers with digs in SoHo and some fancy burbs and around Manhattan. Prices at the outlet are normal; the stores are very expensive.

OK, so the neighborhood isn't the greatest, but this is really part of the new Chelsea. Cab it and don't look back. If you see no taxis upon departure, ask the store to call for you. Or hop a bus to your favorite cross street. Do not shop this area after dark. Possible source for the first apartment, but don't buy too quickly.

THE BIG NAMES IN LINENS

···

FRETTE
799 Madison Ave. at 67th St.

Fine and fancy Italian linen. They also have introduced a lingerie line, so you have something to wear between their fancy sheets.

PORTHAULT
18 E. 69th St.

The most expensive beds in America probably are dressed in Porthault prints from France—a set of king-size sheets with standard cases is well over $1,500. If you have lots of pillows (who doesn't?) and like the shams with scalloped and hand-cut ruffles, figure another $300 a pillowcase. There are Porthault made-in-America designs for Wamsutta, but the really fancy stuff from France is here. Every January the store still has a half-price markdown spree. There are less expensive knickknacks, by the way, and we know some women who treat themselves to one pillowcase a year. As time goes by, they have a delightful mélange of Porthault prints, which they mix with white sheets (always a style classic) and American quilts, and the look is stunning.

PRATESI
829 Madison Ave. at 69th St.

More fine Italian linen. This is the line that advertises that most of Europe's royalty was conceived in its sheets. Not bad, huh. A basic sheet set does costs more than $1,000 (but of course), but then, it's less expensive than Porthault.

Pratesi also has numerous styles that are suitable for the man who doesn't want to be in a bed of roses or a scattering of hearts.

There are twice-a-year sales.

SCHWEITZER'S LINENS
1132 Madison Ave. at 84th St.; 457 Columbus Ave. at 81st St.

This shop has no discount sheets, nor does it have average sheets. Everything is either the special high-end line of a major sheet company (like the Royal Collection or the Versailles Collection) or a European sheet made to look like an even more expensive European sheet. The only Porthault look-alikes we've ever seen come from this shop.

Its small stores feel European and cater to a well-off local crowd that wants top-of-the-line quality. There is a catalog, and they do custom work. A few designer prints are available, but the mainstream here is the subtle print (stripes, dots, bows, flowers) and the European look.

KITCHEN CONCEPTS

••

BRIDGE KITCHENWARE CORPORATION
214 E. 52nd St.

Calling all cooks—this is the favorite address of professional chefs in Manhattan. Whatever kitchen utensils you may need, they will have them.

BROADWAY PANHANDLER
477 Broome, SoHo

This housewares store seems ordinary enough at first, but it has moved into the local legend level and now has new digs to please its regulars. Check out the selection of Wilton cake supplies and professional equipment for fancy baking. Also known for great prices on its equipment.

Please note this is a new address.

DEAN & DELUCA
560 Broadway, SoHo

There may not be a more "in" place in SoHo than Dean & Deluca. This upscale grocery store, greengrocer, and cookware store has the beautiful people (and a coffee counter where you can stare at them) and the beautiful fruit and prices to match. We love it here and insist you visit, but we must warn you that we first spotted pastel-colored (pink, blue, yellow, and lavender) pasta here at $7.98 a pound, but hours later we found the same stuff at an uptown gourmet deli for $1.99 a pound!

HOLD EVERYTHING
1311 Second Ave. at 68th St.

Another division of the Pottery Barn/Williams-Sonoma people, this store sells containers, shelving, and gadgets for kitchen and closet and more. They have several Manhattan locations, and a catalog business.

J. B. Price
36 E. 31st St.

Ever since Patricia Wells started me baking tarte tartin because she found the perfect pan for me, I've understood that the equipment does matter. If you're serious, this is a professional source.

Lechter's
475 Fifth Ave. at 41st St.; 250 W. 57th; 2151 Broadway at 75th St.; and many, many more

For more moderate prices and a gigantic selection of kitchen gadgets and housewares, try this store. Rather an old-timer at American malls, where it has been supplying suburban homes with housewares for years, Lechter's is taking Manhattan by the zester and opening up in every neighborhood. Headquarters for setting up the first apartment or second home.

HOME FURNISHINGS, FABRICS & YARD GOODS

See the section on regular fabrics in chapter 7 and take a look at the small shops clustered on East 20th and East 19th St. near Broadway (around the corner from ABC Carpet & Home). Of the various jobbers, **Beckenstein** is the best known; note that they have moved out of the Lower East Side.

Paterson Silks
36 E. 14th St.; 152 E. 86th St.; 151 W. 72nd St.; and many other locations throughout the five boroughs; mail order:
☎ *800/522-5671*

This is pretty funky and you need a bit of a sense of humor. These guys are mass purveyors of fabrics, curtains, slipcovers, and even fashion fabrics (and patterns). You never know what will turn up on a bolt here. Last time I stopped by, the selection made my skin crawl. After I got used to the stock, and adjusted my sights, I realized there were a lot of simple basics at very good prices. Call the number above for their mail-order service.

SILK SURPLUS
1147 Madison Ave. at 85th St.

Even though it's not a warehouse filled with discount fabrics for the home, this small space does have a number of choices. Among the better buys are the trims. Everything is on a bolt; the sales help is pretty knowledgeable if you ask for direct help. They have several branches around town, as well as their own "boutique" in ABC Carpet & Home.

SOHO CHIC

SoHo is famous for its design stores and the inspiration it can give you. Lately, several furniture stores and furniture makers have moved into the area. There are other sections in the book about SoHo, but here are some of the top design resources. You'll find others as you prowl. Note that more and more lifestyle stores sell a look that covers clothing and home decor. One of my favorite SoHo sources, Yaso, has just added on a home furnishings line.

BARTON SHARPE LTD.
119 Spring St.

If country is your look, then pack your nightie and toothbrush and simply move into this showroom for Shaker-inspired, handcrafted repro furniture. To die for.

GEORGE SMITH
73 Spring St.

Famous for his big, comfy furniture upholstered in kilim fabrics. Perfect for living rooms or dens. English, but they know all about sample sales. One of the best resources for cozy classics.

PORTICO
379 W. Broadway

PORTICO BED & BATH
139 Spring St.

These are two different stores in two different locations around the corner from each other. Both are spacious and gracious. I adore the Bed & Bath space. The home decor store has a rustic Italian feel that mixes with country French, Early American, and even some Arts and Crafts looks.

SHABBY CHIC
See page 218.

TERRE VERDE
120 Wooster St.

Environmentally aware store of home, patio, garden, and even body products. Also lots of bed and bath goods. And, of course, aromatherapy.

WOLFMAN-GOLD & GOOD CO.
116 Greene St.

The table settings make you want to snap Polaroids so you can go home and do it yourself. Class, style, and inspiration, all in one shop. Prices are not low. Don't miss the downstairs alcove.

ZONA
97 Greene St.

This long, narrow store has changed its subtext so that instead of being as Southwestern/Santa Fe as it once was, it now feels a little more country and even European. There are fabulous gift items, a wide range of prices (many items cost $6), ecologically inspired bath soaps, tableware, and more. A very special place.

FLEA MARKETS

Just because you buy it at a flea market does not mean it's a bargain or the price is any better than in a store. Know your prices and comparative values, and keep in mind:

- Most markets are held on weekends; read the fine print carefully, as a few are only held on one day.
- Markets that are held outdoors are held "weather permitting," which means no market in a downpour or when it's freezing.
- Some of the markets do not operate on the weekend between Christmas and New Year's.
- Cash is preferred, especially if you are bargaining.
- Buy with the understanding that this is alternative retail—vendors may tell you any old hogwash in order to get you to buy. We've heard "antiques" vendors say some outrageous (false) things about their wares. Be careful.

There are special-event flea markets, such as the **Pier Shows,** which are sensational, especially when money is tight and dealers want to raise cash. Watch the trade newspapers for announcements of these shows and other markets. See page 236 for more on **Brimfield,** the king of the flea markets.

THE ANNEX ANTIQUES FAIR & FLEA MARKET
6th Ave. and 26th St.

This is one of the best in terms of getting the adrenaline running and the heart pumping fast for a few hours of shopping fun. I must warn you, however, that this place has long been discovered, that it's "in," that prices can be very high, that vendors may not know their stuff. The crowd that shops, however, is as much fun as the dealers and the goods. There's also the chance that it will all go away some day since the real estate is so valuable.

On Saturday there is an outdoor market in two parking lots; on Sunday there is an outdoor market in three lots. There is a $1 admission charge to the main lot only.

On Saturdays and Sundays there is an additional indoor market called **Metropolitan Arts & Antiques Pavilion** at 110 W. 19th St. Hours are 9am to 5pm. The market has free admission and is near the outdoor street market. There are more markets on West 25th St., one of which is in a garage and therefore called Garage Market.

ANTIQUE FLEA & FARMERS MARKET: P.S. 183
E. 67th St. between First Ave. and York Ave.

Don't waste your time.

BRIMFIELD
Held three times per year in May, July, and September. For the dates of the market call the Brimfield market office at
☎ *413/245-3436 or 508/597-8155*

We have done this as a day trip because we are nuts, because it's not quite as long a schlepp from Connecticut, and because it is such a zoo that if you aren't organized, you won't be able to find a hotel room anyway. But here goes: The country's wildest flea market is held three times a year in a small Massachusetts community (near Sturbridge Village) called Brimfield. About 50,000 people show up for each of the three events, which last a week each. The May fair is the most popular, but all three are worthwhile for dealers and pros. If you aren't quick-witted, you'll be trampled to death!

Pros are there when the gates open at 7am and run around like maniacs papering the place with money. We just go for the day and don't do it that way, but you should experiment and find your own style.

Please note that there are several areas where the flea markets are held, and that it really does take most of the week to do this properly, the way a dealer should. Thousands of dealers from all over the country will be in Brimfield for the event; this is truly the largest flea market in the world. Remember, the event lasts 10 days, but most fields are only open 3 days.

Book motel rooms way in advance if you are staying over. Leave the kids at home.

THE CHELSEA ANTIQUES BUILDING
110 W. 25th St.; open daily

This building has 12 floors of stuff to handle and please the crowds swarming to the Annex market (and demanding more). It's a lifetime commitment just to do this one source. Amen. What a way to go.

THE GARAGE
112 W. 25th St.; open Monday through Friday

The Garage offers space to 150 additional dealers.

P.S. 41
Greenwich Ave. between Sixth and Seventh aves.; Saturdays only

This is a schoolyard extravaganza complete with green market. It gets going late; don't arrive before 11am. Part of the glory of the Village.

P.S. 44 FLEA MARKET
Columbus Ave. between 76th and 77th sts.; Sunday only, from 10am to 5:30pm

This is a very varied market with several parts to it so that as a whole it's got something for everyone. There's a small green market—don't miss the pretzels—and there's both an outdoor and an indoor portion.

The outdoor portion is as large as the schoolyard and brimming with colors and energy and fun. There's a large percentage of people who seem to have just returned from some exotic destination and have set up a booth to offer folk ware from wherever they traveled (Ecuador, Mexico, Bali); there's a small percentage of new and basic merchandise (socks, underwear, pet needs). You'll find lots of arts and crafts and, of course, traditional flea-market fare like "antiques." Nothing beats a gorgeous day, a hot pretzel, some money in your hand, and all this color, style, and energy.

Inside the school is a jumble of tables and "antiques"— I get claustrophobic from it all. I'm happy enough with the antiques and used treasures sold outside; on a pretty day it seems like a sin to be indoors. The throngs don't agree with me.

ROOSEVELT RACEWAY FLEA MARKET
Westbury, NY; Wednesday and Sunday 9am to 3pm,; closed for the winter season

I was once heartbroken to give up California and the Rose Bowl Swap Meet. But now I know about the Roosevelt Raceway Flea Market, in Westbury, New York.

The Roosevelt Raceway Flea Market is a full-day trip. Ideally, plan to go with some friends and rent a truck. You can go on the train (from Penn Station, take the Long Island Railroad to Westbury). You can take a city bus or a taxi or even walk to the raceway from the train station. But you'll need to call a cab for getting back to the train, you will be so loaded with packages.

Although the market is held rain or shine and there is indoor space, the event just isn't as much fun in the rain. On sunny days, about 1,500 vendors set up in the parking lot to sell an assortment of everything. Most of it is new—there are no antiques here—and some of it is designer quality. This is where I've bought T-shirts ($5 each), name-brand luggage (Lucas), clothes for Aaron for camp, stationery, wrapping paper, and brand-name shampoo and hair goo.

A few announcements: Many dealers will not take checks or credit cards; be loaded with cash or traveler's checks. The Sunday event feels entirely different from the Wednesday event—there are about 25% more vendors on Sunday, and they are different; it's a more commercial fair those days—not quite so warm and neighborly as on Wednesday. Remember sunscreen or a hat in summer—it can be brutally hot out there. The bathrooms are clean; there are several snack bars for hot dogs, etc. Admission fee is by carload: 50¢ on Wednesday, $1 on Sunday.

SoHo Antique & Flea Market
465 Broadway; Saturdays and Sundays from 9am to 5pm

This is the funkiest of the Manhattan markets—much more like a tag sale than the others, much more casual. Held in a parking lot, the market is "antiques" with an emphasis on vintage clothing, used cameras, and so on. Not worth going out of your way to visit, but nice as part of a SoHo spree.

Tower Records Flea Market
Broadway between 4th St. and Great Jones; Saturday and Sunday from 10am to 7pm

This isn't so much a flea market as a happening for teens. It's a tiny market in a narrow parking lot next to the record store, but it is so undeniably hip that it is the essence of NoHo, SoHo, the East Village, and all that New York youth ever meant to be.

The market can be so jammed that it may make you uncomfortable; if you have a middle-aged mind-set, stay away. All the merchandise is new; there's an emphasis on T-shirts with smart-aleck sayings, ethnic inspirations, tight blue jeans, non-team baseball caps, watches, and homemade jewelry.

Yonkers Raceway Flea Market
Sunday only, from 9am to 4pm. (No flea market when major events are held at the Raceway.)

This is almost as good as the flea market at the Rose Bowl in Pasadena, California. Collectibles shows are also held here, so one weekend we took in baseball cards, jewels, and minerals, as well as the swap meet. Held outdoors on the upper level of the parking lot, weather permitting. More than 200 vendors participate.

AUCTIONS FOR ART & ANTIQUES

There's a war going on in them thar sale rooms, so stay tuned. **Christie's,** hoping to ease past **Sotheby's** and get more business, has lowered the seller's premium. The world waits with bated breath to see who sneezes next.

For buying art, antiques, collectibles, or fancy junk, auctions are a good training ground. If you study catalogs, go to viewings, eavesdrop on conversations, and attend enough auctions, you will become knowledgeable not only in the art of auctioning, but also in the nuances of the items you collect and of those who also collect them.

There are two types of auction houses: big time and fun time. They never get the same kinds of lots; each big-time house has a more casual division.

Things go to auction for two reasons: One, a collector has decided to give up a piece or pieces of his collection; or two, a collector has died and the estate needs to liquidate the assets. Country auctions usually are the best places to find overlooked pieces. These auctions are advertised in local papers as well as in *Antiques and the Arts Weekly,* published by Bee Publishing Company (☎ 203/426-8036) in Newtown, Connecticut. (If you're looking for something more serious to keep you up on the latest of auctions, get a subscription to *Art & Auction,* a glossy magazine dedicated to those who care.)

Previews (also called viewings or exhibitions) are very important and occur the week before the auction. During the auction there is no time to think or change your mind. You must know ahead of time if you are going to bid on a piece; you can even send in a sealed bid or fax your bid ahead of time.

During previews it is important to think about the following questions:

- Are there provenance papers on the item (which give the history of ownership)? All quality pieces of furniture and art will have them.

- What is the condition of the item? How many repairs have been done to the legs? Can you tell if anything has been replaced? Has the piece been refinished recently, and if so, by whom? Can you ask the owner for details? Usually the answer is no. In this case you might consider hiring a consultant to look at the piece for you.
- Can you guarantee authenticity? Provenance helps, of course. We need not tell you about all the fakes that have gone through the auction houses. Quality houses will authenticate as best they can, but even they get fooled sometimes. Authentications will be found in the catalog listing. If nothing is listed, ask why. Very often the auction house cannot risk giving a guarantee unless there is no question as to the origin of the item. We once attended an auction where the auctioneer asked the artist to stand up and authenticate her work of art in person.

Once you leave the preview, take the catalog home and read the fine print. Everything you need to know about how the auction will be run and what the house is responsible for handling is in the front or back of the catalog.

Check to see if the piece you will be bidding on is "subject to reserve." Reserve is the minimum price for which the piece will be sold. It is a confidential price known only to the auction house and owner. However, it is important for you to know if you will be bidding against this price. Sometimes the piece will be taken off the block if the reserve is not met. Sometimes the house will bid on behalf of the consignee to meet the reserve.

Tucked into the catalog, or on the final pages of the book, will be a list of prices for the lot numbers that show what a similar item went for at a previous date, or what the house estimates the sale price to be. This means nothing, but it can give you an idea of where to expect the bidding to fall. One of the reasons auctions are so much fun is that you never know what really will happen—it could go either way.

Once you have done your homework and decided to attend the auction to bid on one or more "lots," there are a few more details:

You may be asked to register when you arrive at the auction house. If the auction involves high-stakes items and you are going to be bidding above $10,000, bring credit references with you. Once you have registered you will be given a "paddle" with your bidding number on it. This number corresponds to your registration. During the auction, names are never used. Lots are assigned to the highest bidder's number.

Don't be shy when bidding. If the auctioneer can't see your paddle, you will lose out on the bidding. Everything you've heard about sneezes, flicks of the wrist, or eyebrow arching is nonsense. While some people bid in a subtle motion, everyone does know what's going on—even if paddles aren't being used.

If you can't be present at the auction, you can name a representative to bid for you, or be on the phone with a member of the auction-house staff. It is also possible to bid by mail. Absentee bid forms are published in the auction catalog, or can be obtained from the auction house by mail.

When figuring price, don't forget to add in the auction-house commission and the tax. Ask ahead of time what the auction house will be taking as its cut. If you thought the price you bid was the price paid, welcome to the cruel world. The auction house gets from 10% to 20% of the sale price. If you are bidding on a large item, figure in the cost of delivery also. The auction houses all have services to help you, but they are not free.

Payment will be asked for at the time of the sale, unless you have an account with the house or have arranged ahead of time to be invoiced. All large auction houses preregister bidders and check references.

Payment for goods will be asked for in American dollars. Although you will see prices being quoted on the currency board in many foreign currencies as the bidding is taking place, it is merely for the convenience of the foreign clientele to compare the price in dollars with their currency. On small items you often can pay with American Express, Visa, or MasterCard.

If you are planning on shipping your purchase out of the country, be sure to obtain an export permit. As in European countries, some items may not be exportable. Check with a U.S. Customs expert in this area.

You will be expected to take possession of your purchase within 3 working days. After that time you will be charged a storage fee.

You need to read the *New York Times* Thursday "Home" section for listings of weekly events. Also check ads in the Friday *Times* and perhaps the Saturday *Times*.

If you are observing but aren't planning to buy, you may be a tad nervous. Relax. You're welcome here, even if you don't bid. Dress like you own a bank, and you'll be fine. Admission to a big-time event is always by catalog (the catalog admits two)—pay for the catalog at the desk before the preview or right before the actual auction or subscribe. Prices range from $2 to $25. Half a catalog does not admit one.

Many big-time auctions are star-studded events and may be black tie. A collection of important jewels, by the way, does have a viewing, but the bidding is done with slides on a screen, as if it were home-movie night. Remember to keep your cool when the really big rocks are screened. Previews are far more casual than auctions; you may even attend in blue jeans, as long as you are wearing Gucci loafers with them. It is better to have been to the preview, but it's not imperative if you are not planning on buying. You will see the items much better at the preview, and can touch many of them. This is a no-no during the auction.

Should you be planning on buying for the first time in the big time, you may want to walk through it all at an auction that is not yours, just to get the lay of the land. There's no reason to be intimidated or unduly nervous when you will have enough on your mind spending your trust fund on a piece of canvas and oil paint.

CHRISTIE'S
Rockefeller Center, ☎ *718/784-1480*

CHRISTIE'S EAST
219 E. 67th St.

Christie's is in hot contention with Sotheby's to be number one and has, in fact, scored enough coups to probably be number one these days. I mean, did you get a load of that Princess Diana stuff a while back? Christie's is a British firm; Sotheby's is based in the United States. People who shop big-time auctions do not prefer one house to the other; they merely choose the auction they are interested in. The difference between the two houses is probably inside, behind closed doors, and is possibly in how they woo potential customers and their estates. Both houses will treat you and your money with equal charm or disdain, depending on your money and your manners. There's a 10% buyer's premium. Call the number above to request a catalog.

Christie's East sometimes sells goods that are less fancy than those sold at the main branch.

PHILLIPS FINE ART AUCTIONEERS
406 E. 79th St.

Phillips is an international auction house of the same caliber as Christie's and Sotheby's. With offices around the world, they are able to acquire lots of good-quality items, some with incredible pedigrees representing centuries of ostentatious buying or conservative wealth poured discreetly into fabulous collections. It is also possible to participate in their European auctions without going abroad.

SOTHEBY'S
1334 York Ave. at 72nd St.

Sotheby's is the world's "other" famous auction house, leading the ranks along with Christie's. They publish a catalog for all sales, national and international. You can subscribe to the catalogs that deal only with your collecting mania (painting, pre-Columbian, furniture, and so on), which is a wonderful way to keep up with the international market in your area.

Sotheby's experts are available for consultation to both buyers and sellers. (Other auction houses also provide this service.) If you have a piece of art that you think is worthy of being put up for auction, you can make an appointment to bring it in or have an expert visit you. I've fallen in love with a few of their experts; they know their stuff and are really fun to be with—especially when you share a common interest.

Sotheby's people make periodic trips to major cities around the country. Their visits are advertised in the local newspapers the week before they arrive; they also have representatives in most of the major cities in the United States.

Sotheby's Arcade Auctions are for those of us who love to buy but can't yet afford an old master. These sales are well within the affordable range and often involve surprise packages. Lots are sometimes sold in groups.

Yes, Sotheby's does have a sidewalk sale when they mark down the unsold items and clear house. The most fun you'll have in years.

SWANN GALLERIES
104 E. 24th St.

Specialists in books and paper goods, movie posters, and ephemera, this upstairs location is low key and funky. Go upstairs in the elevator, don't panic when you see the neighborhood. There's a 10% buyer's premium. Tepper Galleries is at street level; no, I'm not mixed up—Swann is upstairs. And you'll be thrilled when you get there.

WILLIAM DOYLE GALLERIES
175 E. 87th St.

They try to acquire some unusual items not seen in the other houses, and are not quite as intimidating to us as the big-timers. They certainly are more tony than others listed in this category. Doyle's has important auctions and must get your equal attention if you are a serious shopper; but snobs will tell you it just isn't Christie's.

HOITY-TOITY ANTIQUES: THE UPPER EAST SIDE

The Upper East Side is home to the best of the best. If you are looking for a Ming vase, Empire chairs, a Federal hutch, or a Louis sofa and have a well-endowed checkbook, go no farther. These shops are superb in both quality and selection. The owners are knowledgeable and willing to help you find what you are in search of. They will authenticate and help you ship.

Most hoity-toity shops are specialists; many require an appointment and are not even open to the public. (I haven't listed any of those, thank-you.) Seek and ye shall find; shop and ye shall spend. If you are buying, dress however you please. If you are browsing, please look the part and dress up in respect for the artworks and the dealers.

Not to Be Missed

This one is in a category by itself and is one of those "Gee, Toto" kinds of places. They do not have one of these in your hometown, and we don't care where you come from.

NEWEL GALLERIES
425 E. 53rd St.; Monday through Friday, 9am to 5pm

Shocking and wonderful and weird and fabulous and incredible and not to be believed and, well, you just have to go see this for yourself. Newel is an antiques resource of extraordinary proportions. Many pieces are for rent; all are one of a kind. Every variety of antique can be found somewhere in the vast recesses of the six floors of warehouse space. You have to experience Newel to appreciate its unusual nature. If you think this is a pass, you get us wrong. This is theater. This is what you came to New York for.

Specialty Dealers (Open to the Public)

AGES PAST ANTIQUES
450 E. 78th St.

Specializes in blue and white transfer ware, and while I can hardly afford any of this, it is heaven to look.

AMERICA HURRAH
766 Madison Ave.

Quilts, samplers, and hooked rugs are their specialty.

DE LORENZO
958 Madison Ave.

They call it "Twentieth-Century Decorative Arts": art deco, art nouveau, Giacometti chairs. Ah, the things money can buy.

DIDIER AARON
32 E. 67th St.

Important European furniture, mostly French. The New York showroom doesn't look like much from outside, but never judge a book by its cover.

MINNA ROSENBLATT
844 Madison Ave.

Art deco and art nouveau lamps and other items. Tiffany and such.

NOT QUITE HOITY OR TOITY BUT FANCY

In the last few decades, East 60th St. in the 200 block has been many things. Lately, aside from housing a resale shop called Transfer, the area is home to a large number of antiques shops selling mostly Continental antiques not of the

Lord-Rothschild-is-pleased category, but far above the flea market and garden variety.

There are almost two dozen dealers here, so the best thing to do is to walk and wander. Begin at Antiques on 60th (no. 207) and make your way up—a few shops are to the trade only.

And Don't Forget

MANHATTAN ARTS & ANTIQUES CENTER
1050 Second Avenue at 56th St.; 10:30am to 6pm; Sundays noon to 6pm

About 100 dealers with this and that, open daily. I have bought here and used to come here often; now I prefer tag sales and flea markets. These are dealers and they do know what they've got.

NOT-SO-FANCY ANTIQUES

You don't have to grow up in Versailles to want to buy antiques. Even if your budget is limited, you still can find enough selection and specialty items to make the trip worthwhile. Recent college grads and young professionals take note: You can have your cake and eat it, too.

Enjoy Madison Avenue and the East Side and all the gilt trips you can stand, but take your checkbook when you travel to 12th St. or to Brooklyn—these are the areas where designers go to nose through lots of stuff, hoping to find hidden jewels. The shoppers wear blue jeans or are properly dressed professionals, although Brooklyn on a weekend is decidedly laid back.

Atlantic Avenue, Brooklyn

Many of the antique shops that could no longer pay the rent in Manhattan moved to Atlantic Avenue in Brooklyn. The street is incredibly long, and houses many, many antique stores of varying quality and price range. If you're coming from Manhattan, take the F train to the Bergen Street stop. Walk back along Smith Street and turn right onto Atlantic after only 3 blocks. On weekends there's a flea-marketlike affair set up by dealers for locals.

If the F train isn't convenient, there's a big subway station for trains B, D, M, N, Q, R, 2, 3, 4, and 5 called Atlantic Ave./Pacific St./Fourth Ave./Flatbush Ave. You can also get here from Long Island on the railroad (Brooklyn Terminal). It's about 5 blocks from here to the antiques neighborhood; you can always cab it the short distance.

The greatest concentration of antique shops starts at Hoyt St. and continues along Atlantic Avenue for about 10 blocks.

University Place

Between the Village, SoHo, NoHo, and Washington Square and the nether regions of lower Manhattan, University Place is a street just filled with the fun kind of antique shops that I love to prowl. This is on the East Side of Manhattan, just below 14th St.; along with Broadway, which at this point in its life is now on the East Side and it creates its own little neighborhood.

We're talking one resource that may have six floors of great stuff. This is not the home of the $35 bed frame. But this is where affordable furniture can be yours. You should know your market if you are spending a lot of money or think you have a serious piece; otherwise, just enjoy. The area is so well combed by dealers that the diamonds get ferreted out very quickly. You may be forced to make do with rhinestones.

If this sounds like I've just told you about the funkiest little yet-to-be-discovered part of town ever created, think again. Some very sharp dealers have already moved down here and are slowly creating a gentrified zone connected to the renewal of the entire Fifth Avenue area between 23rd and 14th streets and the Gramercy Park area. And if you're the kind who only likes the high and the mighty, honey, this ain't for you. Home, James.

Chapter Ten

....

NEW YORK BARGAINS

BARGAIN CAPITAL USA

....

I don't really know why they call New York "The Big Apple"—
I think it's the Big Markdown, or maybe it's really the Big
Markup and then you have to search for the big markdown
and that's why it's so much fun. I always say it's all in the thrill
of the chase. Hmmm, this could get philosophical in a minute.
In a New York minute.

There's no question that everyone wants a bargain these
days. It makes sense that New York, with so many retail
opportunities, also has a lot of bargain opportunities. But retail
has been hard hit by the struggle for financial recovery and
retailers who have survived are a very savvy bunch. It's a lot
harder to find a real bargain and a lot easier to get taken these
days.

If you're visiting from overseas, no doubt you think New
York at regular retail is indeed a bargain mecca. Compared to
regular retail prices in Britain or France, it is. But, you haven't
been to **Woodbury Common** yet. You haven't even heard the
controversy surrounding **Jersey Gardens.** Don't know about
Filene's Basement or **Loehmann's,** which are in bankruptcy pro-
ceedings but are still open in Manhattan as we go to press. If
you're British, you probably know about **TJ Maxx,** but maybe

not. And you surely have never heard of **Century 21.** Don't even know to thank Sy Syms and his firm, **Syms,** in your nightly prayers. Read on, read on.

While there is a chapter in the beginning of this book for foreign visitors, I still urge all international visitors to New York to read this chapter and highlight the good parts. If your English is spotty, get a dictionary. This is the part where I tell you about the *gangas* (that's bargains in Spanish and, yes, it was one of the first words I learned in Spanish).

NONTRADITIONAL RETAILING

New Yorkers pride themselves on being able to get around the high cost of living with a sixth sense called "street smarts." Most New Yorkers depend on various nontraditional methods of retailing to keep up their standard of living. Even with the stock market boom and money flooding the streets, people still want a deal.

Vintage clothing continues to be popular; jewelry and accessories are frequently bought off the street or from marts that sell their low-cost wares off pegboard; trips to New Jersey for bulk shopping—yeah, yeah, I'm going to tell you all about what's going on with **Jersey Gardens** where you won't have to pay a sales tax on many items.

The entire concept of chic has changed in New York so that "Cross Shopping" has become the big phenom that the trade is talking about—shoppers will now combine their good clothes and luxury brands with items bought from catalogs, discounters, off-pricers, street vendors, and private sales—and get away with it. Go to one private pashmina party in someone's Upper West Side apartment and you're hooked forever.

DEPARTMENT STORE SECRETS

....

These days, some of America's best deals are to be found in her most famous department stores. And those are deals on everything from bed linen to Chanel. And I don't just mean No. 5. New York is the king of the department store flagships, so even if you have a branch of these stores in your hometown, you owe it to yourself—and your bottom line—to visit the Manhattan branch.

You'd be surprised at just what kinds of bargains and treats you may find in New York's department stores. Besides offering fantastic sales, look to department stores to offer promotions and customer services you just can't find anyplace else. A large department store once gave away a second strand of pearls to customers who bought one strand (a Mother's Day promotion). Cosmetics and perfume gift-with-purchases deals and giveaways are commonplace. The big thing now in this business is the extra bonus—bring in a coupon to get a free product, turn in your old lipstick and get a free new one. In New York, there might not be a free lunch but there is a free makeover. Extras are offered every place you turn in a department store.

Department stores also have restaurants, exercise studios, day spas (the newest thing), makeup artists, fashion shows, translators, shipping services, and special shoppers to coordinate choices for you if you are too busy to shop on your own. Department stores offer a kind of value not seen elsewhere.

When it comes to color, ambiance, entertainment, and cachet, a with-it department store has mouth-watering appeal. And great markdowns.

When it comes to bargains, remember that department stores have to unload merchandise just as every other retailer does. They do this through the rather staid old method we all love best: sales. But when the sale merchandise isn't all sold, what happens to it? It does not go to retail heaven. Usually it goes back to the warehouse, to be held for the annual department store warehouse sale—or to the "factory outlet store."

Yep, department stores now have factory outlets. They are all located outside of Manhattan, out of respect for regular retail, but they aren't hard to get to.

BARGAIN BASEMENTS: DISCOUNT STORES & OFF-PRICERS

You may not remember Korvettes, Fifth Avenue's first discount store, but you'll have no trouble remembering the new generation that's come to town, which includes everything from **Kmart** to **Filene's Basement.** New York is filled with bargain basements: Some are readily identifiable as such; others are secrets.

The most important thing to remember is that many places that look like bargain basements merely offer inexpensive merchandise—it may simply be cheap. Quality is everything or a bargain isn't a bargain. I delight in expensive merchandise at low, low prices. Don't you?

So what's the difference between a discounter and an off-pricer? The discounter sells some brand-name merchandise and some private-label merchandise at a 20% to 25% discount from prices in department stores. The off-pricer sometimes sells current merchandise that is gleaned from a warehouse close-out but often sells older merchandise at a deeper discount.

Target, Kmart, and **Bradlee's** are some of the more famous discounters, although Bradlee's might be leaving Manhattan soon and our Target is in the burbs. **Filene's Basement, Century 21, TJ Maxx,** and **Daffy's** are off-pricers. I actually think that Loehmann's functions as both and that they have their own special thing going.

Off-pricers offer the most savings. They usually specialize in certain categories of merchandise, such as women's or children's ready-to-wear, appliances, beds, and the like. Many off-price stores sell designer merchandise. These stores can be smaller and less fancy than discounters, or as big as a warehouse and very nicely decorated. Have you been to **Century 21** lately? The Manhattan store is as fancy as any department store. There are so many different types of off-pricers that it is impossible to suggest there is only one way of doing business.

When shopping the bargain basements, remember:

- Bargain basements may or may not have new merchandise. Some get their goods at the beginning of the season; others don't get new merchandise until stores have dumped their unsold merchandise. Old merchandise always is less expensive than new merchandise.
- Look for damages.
- Know the return policy before you buy.
- Try everything on; actual sizes may be different from the marked sizes.
- If you are shopping in a chain, understand that another branch of that chain will have some of the same merchandise and some different merchandise; the better the zip code, the better the choices. Factory outlets can have entirely different merchandise in the exact same time frame.
- Expect communal dressing rooms and sometimes primitive conditions.
- Be prepared to check your handbag and/or your shopping bags. Security can be offensively tight at a bargain basement.
- Few bargain basements mail packages for you.

Shop a department store before you get to a bargain basement. At various well-known (and listed in this book) bargain basements, I saw the same designer blouse on the same day for several different prices, with a range of more than $100. The Saks Fifth Avenue price was $230. I saw it at different outlets for $180, $163, $142, $109, and $93. It is impossible to know which bargain is the best bargain when you are shopping, but try to do a little homework first.

Some bargain basements don't have bargains. Try this notion on for size: I was just shopping at my beloved Filene's Basement where I found a truly fabulous, stunning skirt by a Belgian designer that most people in America have never heard of (and cannot pronounce her name)—the Filene's Basement price was $49. A sensational bargain. But wait: The Neiman Marcus price tag, still attached, showed all the markdown prices that Neiman's had used in order to sell this little skirt. The last price on the floor at Neiman's was $51! While both prices are great bargains, there ain't much margin here and department stores very frequently offer as good as it gets.

Let the shopper beware.

In the past, discounters and off-pricers have been fearful of Manhattan: high rents, concentration of department stores and clients to please, and sophisticated shoppers. Now, several off-pricers have had financial difficulties and may disappear from the city—but that doesn't mean you won't find bargains in the Big Apple.

Big brand-name off-pricers have struggled in Manhattan because of a system that limits what off-pricers can sell in certain areas: While off-pricers with branch stores usually distribute their high-end goods according to zip codes—wealthy zip codes get the best merchandise—Manhattan never got the same stock as other well-off cities because department stores and certain makers prohibit sales within certain areas. Thus Filene's Basement is not allowed to have its famous Brooks Brothers sale in its Manhattan stores because New York is Brooks Brothers territory.

Still, you won't go naked.

Easy Access Bargain Basements

BOLTON'S
27 W. 57th St.; 1180 Madison Ave. at 86th St.; 4 E. 34th St.

I bet I am not the only woman in New York who shops Bergdorf's and Bolton's but buys at Bolton's. Bolton's is a chain—this is where you get very serviceable fashion items for a lot less money. They claim to get big-name designers, but frankly, Scarlet, I've never seen any big-name designers at discount.

When I discuss Bolton's, I'm not talking the same quality as Filene's Basement or even the same kind of names. My best finds at Bolton's have been names in the midrange, such as Kenar, and on hats. You won't believe this, but I saw a hat similar to one shown by Karl Lagerfeld at Bolton's for $30!

There are also good standard basics.

I like the West 57th Street store, since I am most often in that neighborhood, but Bolton's shops are seemingly everywhere. The addresses listed here represent a few conveniently located stores. Check the phone book for more options.

CONWAY
1333 Broadway at 35th St.; 11 W. 34th St., 49 W. 34th St., and 225 W. 34th St.; 450 Seventh Ave. at 35th St.; 201 E. 42nd St.; 45 Broad St.

Conway has so many different branches and parts to it that to get the real flavor, you must shop at the store in the block after Macy's. The other stores are ordinary and bland and ready for prime time basic bargain basements. The store at 1333 Broadway, next to Macy's, is a real Turkish bazaar in an air-conditioned haven of tables piled high with merchandise—out-of-season, discontinued, unloved styles and designer overruns. It's the souk of your dreams, but you have to like the jumble.

There are actually more than five different branches in the same neighborhood; some are quite upscale. If you like cheap clothes for your kids, inexpensive towels for summer camp, or discounted household goods, you just might have a good time here.

Now then, for the warning: The main store is not for everyone. This is not Bendel's. This is a bargain basement in the truest sense of the word; all it lacks is basement space. Only for the strong-hearted. Its West 34th St. stores are quite average and you will wonder why the warning.

International shoppers get a discount when they show their passports at the cashier.

DAFFY'S
111 Fifth Ave. at 18th St.; 335 Madison Ave. at 44th St.; 1311 Broadway and 35th St.; 125 E. 57th St.

Daffy's does get some names sometimes and you can do rather well for yourself. For some reason or another, I always do better with men's clothing—an Alexander Feza blazer for $50; a pair of cords for $13. But wait, I have bought Armani here! Shhh! Don't tell anyone.

The store on Madison is convenient for midtown shoppers, although the downtown store is much bigger. The East 57th St. store is the most convenient for visiting tourists—and is also the fanciest and easiest to shop. The downtown store has three levels of fun with a larger men's department as well as a luggage department and much better selection of women's accessories. There are shoes for men and women.

The West Side store, near Macy's, is a many-level splendor inside a mall: It is truly overwhelming. And I am not overwhelmed easily. This branch is my least favorite.

It's very much hit or miss at Daffy's, like at all these places.

FILENE'S BASEMENT
2222 Broadway at 79th St.; 620 Ave. of Americas at 18th St.

Here's the truth about Filene's Basement—Boston stores are better because there aren't as many prohibitions against them. That doesn't mean you should ignore the New York branch stores—heaven forbid—it just means that New York can be spotty. You have to get lucky. Also, because of financial reorganization, sometimes they don't get the merchandise or brands they used to get. You may want to make a day trip to Boston's flagship to have a really good time. New York may be worth only a quick look.

Filene's Basement sells overruns and unsold designer goodies for men and women in various categories from shoes to underwear. It has a small petites department and a plus sizes department as well.

In order to raise cash, The Basement often does coupon mailings and promotions giving you 15% off; get on the mailing list!

FORMAN'S
82 Orchard St.; 59 John St., financial district; 145 E. 42nd St.; 560 Fifth Ave. at 47th St.

Forman's is one of the oldest and most established discount sources in Manhattan; for decades they were famous for their stores on the Lower East Side. While they still have a store there, this company has changed its approach and opened stores in many key shopping districts—even on Fifth Avenue!

Now then, this is tricky because I can't quite figure out the deal. The store on Fifth Avenue appears to have no discounts whatsoever. The store on East 42nd St., which is one I visit a lot, has a variety of deals and it's hard to know when to pounce.

For example, Forman's sells a lot of Jones New York, a brand I like and often buy. This brand sells trousers for $119 in all area department stores. If you can find them at Loehmann's, they sell for $89. At Forman's they cost $109—a mere $10 discount. This is not impressive, but it's something. Hmmm.

They carry brands you like—Ellen Tracy, Polo, and so on. There's also petites, coats, some accessories, and other items. End-of-season sales offer better deals; they also send out postcards to those on the mailing list giving special discounts and deals.

LOEHMANN'S
106 Seventh Ave. at 17th St.

Loehmann's has finally come to New York but is in serious financial trouble and will probably close its New York store, since it's a rather weak link. The store is clean and modern and multileveled and sells men's and women's accessories and designer stuff. You have to get very lucky to get good designer stuff.

TJ Maxx
620 Ave. of the Americas at 18th St.

This off-pricer is like a minidepartment store in that it sells a little of everything—clothing for men, women, and children, underwear, shoes, luggage, home accessories, and bed and bath products. It carries some big-name designers every now and then; I have seen DKNY.

I find the store is great for home items, dishes, picture frames, and the great gift in the $10 to $15 price range. Every now and then I luck into lingerie or a nightie or two.

It's located above a branch of **Filene's Basement,** just as it is in downtown Chicago. Comparison shop the two!

Slightly Inconvenient Sources

Aaron's
627 Fifth Ave. (17th to 18th sts.), Brooklyn

Perhaps I am partial to this store because my son is named Aaron. I think I just like it because the bargains are very nice. Paul and I recently took off a day to shop several bargain basements in order to compare merchandise, selection, ambience, service, and schlepp. Therefore, with some authority I can say, if you are only going to go out of your way for one resource, this is it.

"If your husband isn't in the business," says the sign near Aaron's, a Brooklyn bargain basement that is worth the trip a thousand times over.

You do need to be organized to get to Aaron's, but it's far more worthwhile than the Lower East Side and certainly simpler than renting a car and driving to a factory outlet village in upstate New York or in New Jersey.

Don't mind that it's 20 to 30 minutes away on the subway; it's worth the trip. The Brooklyn subway station is clean and nonthreatening; the 1-block walk from station to store is safe and simple. You may have hot flashes when you get inside: The amount of stuff is a little overwhelming.

Aaron's has about 10,000 square feet of clean, well-lighted space with neat racks and handwritten cardboard signs that name many of your favorite designers. Stock is kept in the back, so if you don't see your size, ask. It can be brought forward. The sales help is nice; no one is too pushy. The tags are marked down 20% to 25% off regular retail, which might not be the bargain of the century, but there's a lot of stock and selection. Often, there are further discounts.

The variety of names ranges from the traditional (Jones New York) to the expected and to the big time (Adrienne Vittadini). Clothes I've never seen discounted elsewhere are sometimes carried here.

Aaron's opens at 9:30am, which makes it a good first stop. Leave your hotel at 9am, and avoid rush-hour traffic.

Directions: Take the N or R train (going in the Brooklyn, or downtown, direction), and go to the Prospect Avenue Station in Brooklyn. You'll get off at Fourth Avenue and 17th St. Walk 1 block east to Fifth Avenue. It's easy, you can't miss it. Aaron's charges $5 to send a large package out of state. Its refund policy is posted.

You can also get there via the B train to Pacific St., Brooklyn (or D or Q train to De Kalb St., Brooklyn)—then simply walk across the platform to get the same N or R local. This saves at least 10 station stops from midtown, and crosses the East River via the Manhattan Bridge rather than a tunnel.

CENTURY 21
22 Cortlandt St., financial district; 472 86th St., Brooklyn; 1085 Old Country Rd., Westbury, Long Island

Words fail me and my palms get sweaty when I think about Century 21. There is no question that this is one of the best bargain resources in Manhattan. I find getting to the downtown store a real pain. Getting to the Brooklyn store is an even bigger pain. But, and this is a big but, this is such a wonderful shopping experience that it's simply a must-do.

What we do for a bargain.

Now then, let's begin at the beginning. Century 21 has a very fancy department store kind of place in lower Manhattan in the financial district; it has a shabby store in Brooklyn in the middle of real people Bay Ridge and it has a gorgeous new store in Long Island which is not that far from the Roosevelt Mall and is next door to a terrific source for donuts.

Century 21 sells name brands at discounts, and, my friends, oh what names. I've seen some heavy-duty names at Century 21 (Armani, Lacroix, Prada, Sonia Rykiel, JPTod's) that I've never seen at The Basement, or elsewhere.

The Manhattan store—which is rather similar to the Long Island store—has several stories to it; the Brooklyn store sprawls over several store fronts.

Century 21 sells men's, women's, and children's clothing, linens, shoes, cosmetics, luggage, small electronics, and name-brand perfume and cosmetics.

Its women's underwear selection is pretty good; there is a small department for plus sizes. The shoe department separates out the JPTod's from the normal shoes. They have few size 11, but are well stocked up through size 10. In terms of designer ready-to-wear, the store isn't allowed to name names but I have found every major Italian and American brand in this store. Prices for the most part are 40% less than retail, they range from 25% to 75% off, depending on just what it is.

I am addicted to designer sunglasses, which I buy here for about $50 a pair (instead of $175), you can get Euro designer ties for $40 to $50 each (saving about $70 per tie) and even Annick Goutal perfumes. Now then, the perfumes and cosmetics are not discounted, but the store has an incentive system so that the more you buy, the larger the amount of the gift coupon you get for a purchase on any item in the store.

Good luck getting a parking space; take the subway or move into the Millenium Hilton.

KLEINFELD'S
82nd St. at Fifth Ave., Brooklyn

If you ever thought that Brooklyn was too far to go for a shopping expedition, consider that the store wouldn't be a legend in its time if some people didn't think it was worth the trouble. Kleinfeld's is famous for dressy-dressy clothes, and provides many a wedding gown. All sorts (and all lengths) of dresses are available, at prices from 30% to 70% off regular retail. One store sells wedding dresses, the other store (across the street) sells bridesmaid's dresses.

The store is closed on Sunday and Monday. It opens at 11am other days, and stays open until 9pm on Tuesday and Thursday. On Wednesday, Friday, and Saturday, it closes at 6pm.

Directions: Take the R local train to Brooklyn and get off at 86th St. station (at Fourth Avenue). Walk 1 block east to Fifth Avenue, then 4 blocks north to 82nd St.

Please note: I know a bride who wished she had paid full retail rather than deal with Kleinfeld's. Service may not be their best thing.

LOEHMANN'S (THE BRONX)
5740 Broadway at 236th St., Riverdale, the Bronx

Note that this listing is for out-of-the-way locations; the new Ladies Mile Loehmann's in Manhattan is listed on page 258.

Naturally, you've heard of Loehmann's and probably shopped in one of its many stores. The Bronx store has been its flagship.

It's in a former ice-skating rink in a lovely section of the Bronx called Riverdale-Kingsbridge. You can't miss the structure: Its domed roof is easily spied from afar. The store itself is clean and spiffy, complete with bench for husbands to sit on and Back Room—all carpeted and pretty and swank, with the usual big-name bargains. There are other bargain shops, off-pricers, and discounters nearby so that you can make a day of it.

While this Loehmann's is nice, it's not immensely different from the Loehmann's in your own neighborhood, and might not be worth the trip if you are visiting from out of town. However, I have found designer clothes in this store that weren't in other branches. Impossible to know.

Hours are Monday through Saturday 10am to 9pm; Sunday noon to 5pm.

Flash: They now have a free bus from Manhattan straight to Loehmann's in the Bronx.

To get there by subway, take the no. 1 train to the 238th St. station. By bus, take the regular BX 9 to West 236th St. (at Broadway), or Liberty Lines express bus BMX no. 1 at Third Avenue and 34th Street in Manhattan to West 239th St., or BMX no. 2 (express bus) at Sixth Avenue and 34th St. in Manhattan to the same stop in the Bronx. By car from the West Side: Drive north on the Henry Hudson (toll); exit at West 239th St. Doug says it's easier going from the East Side; just take I-87 North (Major Deegan Expressway) exiting at West 230th St. or Van Cortland Park South (West 240th St.), then head west a block or two to Broadway. For more specific directions, call ☎ 718/543-6420.

Menswear Off-Pricers & Discounters

ARTHUR RICHARDS
85 Fifth Ave. at 16th St.

From my days at *Gentleman's Quarterly* I know that Arthur Richards makes a good suit, so I continue to follow his sales and retail practices with interest. The twice-a-year clearance sales are great events, and since the store is near Barney's, the two can often be put together in a one-stop shopping spree. Because this is a showroom, the business opens at 9am, which I love. Choose from just about 10,000 units: traditional suits, silk sport coats, and summer-weight suits. Arthur Richards is a manufacturer, so that's not really a private label you see there. These are good suits I have known for years; women's suits and blazers as well.

DOLLAR BILL'S
99 E. 42nd St.

I'm not sure what you would call Dollar Bill's—sort of a general store, jobber, and discounter. He sells everything and anything. He's also located near Grand Central Terminal, so he's conveniently placed. But best of all, he sells major, major designer clothes at low prices. The merchandise varies from week to week, and Bill's loudly proclaims that they can't advertise the names of the designers whose goods they are unloading and they've even told me that they would appreciate it if I didn't name names. Gee guys.

Dollar Bill's is a matter of perspective and location. For the businessman who just has 1 hour between meetings in New York, this could be a good source to know about. While the stores sells some women's things, it's a much better source for men's. The good stuff is downstairs.

HARRY ROTHMAN
200 Park Ave. South at 17th St.

Also known as Rothman's at Union Square. The old Harry Rothman store on Fifth Avenue is gone, but this new store, on Park Avenue South, is run by Harry's grandson. There's quite a little cache of discount stores in this block, flanking Harry. So women can shop while men take in the glories of Harry's and the discounts on big-name designer clothes and suits. A wide variety of sizes, so that any man can be fit. Also near the Green Market and all the excitement at ABC Carpet & Home and then Ladies Mile. You can't afford to miss it.

MOE GINSBURG
162 Fifth Ave. at 21st St.

Moe Ginsburg is a one-stop discount department store. It is on several different floors, so ask for what you want when you get there. Suits retail from $110 to $170. Shoes are on the fourth floor; tuxedos are on the third. This also is a downtown location, so you can get to several other big discounters on the same day.

Hours are unusual, 9:30am to 7pm weekdays except Thursdays, which are late nights, open until 8pm. Saturday and Sunday, 9:30am to 6pm.

SALES

Like all parts of the United States, New York has two big sale periods: Spring and summer merchandise are sold at rock-bottom prices from mid-July through August; fall merchandise goes on sale right after Christmas or in January.

You can get a good bargain at any good store, but in New York you get incredible selection during a sale time. Since many department stores carry the same merchandise, you may be able to add to your wardrobe as you continue to shop, buying part of an outfit at one store and finishing off with a missing part from another store.

Some stores have cyclical sale periods—they clean house every 60 to 90 days and mark down automatically, with or without big sale announcements. Or they may have private sales for charge or preferred customers. If a store needs cash, it may host a 1-day sale, with hours from 8am until 11pm (or so), just to bring in as much traffic as possible and bring up the bottom line.

All sales are announced in local newspapers; some special sales are written about editorially, as in *New York* magazine's "Sales and Bargains" column. Even factory outlets have sales. Sometimes a store runs a coupon ad in the newspaper that corresponds to a sale—you get a 15% or 20% discount with the use of the coupon. This is not as low rent as it sounds; some of Manhattan's biggest department stores do it regularly, especially around holidays when they want to jump-start the shopping seasons. For more sale information call Find-a-Sale at ☎ 212/ 55-SALES or go to www.findasale.com.

Sales in New York come in all different flavors. When Chanel runs a sale it prints an invitation in the *New York Times* telling customers that they can "refresh their wardrobes at reduced prices." How's that for genteel? My friend Polly convinced me that we had to cover the Hermès sale for academic purposes and, my God, what an event: hand-drawn poster board on the floor of Hermès with arrows pointing to the upstairs salon; silks in clear plastic garbage bags piled on the floor; ladies' room closed to sale shoppers. Enter this door; exit this door; stand here, Madame; yes we are sold out of silk scarves; no, Madame, we do not give boxes or gift wrap sale merchandise.

The conditions of the sale are posted in the store during the sale. Yes, even at the Hermès sale they do this. Some stores specify a no-return policy during sale periods. If an item is not returnable, the clerk must tell you that it is not returnable, and the sales slip also must so state.

One final tip about sales: I've noticed that the after-Christmas sales fall, well, after Christmas—either the day after or right after New Year's Day. These events, however, are usually held at American stores and department stores. The European designer boutiques have their sales much, much later in January—the third or fourth week in January, to be exact. I mention this because if you are flying to New York specifically to shop the sales, do not assume that December 26 is the magic day. It may indeed be January 26! Also note that the July sales are now held the last week in June.

FACTORY OUTLETS

The factory outlet business has become so attractive (that means profitable) that many makers are overproducing perfect merchandise to fill factory outlets. This capitalizes on the designer's well-known name and expensive advertising campaign, which has already been paid for, and reaches a totally different segment of the market, so it doesn't compete with traditional retailers.

At least, that's the theory. But the big squawk in New York is that our newest outlet center, Jersey Gardens, is too close for comfort, breaks the rules, violates trust, and is in deep trouble with everyone (but shoppers). The mud slinging has been so serious on the trade level that plans for two other outlet centers have halted. Stay tuned.

The prices in factory outlets are usually the same as at discount stores or department store sales—retail less 20% to 25%. A dress that has a $100 price tag usually sells for $79 at a factory outlet. But it can sell for $50, and certainly will be marked down to $50 as the season draws to a close. The discount may vary on a per item basis, since irregulars should be less expensive than overruns.

Outlets may or may not offer a better deal than off-pricers. Generally speaking, an off-pricer has a better bargain than an outlet store, unless you hit a sample sale or special promotion. On the other hand, if you have the opportunity to spend a day at **Woodbury Common,** an entire city of outlets, you may indeed do all the shopping, and saving, you might ever crave.

There are several factory outlet villages in the greater New York area that offer a different type of shopping center to the eager public; one of them is the controversial **Jersey Gardens**— the newcomer as we go to press. More are expected after the controversy in Jersey dies down. Watch Seacacus for more news.

All of the outlet malls and villages and spreads are different, although **Woodbury Common** and **Liberty Village** are owned by the same company and have some similarities. But wait, the similarities are a lot less than they were a few years ago, so don't jump to conclusions.

I feel very strongly that no trip to New York could be called a proper shopping excursion without a visit to at least one of the outlet malls. If you're only going to one, there is no doubt in my mind that it should be Woodbury Common, but because of the high rate of tax in New York State, you'll find people who can argue in other directions.

Secaucus, New Jersey Warehouses

Secaucus has an industrial zone more or less devoted to outlet stores but in no way similar to any factory outlet or discount village you have ever been to. A large outlet village is being discussed, but it has environmental problems in the wetlands and now the Jersey Gardens business has really muddied the mud.

Meanwhile, it is what it is. This is industrial space with two small commercial malls that fit the profile of what you are thinking of when I say "factory outlet mall" and then a single strip center of outlets; the rest are freestanding units dotted all over the place—you must shop and drive. There are a series of showrooms, some of them 20,000 square feet, new, clean, and well lit. There are no dumps here, but it's very industrial. Of course, that is the point.

The outlets are in three main areas: Harmon Cove, Industrial Park, and Castle Road.

A few tips:

- Never, never attempt to go to Secaucus and Flemington (home of Liberty Village outlet mall plus many other outlet stores) in the same day, unless you are a masochist.
- Avoid bringing young children with you, if possible.
- Wear comfortable shoes—you'll do a lot of walking.
- Carry high heels in a tote bag if you need them to get the right look for clothes you may try on.
- Drive if you can; it's worth the price of a rental car. The distances between the various warehouses are not lots of miles, but we are talking a walk this way, a walk that way, and an area that is bigger than Disneyland (and much more fun). Be prepared to move your car constantly—at least three different times, even if you walk to three times as many outlets from one parking space. I once saw bargains at the Calvin Klein outlet that were so great that I firmly believe if you are a big spender, it's cost effective to hire a car and driver to come to Secaucus just for the Klein outlet.

- Try to eat at off-peak hours—there are not enough restaurants around. It's worth it to get in your car and drive over to the Hilton's coffee shop, where there's free self-parking. There is a food court in the **Harmon Cove Mall.**
- Regular hours usually are 10am to 5pm; most stores are open until 8 or 8:30pm on Thursday.
- Remember that Sunday hours are noon to 5pm, so you don't get in as much shopping.
- Weekends are very crowded; a weekday is preferable if possible.
- Read the locally printed broadside that is free at your first stop. There's also a map, so you can take some time to plot your day.
- There is some give and take with outlets—they do open and close; I am amazed at the amount of turnover in any given year. The giveaway newspaper will help you better than any guidebook when it comes to catching the newest openings.
- Most stores take checks; no hassle for out-of-state checks. You must have a driver's license and two IDs. Traveler's checks are accepted; some credit cards are taken.
- Return policies are carefully posted; read the signs before you buy. The rules vary from store to store, but most warehouses allow returns in a 7-day period.
- Each warehouse has a mailing list. Out-of-state addresses will be honored; addresses out of the United States may not.
- Don't judge a book by its cover. While all the outlets are attractive in that they are clean, some of them bear decidedly uncute names.
- If someone is carrying an interesting shopping bag, ask questions. Discount shoppers love to help others.
- Do not assume a bargain or a best-price-in-town price tag. The Armani and Ungaro were less expensive (exact same styles and same time period) at **Century 21.**
- Go with a friend; share driving if you've come a long way. You will be exhausted at the end of the day. Pace yourself for a long drive or traffic on the way home. This kind of shopping is more fun with a friend, anyway.

- There are kids' clothing outlets but no toy outlets. If you are bribing your kids into good behavior, be prepared with your own bribes.

Welcome to Woodbury Common

Woodbury Common has changed so dramatically in the last few years that I don't know where to begin. I guess the most important thing I should blurt out is the warning that the area is now too big to do in a day and you might want to consider spending a night nearby. If you get overwhelmed easily, do research when you arrive so you can just visit the places that interest you. The "village" is larger than the space downtown takes up in the city where I live. I swear.

Visually speaking, Woodbury Common was the most attractive of the outlet villages. Its core is a fake colonial village; each shop is a different pastel shade; you may want to move in. With the new additions, the village has grown a little wild—it sprawls here and there and you could well do with a golf cart to get to all the outlets.

Consider moving your car once or twice, although this is impossible on weekends and could be impossible any day—the later in the day it gets, the less easy it is to find a parking space. The new additions are not as cute as the center part. They aren't uncute, they're just more economically built.

Woodbury Common was once extremely similar to Liberty Village (same developer), but the new additions at Woodbury Common make it so exciting that it cannot be compared to its sister in New Jersey. Or any other outlet village in the world. This is, hands down, the king.

The drive to Woodbury Common is easy (on a gorgeous highway) and beautiful almost any time of the year, especially in the autumn. It takes approximately 1½ hours from Manhattan. If you are visiting from Connecticut, not Manhattan, you may wonder about the best route because of the limited number of bridges across the Hudson River. Again, it depends on which part of

Connecticut you are coming from, but we saved a half hour by using the Tappen Zee Bridge in our drive from Fairfield County.

If you are choosing only one outlet village to visit, Woodbury Common is probably the one to pick. It's easy to get to and it's easy to shop. It also has more high-end stores than any other outlet mall.

So welcome to Woodbury Common, a wise choice for anyone—a sound choice for a day of stocking up on everything, or better yet, for holiday shopping. If you are a foreign visitor to the United States, you'd better take notes or videotape—your friends at home just won't believe this place.

Bring your station wagon, bring your van, bring your pals. And for heaven's sake, bring your credit cards.

Shops in Woodbury Common are open 7 days a week, so merely hop on the New York State Thruway (Interstate 87) and get off at Exit 16. Almost immediately after going through the tollbooth, you will see the mall to your right. There's free parking. But wait!

The mall space is now so large that what I do is circle the entire parking lot looking at the buildings and deciding where I want to be. Get an overview before you get too excited because if you are blinded by the first buildings you see, you might not even realize there are other sections to this mall.

Bus tours to this outlet have become easier than ever, thanks to a program offered by Gray Line. You get this bus at 54th St. and Eighth Avenue in Manhattan, which means you avoid the Port Authority Bus Terminal, which many people feel is worth avoiding. There is one morning bus and two return buses each day; all riders get a discount coupon booklet. The cost is about $30 per person. Call Gray Line at ☎ 800/669-0051 or 212/397-2620 for details.

There are more than 200 outlets in the village, including many big-name shops like Armani, Burberry, Brooks Brothers, Cole-Haan, Calvin Klein, Barney's, J. Crew, Gucci, Carole Little, Harvé Benard, Ellen Tracy, Ungaro, and Versace.

There's also outlets that don't have a lot of other outlet stores, such as Judith Leiber and Prada!

There is an information center, a free map and newspaper, and several clean rest room stations placed at various intervals in the structure. Of course there are places to have coffee or eat. What they really need is a hotel on premises.

Hours are Monday through Saturday 10am to 6pm; Sunday 11am to 5pm. Open until 9pm on Thursday and Friday evenings from May 1 to December 31. Closed from 3pm on July 4, Christmas Eve, and New Year's Eve. Closed all day on Easter, Thanksgiving, Christmas, and New Year's Day. Call ☎ 914/928-6840 for information.

JERSEY GARDENS
651 Kapkowski Rd. Exit 13A on the New Jersey Turnpike, Elizabeth, New Jersey

Jersey Gardens is a relatively new outlet mall that sprang up near Newark Airport and near existing big-box stores; stores that heretofore attracted shoppers from the tristate area—like IKEA. The reason designers and manufacturers and retailers are fighting it out now is that the mall is very, very attractive and is drawing traffic from regular retail—several other Jersey malls report business is down 20% in some categories and they are furious.

This mall has more than 1 million square feet of shopping and includes a mix of outlets and value-oriented stores as well as restaurants, entertainment centers and stuff to keep the whole family dizzy. In fact, it's more like an amusement park than an outlet village.

The architecture is hot and spiffy—however, some of the outlets are the bare bones type and others are really decked out. The style of the mall reminds me of the malls in The Mills Group, which does not happen to own this mall.

Among the tenants are several department stores with outlets, such as Saks' **Off Fifth** and Neiman-Marcus's **Last Call.** There's also off-pricers such as **TJMaxx** and **Daffy's.** For main street brands, there's everything from The Gap to Banana

Republic. In total, there are 201 stores (220 in Woodbury Common). All stores are indoors in this mall (they are outdoors in Woodbury Common).

There are shuttle buses from New York and from Newark Airport; the bus service from Manhattan doubles up on weekends, although the crowds do too.

STREET MERCHANTS

The street merchants in Manhattan may be fabulous, but they are really best for beads and trinkets and should only amuse you, not take your shopping budget. In good weather, there's a guy at every other corner selling a small selection of something—watches, sunglasses, books, pearls, ties, sweaters. In bad weather, there are guys selling umbrellas, gloves, mufflers.

The quality of all this merchandise is suspicious, but if you take it with a grain of salt, you may find that the shoe fits. The umbrella will last long enough to get you through the storm, the pearls won't turn, and watches may work for quite some time.

Street hawking, especially of fake or counterfeit merchandise, is essentially illegal, so most hawkers are on the lookout for the police and will roll the merchandise into a ball and be gone in less than 30 seconds should anyone look at them suspiciously. Depending on the police reaction at any given time, street hawkers are abundant or scarce. They try to work popular areas and to attract tourists—Fifth Avenue, in midtown, boasts a fair number; Sixth Avenue in the Village (near Bleecker) and lower Broadway (near Astor Place) are other good places to find street merchants. I've also noticed there are more guys out on the streets on weekends than on weekdays.

I've found it so hard to find these guys when I'm actually looking for them that when I need something fake, I simply pop in the subway and go to Canal St., where prices and selection are superior anyway.

Counterfeits & Imitations

If you're talking street merchandise, you have to be thinking of the most nontraditional retailing ploy of them all: counterfeit. Or stolen. Or merely "lost." The watches are no doubt counterfeit, while the sweaters may have just gotten lost from their original warehouse. It's so hard to keep track of all those trucks, you know.

There is some room for debate as to when an item becomes a counterfeit, a copy, or a knockoff, and at what point it's all illegal. If the intent is to defraud the true maker, the item is a counterfeit. Thus all those $25 Gucci, Rolex, Dunhill, and Cartier watches that the street merchants sell are counterfeits. It is illegal to sell them and probably illegal to buy them. Despite that fact, there are waves of fashion in fakes—Chanel fakes are harder to find these days, while Dolce & Gabanna fakes are the rage. Coach is also hot.

Most brand names that are sold on the street are frauds; look carefully at the way the signatures are made. Some Gucci fakes look like Guccis from afar, but a careful inspection reveals that those aren't even G's in the pattern. That's not a fake. It's an attempt to take advantage of your bad eyesight or inattention to detail. But it's legal.

New York does not have nearly the sophisticated counterfeits that can be found in Italy or Bangkok—most U.S. fakes scream "fake" and are just for fun. A few of them are cute enough as joke presents, even though they don't really look that much like the real thing when you inspect carefully.

I would never, ever give a fake and attempt to carry it off as the real item.

Blatantly fake merchandise is rather easy to spot. It looks cheap, feels cheap, and may even smell cheap. Good copies take a more practiced eye:

- Know what the real thing looks like and feels like.
- Know if the real maker even has the same style. Those phony Chanel-style sunglasses sold on Canal Street? Sure they look cute, but as it turns out, Chanel sunglasses don't

even come in that particular style! See those silly Chanel-style earrings that are studs for pierced ears? Chanel does not manufacture studs.

- Check the weight of goods, the hand (texture) of the fabrics, the lining, the stitching, the make of the label, the way the trademark is made. Real Ray-Ban sunglasses not only say Ray-Ban on them (as do the fakes), but have little RB initials smoked into the lens near the temples. This is difficult or impossible to fake.
- Ask if the product comes with an ID card. Ho, ho, ho. Real designer goods now come with their own credit cardlike ID card, some with a serial number. Even a tie at Prada comes with such an animal. They don't have ID cards in the Prada-style bags sold on Canal Street.
- Look carefully at the hardware. Most big-name designer goods have the name of the firm etched into the mold for the hardware. It says Gucci or Hermès right in the brass. Fixings and hardware are good clues to fakes, even in terms of quality if not in terms of engraving. Look at the clasp of a necklace. Check the weight and, in watches, how thick the watch is. Good watches are very thin these days.

If you are purposely choosing an imitation, consider the light in which your fake will be shown. If all your friends have the real thing and you are wearing the fake, you'd better believe that sooner or later someone will discover your secret. However, if you are making a one-time appearance at the Oscars, or if your gemstone will be seen only by candlelight, no one will know the difference unless you tell. Do remember, however, that high-quality fakes are not cheap, and that inexpensive fakes always look fake.

SAMPLE MADNESS & SPECIAL SALES

A few designers and manufacturers keep their samples in an archive. They lend these clothes out to friends or family (many of the evening clothes you see photographed in society pages are loaners), but they do not sell them. Other designers figure any amount of cash they can bring in is worthwhile, and realize that the cost of storing decades' worth of samples can get to be exorbitant. What to do?

They have sample sales. New York is home to so many sample sales these days that there's a monthly newsletter or two announcing them, and New Yorkers are proud of this facet of the city lifestyle. Only in New York.

Once you have ventured forth to your first sample sale, you may find yourself a victim of "sample madness." You end up going to sample sales because they are cheap and buying things you don't need and may not even want—you just get carried away with the prices and the fun.

Many sample sales require cash; a lot of the big ones take credit cards. Note that some sample sales are held in boutiques (Eileen Fisher, Norma Kamali, Dolce & Gabbana), some in corporate offices (Fendi), some are done as private parties or shindigs for best customers or fashion elite (Chanel, Yves Saint Laurent), some are held in hotels (Vera Wang)—others, at FIT or Parsons School of Design in the auditoriums (Escada). I even read about one sale (TSE Cashmere) being held at the Chelsea Market!

Sample Savvy

To get lots of details on sample sales, subscribe to the *S&B Report* (it stands for sales and bargains). Please note that the subscription rate goes up every year; a subscription presently costs $60 a year. What you get in return is a booklet with names, addresses, and short descriptions of what's for sale. For information call ☎ 877/579-0222. You can buy a single issue for $10 if you are visiting only once a year. You can also visit the Web site (which does have e-commerce!) at www.lazarshopping.com. Note that there's also a Black Belt Shopper's Edition, which costs $125 per year and gives you access to specialty events.

If you don't want to subscribe to the *S&B Report,* or you are just in town for a few days but still want to get in on the action, try these tips:

- Walk down Broadway or Seventh Avenue near the Garment District and you will more than likely be given handouts touting a variety of sample sales.
- The best way to find a special sale or a sample sale is simply to ask. Call your favorite designers, especially in April and October, and ask, "Do you sell samples or extra stock to the public?" If the answer is no, you might next ask, "Do you have a factory outlet where you sell samples or extra stock?" It never hurts to ask.
- Read the local events magazines like **New York Magazine** and **Time-Out.** Both announce many sales; *New York Magazine* has totally redone its shopping coverage and its bargain announcements and many sales are listed there each week.
- *Fashion Update* is a publication that competes with the *S&B Report;* call ☎ 718/377-8873 for details. Or click onto www.nysale.com, a free connection with thousands of sale listings, or www.inshop.com, which will send you e-mail whenever there is a designer sale. Then there's The Bargain Hotline ☎ 212/540-0123, which charges $2 for the first minute and 75¢ for each additional minute.
- Watch advertisements in the *New York Times* for the latest sales; pay close attention around gift-giving seasons. Almost all big sample sales are advertised.
- Sign up for mailing lists—ask about future shows.

And while you're at the sale, remember these tips:

- Try to avoid the lunch hour crush; get there when the doors open, if possible.
- Whenever possible, try it on.
- Don't give a sample sale gift to someone in a box from a real department store. The items are usually coded.
- Don't buy something just because it's cheap.

USED MERCHANDISE

··

In New York, many people give their cast-offs to charity to get a tax deduction for the donation. But often they put perfectly good pieces of furniture out on the street for garbage collectors to haul away. Honest. I happen to have pieces of furniture in my home that were rescued from the curbs of New York City.

If you are looking instead for goods that were donated, scads of thrift shops and charity-related stores sell previously worn merchandise. I happen to like the Posh Sale (see page 284) because of the high quality of the designer merchandise, but many good items end up at other good charity stores. I must also note that some of my younger friends—women age 25 to 35—tell me that the clothes sold at the Posh Sale are too matronly for them.

Not to worry. These days used clothing is so chic it's called "vintage" and even Saks Fifth Avenue sells it. For the young crowd there are plenty of East Village sources and even flea markets for vintage. For those who want gently used designer clothes, there are resale shops galore.

Resale

Manhattan's resale shops are a special breed unto themselves, each with rules and regulations and insiders and secrets. I'm convinced that the rules are different for different types of donors, but herewith I tell the tale from both sides. I've been buying at resale shops for years; I have now even tried to sell something through a resale shop. Ho hum.

Generally speaking, the resale shops pride themselves on fashionable merchandise that is only a year or two (at the most) old. I find that well and good and applaud the notion, but excuse me, how come there are so many Adolfo suits in these stores? Adolfo has been closed for more than 2 years, so puh-leeze. All things considered, if you want to wear Chanel, resale is the only way to go. Well, it's not the only way to go, but it's the only way that I can contemplate.

Also note that with the turn in the century, and the revival of many sixties and seventies fashion looks, it's getting harder and harder to tell vintage from resale. Try both.

A Second Chance
1133 Lexington Ave. at 78th St., 2nd floor

Midpoint between other sources while you are out making the rounds, this resale shop has the usual luck of the draw with some designer names, although the mass of the names are bridge designers rather than big-name designers. Still you may find a Ralph Lauren, Mondi, or Adolfo label. Opens 11am except on Sundays, when they open at noon.

Designer Resale
324 E. 81st St.

It's small, but the clothes are frequently brand-new and there are indeed designer names to be found. They sometimes have a color-coded sticker so that when you go to pay, the price turns out to be much less than you thought it was. I let go a Donna Karan skirt that didn't fit me and was marked $55. Too much money for a skirt that didn't really fit. Turns out it was half price. Ask! Hours are Monday, Tuesday, Wednesday, and Friday 11am to 7pm; Thursday 11am to 8pm; Saturday 10am to 6pm; Sunday noon to 5pm.

There's a men's branch across the street.

Encore
1132 Madison Ave. at 84th St., 2nd floor

This store got attention about 30 years ago when it was rumored that Jacqueline Kennedy Onassis was turning in her used clothes here. I had a spate of years of coming by here and finding zilch, then suddenly, I hit pay dirt. The last year or so, this has been one of my regular sources.

Would you like to hear about the Yves Saint Laurent Rive Gauche dress for $90?

Some dressy gowns, some shoes and handbags; there is another floor above with more casual items. There are always a few Chanel suits priced from $500 to $750. A Chanel suit at $500 is really an outstanding buy, as the average price for a used suit is usually higher. (The average price for a new Chanel suit is $4,500, in case you were wondering.)

If you've ever dreamed of interlocking C's, this could be the start of something big.

MICHAEL RESALE
1041 Madison Ave. at 80th St., 2nd floor

For the long haul, I've personally done better at Encore, but last time I did some "thrifting" at these stores, I had a ball at Michael's, got a whole new wardrobe for about $90, and found nothing at Encore. That's life in the big city. This store is close enough to Encore that you can hit both in the same trip.

Michael also has Chanel and Adolfo; I bought a Rive Gauche Yves Saint Laurent black lace tank top for $40. I saw a pair of red and white Chanel sling backs that I'll never get over as long as I live—they were worthy of a museum. I'm shrinking my feet as we speak. They do have a lot of plain old regular big-name designer goods that just keep on keeping on.

They now sell wedding gowns upstairs.

TkANSFER
594 Broadway (at Houston), Suite 1002

The store specializes in used samples from the catwalks or from photography as well as castoffs from celebrities and a few of the rich and famous. They don't have a huge selection and most of the sizes are tiny, which is why everyone in Japan knows about this shop. I saw a Kate Moss dress that Chanel had made for her; it didn't even look like a size 2. I am a size 42 (when I'm lucky) and there were only two things big enough to try on the day that I happened by. I did get a Chanel jacket for $700, but I later found the exact same jacket in Cannes for less money in a resale shop there.

Specialty Resale

CHILDREN'S RESALE
303 E. 81st St.

This is the neighborhood for zillions of resale shops. Just prowl! Infants, toddlers, and sizes up to 16.

GOOD-BUYS
230 E. 78th St.

Another of the neighborhood finds for the uptown crowd. Consignment, up to size 12.

PRETTY PLUS
1309 Madison Ave. at 92nd St.

At last, a resale shop that specializes in large sizes. Second floor. Not a lot to write home about, but it's nice to know it's here. Seemingly many leftovers from bar mitzvahs and weddings.

SECOND ACT CHILDREN'S WEAR
1046 Madison Ave. at 81st St.

Fabulous fun although not dirt cheap—at $16 for a Gap dress, I could have waited for the Gap sale. Nonetheless, this one is a winner. It's on Madison Avenue near the other big resale shops. The upstairs showroom is jammed but packed with boys' and girls' clothing arranged by size. A wall of party shoes. A rack of raincoats. Not only clothes but games and toys, too, and some maternity clothes. Not for the claustrophobic.

Sample, Resale & Discount

FIND
361 W. 17th St.

The hottest new find in the biz; Find specializes in samples and overruns from the hip and hot designer brands, many of whom you might not have even heard about. This is truly an insider's source and is not for everyone. Helmut Lang, anyone?

LE FIRMÉ
37 W. 57th St., 4th floor

Italian designers on racks, discounted 20%. Big names, big time. Some private label. Don't miss the side room with the older merchandise and the big markdowns. Alterations available.

SSSSAMPLE SALES
134 W. 37th St., 2nd floor

OK, so I wasn't impressed when I came calling, but you might want to pop in as you never know, and I've heard tell of shoppers who have done great, especially with young and hip merchandise from names like Betsey Johnson.

Thrift Shops

Stores that specialize in upscale used merchandise consider themselves either resale shops or consignment shops; those that take whatever donations people choose to give in the name of charity are thrift shops, and they are run for the benefit of a specific organization. As a result, most schools, hospitals, and disease care and research organizations have their own thrift shops.

By definition, a thrift shop is only as good as you are lucky. It's impossible to review them, since the merchandise comes and goes and one can never be sure. I've seen that over the years the thrift shop is coming back into its own; aside from the young people who are into grunge, there are plenty of well-off middle-class people who are looking for high quality at a worn price.

Do note that prices at these places can be very high. Especially if you are used to out-of-town thrift-shop prices. A few basic rules hold true for most thrift shops:

- Many thrift shops take credit cards; few will take checks.
- You can sometimes bargain a little if you buy a lot.
- Most stores open at 11am; Saturday hours may be strange. Few are open on Sunday.
- A lot of the thrift shops are located on the Upper East Side; I've grouped together several that make the expedition worthwhile for us.
- If you are used to the high quality and good prices at stores like **Encore** and **Michael's,** you may be turned off after checking out a few thrift shops.

Final note, there are some thrift shops that specialize in home decor. You might want to look at **Housing Works Thrift Shop,** 202 E. 77th St.; 136 W. 18th St. Other spots include:

CANCER CARE THRIFT SHOP
1480 Third Ave. at 83rd St.

GODMOTHER'S LEAGUE THRIFT SHOP
1457 Third Ave. at 82nd St.

IRVINGTON INSTITUTE
1534 Second Ave. at 80th St.

MEMORIAL SLOAN KETTERING THRIFT SHOP
1440 Third Ave. at 81st St.

OUT OF THE CLOSET
220 E. 81st St.

SPENCE CHAPIN THRIFT SHOP
1430 Third Ave. at 81st St.

SPECIAL-EVENT RETAILING

....

An event just wouldn't be special if you couldn't buy anything, would it? Museums have gift shops, circuses have vendors, and New York City has all sorts of special events that revolve around the selling of something or other.

The best of these events are charity related, especially when it comes to support for AIDS research and events such as **Seventh on Sale,** when designers donate clothing to be sold flea market style. The shoe industry also does an annual bash, sponsored by QVC.

Some events are food-related—the Ninth Avenue Association has an annual block party that allows you to roam through throngs of people as you explore a variety of ethnic food stands. There are similar festivals in Little Italy; there's Chinese New Year in Chinatown.

Check with your hotel concierge or *Where* magazine to find out if such events will be held when you are in town. The Visitors Bureau also sends out a quarterly list of all special events in Manhattan.

Also investigate traditional charity events: For antiques and furniture, there's the twice-a-year sale at the Armory on Park Avenue at 67th St. (the Seventh Regiment Armory Antiques Show) as well as a raft of shows on The Piers; see the Home Furnishings chapter for more on these.

For clothes, try the **Posh Sale,** a benefit for the Lighthouse for the Blind, also held at the Armory. Twice a year the great ladies of New York society clean out their closets (designers do this, as well) and send their tired, their poor, their wretched excesses to the Posh Sale, where we are yearning for them to be free but will pay $30 to $50 for them. Call the **Lighthouse for the Blind** or check magazine listings— there's a spring and a fall sale. By way of nothing, The Lighthouse also has a very nice boutique with a combination of types of merchandise, some related to large type or large size print for those who don't see so well, but many other items more along the lines of what you would find in a museum store.

Special Visitors

For a clothes encounter of the bargain kind, also check for listings about special visitors from foreign retailing establishments. The British are particularly adept at flying to New York for a week, taking a suite in a midtown hotel, and visiting with private customers, to whom they sell at wholesale or rock-bottom British prices.

To become a private customer one needs only sharp eyes—ads usually run in newspapers or selected magazines such as *New York* or *Avenue*. Tailors often employ this method, but so do manufacturers and even entire department stores. A representative from **Harrods** used to come over to sell from the store catalog on a regular basis; now there's **Harrod's online** for U.S. shoppers. **Chinacraft** comes to all major U.S. cities and takes hotel space for a few days. The hotels get a good bit of this business, so we've gotten into the habit of asking the concierge if any sales in the meeting rooms are open to the public.

THE SAME BUT DIFFERENT

....

Every now and then, you find a retailer or a manufacturer who isn't in love with the idea of outlet stores and who goes for a different version of the lower priced gimmick. The two best examples are **The Gap** creating its lower priced line, **Old Navy,** which is almost an icon in brands now—and Ann Taylor, creating **The Loft,** which was originally a branch of outlet stores in outlet malls but has now opened in midtown Manhattan offering the Ann Taylor look at 30% less. The Loft customer is also younger than the regular Ann Taylor customer.

TRADE SHOW SHOPPING

Inveterate shoppers usually shun the standard shopping services and go on the prowl themselves. Trade shows are one of their favorite haunts. Manhattan hosts almost 1,000 conventions a year. Not all of these will interest you. But events such as the Gift Show, the Stationery Show, and the Linens Show are not only fun to attend (you get a sneak preview of next season's wares) but also fun to shop—on the final day of the show, the representatives of the company often will sell the samples right out of the booths rather than pay to truck the merchandise home. You will pay wholesale, sometimes less. You also may get a lot of small-time freebies.

To shop a trade show:

- Get a list of the week's trade shows from your concierge, a magazine such as *Where,* or the Visitors Bureau.
- Find out the last day of the show and the hours.
- At about 11am on the final day, go to the convention hall and fill out the papers for accreditation. Attendance at a trade fair may be free, or there may be a charge ($10 to $25); either way, you must have some business credentials. This is what business cards are for.
- Your business card should be related to the business of the trade fair whenever possible; it should have some kind of company name rather than anything too cute. Your name should also be on the card. Have other ID including photo ID. I recently had a very hard time getting into a trade show, they wanted all sorts of extra ID and business letterhead or checkbooks, and so on.
- Be prepared to answer a few innocent questions about your business, such as what you do. Having a gift-buying service or being in the party-planning business are two good entrées to just about anything.
- When you see something that interests you, introduce yourself—with your professional demeanor and company

name—and ask if samples are being sold. If the answer is yes, pay in cash. No one wants your check. No one will change a traveler's check. No one has American money for lire. Cash and carry. Heavy-duty shopping bags.

- Every now and then, before the last day of the show, you can get a maker to run a personal for you—but you still must meet a minimum order. Sometimes this is only $100. Shipping will be extra.

If you are prepared to do your Christmas shopping in July, your Halloween shopping in May, and your kiddie birthday shopping by the dozen, you can get some great bargains—and save a lot of time in future months when all your friends will be frantic and you'll be cool as can be. Trade show shopping takes organization, storage space, and extra cash resources, but it's the best way to save money and time and still give fabulous gifts.

CORPORATE DISCOUNTS

There are corporate discounts offered by regular, traditional retailers. **Tiffany & Co.** has one of the most famous corporate plans; if you qualify (you must be incorporated), you can get a very nice discount (usually 10%) on its merchandise.

Some corporate discounts are based on location: A fancy jeweler on Madison Avenue gives a discount to businesspeople who work in the neighborhood—he wants their business. A certain camera shop offers a discount to photographers who work for Time, Inc., because he likes to tell his regular customers that all the *Life* magazine photographers buy from him. And so it goes.

If you are visiting your corporate headquarters, it pays to ask a local company representative which retailers offer corporate benefits. You just may be surprised at the choice.

AUCTIONS FOR BARGAINS

....

Auctions service the high-, mid-, and even lower midmarket for art and home furnishings. There is another type of auction business in unclaimed merchandise: Police departments and the U.S. Postal Service, as well as the U.S. Treasury Department (Customs), all have auctions on confiscated and nondelivered or unclaimed merchandise. (Drugs are not sold.)

There's a **Post Office auction** about once a month; call ☎ 212/971-5180 for details. It's held at what we call the Big Post Office, which takes up about a city block just west of Madison Square Garden, at 380 W. 33rd St. There are viewing days, and there is a catalog. You bid by use of a paddle, which costs $20 (it's refundable or can be applied to the first purchase), and you must pay in cash.

For the **Police Auction** at One Police Plaza, New York, call ☎ 212/406-1369. They have a catalog and a viewing period, although you do have to tramp around to various police warehouses—not our idea of safe or fun. You can get a great buy, although we hear that the police keep the really good cars to use as unmarked vehicles for stakeouts.

The schedule for **Customs auctions** is released about a year ahead of time, with big auctions held twice a year at various regional offices. Call ☎ 212/466-2924 for dates and details. The Los Angeles date may be different from the New York date. You also need a paddle for this auction (the $25 fee is refundable). The items for sale are usually the things people refused to pay duty on. Items that were confiscated usually were seized for legal reasons, so they are seldom sold—this is not the place to buy the leopard coat you have been dreaming of. This is great rainy-day fun. Ask to get on their mailing list.

For more on the more traditional auctions, see chapter 9, which deals with the home. There are auctions for vintage and designer clothing, even movie star clothes held at the big houses, which compete to get the collections and the estates.

Each now has its own fashion expert who is out there tracking down Puccis and the like. William Doyle has tried to make a mark in the vintage auction business, but the bigger names are moving in.

OFF-PRICE BY MAIL

Although Saks Fifth Avenue has its own grouping of outlet stores, Off Fifth, they also have a discount and off-price system called Folio On Sale through mail-order.

You can shop via the pages of this seasonal four-color catalog and get the same bargains that will be for sale in Sak's chain of outlet stores. Simply call ☎ 800/345-3454 for your copy of the catalog. You need not have a Saks charge card in order to buy.

There are no steals or deals. There is simply solid wearable fashion and basic style for a solid middle-of-the-road price. That's what regular retail used to be about.

HAIR DEALS

If you're young at heart, have a good sense of humor, little in your bank account, or just an adventuresome spirit, you may want to take advantage of some of the best deals in Manhattan: free or low-cost beauty services offered through training classes. I used to get my hair marbleized by Clairol for free, back in the dark ages when I was about 22. Clairol still has that studio; other salons also have deals.

CLAIROL
345 Park Ave. at 52nd St., ☎ *212/546-5000*

Clairol is constantly testing its hair color products and processes. If you're looking for a new you, or need to have a terrible mistake corrected, call for an appointment.

VIDAL SASSOON
767 Fifth Ave. at 58th St., ☎ *212/535-9200*

Sassoon used to have a freebie night when apprentices could practice on you; now you pay a small charge. They prefer that you have some hair and, of course, you have to agree to let them do what they want, but it's great fun. You can call for more info or show up on Wednesday evening at 6:30pm for a free consultation when they will decide if they can use you. Then they make a regular appointment at which time you will pay $14 to $18 depending on your hair and the skill level of the technician.

Chapter Eleven

....

MANHATTAN SHOPPING TOURS

MAKE MINE MANHATTAN

....

This is a city for walking—it is dense with neighborhoods and fabulous retail. I hope this book has already made that perfectly clear. Any walk or wander can be a tour. But if you're in a hurry, see Chapter 1, "The Best of New York," for some specific suggestions, or try one of my jam-packed tours below.

TOUR 1: THE SHOOT-FOR-THE-STARS TOUR

Lace up those Hogan's or slip into your flats, because you are in for a lot of walking.

Please wear nice clothes, no blue jeans (unless you are doing "The Look"—blue jeans with a $500 handbag and $500 shoes and Rolex watch and Hermès scarf in your ponytail). You can wear a simple black nothing, but do look chic please.

If you think you will be buying (of course you will be buying!), put your regular-height heels into a shopping bag or tote bag.

1. Leave your hotel by 8:30am if you can (do eat a good breakfast—this is going to be a killer day). You are headed downtown on the subway; since this is rush hour you needn't worry about your safety. If you can't stand crowds, 9am will be less crowded—but you're losing shopping time here.

The Shoot-for-the-Stars Tour

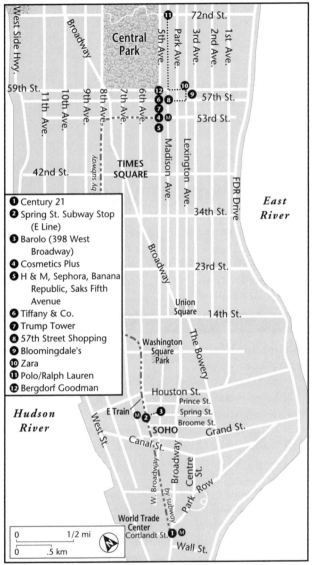

① Century 21
② Spring St. Subway Stop (E Line)
③ Barolo (398 West Broadway)
④ Cosmetics Plus
⑤ H & M, Sephora, Banana Republic, Saks Fifth Avenue
⑥ Tiffany & Co.
⑦ Trump Tower
⑧ 57th Street Shopping
⑨ Bloomingdale's
⑩ Zara
⑪ Polo/Ralph Lauren
⑫ Bergdorf Goodman

West Side Hwy.
Broadway
Central Park
72nd St.
5th Ave.
Park Ave.
3rd Ave.
2nd Ave.
1st Ave.
59th St.
11th Ave.
10th Ave.
9th Ave.
8th Ave.
7th Ave.
6th Ave.
Madison Ave.
Lexington Ave.
57th St.
53rd St.
42nd St.
TIMES SQUARE
by subway
East River
FDR Drive
34th St.
Broadway
23rd St.
Union Square
14th St.
Washington Square Park
The Bowery
Houston St.
Prince St.
Spring St.
Broome St.
E Train
SOHO
Grand St.
Hudson River
West St.
Canal St.
W. Broadway
Broadway
Centre St.
Park Row
by subway
World Trade Center
Cortlandt St.
Wall St.

0   1/2 mi
0   .5 km

You are headed for the Big Bargain: Century 21 on Cort-landt St. You can take the 1, 9, N, or R trains to the Cort-landt St. stop. The store opens at 8:30am and you want as much early hours shopping as you can squeeze in.

2. By 11am you are on your way to SoHo. The most effi-cient way to get there is to pop into the subway at the World Trade Center, take the **E train** in the uptown direction and get off at **Spring Street.** This will take you to the edge of SoHo and is just where you want to be. The problem here is that you might have too many packages from Century 21. Depending on your ability to deal with the load, pick and choose your method of transportation. Of course, if you are brilliant, you are staying at the Hilton Millenium next door to Century 21 so you can drop off your pack-ages before you head uptown.

3. Poke around SoHo and if you are hungry, you can eat lunch at **Barolo,** 398 W. Broadway (☎ 212/226-1102), or **Balt-hazar,** 80 Spring St., which is not only the in-spot of downtown, but an awfully cute place to be. See "SoHo Made Simple" on page 296, for more on exploring this area.

4. Once finished with your SoHo sojourn, you are back on the E train headed uptown. Alight at the **Fifth Avenue** stop, which will put you at 53rd St. As you exit the station, you will notice there is a branch of **Cosmetics Plus,** a dis-counter, right there under the 666 Fifth Avenue building at the station. Shop to your heart's delight, but don't get too carried away because in a few minutes you will be in New York's flagship Sephora, the French grocery store for makeup and beauty aids.

5. Walk half a block east to Fifth Avenue and turn right with-out crossing the street. Now you are walking downtown. Continue down Fifth Avenue, window shopping until 52nd St.—that's all of one block. Then hit **H&M,** for teen thrills (640 Fifth Ave.), or skip right over to 51st and Fifth for **Sephora** (630 Fifth Ave.). Then see the new **Banana**

Republic lifestyle store and cross Fifth Avenue to go into **Saks Fifth Avenue.**

6. Leaving Saks, stay on the Saks side of the street (the east side) and walk uptown, toward Trump Tower. This is only 7 blocks. Look in windows or shop until your charge cards wither and die. Pass Trump Tower to dash into **Tiffany & Co.,** where you owe it to yourself to see the table settings and upstairs floors even if gemstones bore you.

7. Then, go next door to **Trump Tower.** If you go to Trump first, you will be too exhausted to go Tiffany & Co. and you will miss one of the best stores in New York.

    Be careful as you enter Trump Tower, especially if it is or has been raining. The marble floor is very, very slick. There are about 50 shops in the atrium, but don't stay very long; gawk and leave.

8. Exit and turn right; go east on 57th St. This will take you right past all the weird and wonderful retail happenings on 57th St. from the **Warner Brothers Studio Store** to **Levi's** and to **NikeTown** and yes, even to **Chanel** and **Hermès,** two of my favorite stores. (You don't have to buy anything, you know.)

9. Walk east 3 blocks to Lexington Avenue, cross, and walk uptown to **Bloomingdale's.** Spend an hour in Bloomingdale's. You may need coffee at this point. Or the stores could be closing. This is a very busy tour!

10. Exit Bloomingdale's on the Lexington Avenue side at 59th St. and walk across the street to **Zara,** and then west to Madison Avenue. Turn right and walk uptown on Madison Avenue. Mostly you only have time to look in windows and soak up atmosphere, but shop and adjust your schedule accordingly.

11. After the **Ralph Lauren** shop, on the corner of Madison Avenue and 72nd St., cross Madison and walk downtown. As you get to 60th Street, you'll see all of Manhattan's newest big-time retailers, including the Donna Karan **DKNY Store.**

12. Turn right at 57th St. and walk west until you come back to Fifth Avenue. Go to **Bergdorf's,** where you can get coffee and be dazzled by the best and the brightest. If you haven't had your coffee break yet, you may want to do the tea service in the Rotunda at the **Pierre Hotel.** It is to die for. After this kind of day, you may be ready to die.

TOUR 2: THE SOHO-SO-FINE TOUR

There are several different subways you can take to SoHo; this tour starts at the Green Market at Union Square, so you can take in NoHo and SoHo, end up at Broadway and Prince (by subway or foot), and make your first store **Sephora,** 555 Broadway. This starts you off with the most commercial part of SoHo and then moves you into the funkier parts. And SoHo has a lot to do with vibes. The Sephora in Rockefeller Center is better, but this is a good place to get grounded, and it's next door to Kate's Paperie, one of the best stores in New York. You can taxi to that address, or walk from Union Square where this tour officially begins.

1. Because we actually start at the Union Square Green Market, it's best to do this tour on a Saturday. You can reach Union Square on the L, N, R, 4, 5, or 6 train. Make sure you are wearing comfortable shoes—this is a walking tour! After exploring the market:

2. Walk down Broadway (or take the N or R train downtown to Prince St.) to reach **Sephora** shop at 555 Broadway.

3. Cross the street from Sephora to get to **Dean & Deluca** (560 Broadway), where you may want a stand-up coffee at the bar so that you can gaze out the window and properly observe the scene. Across the street (561 Broadway) is **Kate's Paperie.** Congratulations, you've now just seen three of the keystones to the SoHo experience.

SoHo Made Simple

I used to get lost in SoHo. I used to get confused in the walk from Canal St. and in trying to remember which of the many subway stops was the right one. Then Bill Mindlin taught me this trick, which simplifies everything to one sentence—and you never get lost.

Take the E train to Spring Street. That's the whole trick. Get off at Sixth Avenue and Spring St., and walk on Spring St. without making any turns. In 1 block, you are in SoHo. Go up one side of Spring and down the other. If you want to explore the cross streets—where all the really good stuff is— you can do so. But you'll never get lost or confused if you stick with Spring St.

To get the most out of your SoHo wanderings, learn the litany. This helps so you don't get lost. Going downtown, it's Prince, Spring, Broome, and then Grand—after Grand the cool stuff has ends, pretty much by Canal St., or when you see the entrance to the Holland Tunnel. Intersecting the streets above (heading east to west) you've got Broadway, Mercer, Greene, Wooster, and West Broadway.

Remember that Broadway is not West Broadway—they are two different streets. You'll want to work your way around Broadway and then begin weaving among the cross and parallel streets, which host the best shops. You don't really need to follow our directions; you can follow your nose. Also remember that there is some alternative retail on the streets—this marvelous woman who sells homemade sunglasses with plastic palm trees glued to them; some people selling hair doodads; and then there's a tiny flea market for T-shirts and fashionable (but poorly made) threads.

4. One of the routes I take to see the most of the neighborhoods is this: Follow Broadway to Spring St., turn right

The SoHo–So–Fine Tour

1. Union Square Green Market
2. Sephora
3. Dean & Deluca, Kate's Paperie
4. Portico Bed & Bath
5. West Broadway Shops
6. Zona
7. Subway Stop

on Spring, and walk across town till you reach West Broadway, taking in all the miracles of retailing along Spring St. as you gawk. Don't miss **Portico Bed & Bath** on Spring right after Mercer.

5. Turn right on West Broadway and shop your way back to Prince, cross the street, and go back down West Broadway and all the way to Canal St. West Broadway is chockablock with designer names, hipsters, and breakthrough talent. Backtrack along West Broadway but cut over on Broome St.

6. Take Broome to Wooster, then weave over to Greene, working your way uptown so you finish with **Zona** and then **Wolfman Gold & Good** and ending up at Greene St. between Prince and Spring streets. Take Prince back to **Dean & Deluca,** where you started. By now you'll certainly want that coffee.

7. Duck into the subway right there at Broadway and Prince or flag down a taxi. Unless you are doing the tour in reverse and want to walk uptown on Broadway to the Union Square Green Market. Or leave via Spring St.; see "SoHo Made Simple," above.

One modification: You can keep walking south on Broadway until you hit Broadway and Canal. This is the edge of Chinatown and the heart of the Asian-made designer fakes. This is where I buy those fake Mont Blanc pens that I hand out as business gifts. I am not big on copyright violations, but these fakes are all quite blatant and the cheap ones are a goof. Handbags, scarves, and serious attempts at forgery are a waste of your good sense— and cents. There are two more subway stations here for easy exit back to the real world.

Another modification: Follow Spring St. east to Elizabeth St. so that you can check out NoLiTa. The action is between Houston and Prince on Elizabeth and then cut back toward SoHo by exploring Mott, Mulberry, and Lafayette.

TOUR 3: THE DOWNTOWN-IN-A-DASH TOUR

For maximum effect, take this tour on a Wednesday, Friday, or Saturday when the Union Square Green Market is open. Traffic is heavy on Saturday.

1. Take the bus downtown on Fifth Avenue, get off at 23rd St., stare at the Flatiron Building, and then walk downtown on Fifth Avenue, stopping in such chain stores as **Banana Republic** and **The Gap** and high-fashion hot spots like **Street Life** and **Paul Smith.** There're big names like **Emporio Armani** and not so big names like **Barami Studio** (with six other locations in Manhattan for made-in-Italy fashions). For discount, there's **Daffy's.**

2. Shop your way as close to 14th St. as you desire, then walk east on 16th St. There are plenty of places to eat in the neighborhood, by the way, and you will pass several now. Or you may want to snack your way through the **Green Market,** which you'll see directly in front of you at Union Square.

3. When you're finished at the market, walk through the park, cross 14th St., and walk downtown on Broadway. You can quickly take in the combination of comics at **Forbidden Planet,** discount best-selling books (and more, of course) at **The Strand Bookstore,** and any number of antique dealers, including the famous **Howard Kaplan,** who has made country French his middle name.

4. When you get to 10th St. or so (do note the china cup mosaics encrusted on the street lamps), you must decide if you will stay on Broadway and continue downtown for NoHo and SoHo or turn around. Let's save SoHo for another day and head for ABC-land, which is what I sometimes call the area surrounding **ABC Carpet & Home** on Broadway and 18th St.

5. Backtrack along Broadway past Union Square so that you are now going uptown on the East Side. Around

18th to 20th streets you'll find a whole bunch of goodies, including the most famous resident of the neighborhood, **ABC Carpet & Home.** Anyone who enjoys visual splendor just has to visit ABC Carpet & Home. Finish up this portion of the neighborhood with a trip to **Fishs Eddy,** again if only to see what it looks and feels like.

6. Now head west to the part of town called Ladies Mile; Sixth Avenue and 18th St. is a good place to start at the **Old Navy** store, run by your friends from The Gap. Then hit the big off-pricers like **Filene's Basement** and **TJ Maxx.** And, of course, Manhattan's first **Loehmann's.** Who needs uptown shopping, anyway?

Size Conversion Chart

Women's Clothing

American	8	10	12	14	16	18
Continental	38	40	42	44	46	48
British	10	12	14	16	18	20

Women's Shoes

American	5	6	7	8	9	10
Continental	36	37	38	39	40	41
British	4	5	6	7	8	9

Children's Clothing

American	3	4	5	6	6X
Continental	98	104	110	116	122
British	18	20	22	24	26

Children's Shoes

American	8	9	10	11	12	13	1	2	3
Continental	24	25	27	28	29	30	32	33	34
British	7	8	9	10	11	12	13	1	2

Men's Suits

American	34	36	38	40	42	44	46	48
Continental	44	46	48	50	52	54	56	58
British	34	36	38	40	42	44	46	48

Men's Shirts

American	$14^{1}/_{2}$	15	$15^{1}/_{2}$	16	$16^{1}/_{2}$	17	$17^{1}/_{2}$	18
Continental	37	38	39	41	42	43	44	45
British	$14^{1}/_{2}$	15	$15^{1}/_{2}$	16	$16^{1}/_{2}$	17	$17^{1}/_{2}$	18

Men's Shoes

American	7	8	9	10	11	12	13
Continental	$39^{1}/_{2}$	41	42	43	$44^{1}/_{2}$	46	47
British	6	7	8	9	10	11	12

ABOUT THE AUTHOR

Suzy Gershman is an author and a journalist who has worked in the fiber and fashion industry since 1969 in both New York and Los Angeles. She has held editorial positions at *California Apparel News*, *Mademoiselle*, *Gentleman's Quarterly*, and *People* magazine, where she was West Coast style editor. She writes regularly for various magazines, and her essays on retailing are text for Harvard Business School. She frequently appears on network and local television; she is a contributing editor to *Travel Holiday*.

For updates on Suzy's travels, tour information, or Born-to-Shop Bulletins from over 25 cities, go to **www.born-to-shop.com**.

INDEX

303

Frommer's Born to Shop guides are available from your favorite bookstore or directly from IDG Books Worldwide, Inc.

To order by phone and pay by credit card, call 1/800-434-3422 (AMEX, MC and VISA cards are accepted).

Otherwise, fill out the order form below.

Name _____

Address _____ Phone _____

City _____ State _____

Please send me the following **Frommer's Born to Shop** guides:

Quantity	Title	Price
_____	Born to Shop France ISBN 0-02862360-6	$14.99
_____	Born to Shop China ISBN 0-02863671-6	$14.99
_____	Born to Shop Italy ISBN 0-02863142-0	$14.99
_____	Born to Shop London ISBN 0-02863143-9	$14.99
_____	Born to Shop New York ISBN 0-02863599-X	$14.99
_____	Born to Shop Paris ISBN 0-02863141-2	$14.99

Total for **Frommer's Born to Shop** Guides $ _____

Please include applicable sales tax

Add $4.50 for first book's S & H, $1.00 per additional book:

$ _____

Total payment: $ _____

Check or Money Order enclosed. Offer valid in the United States only. Please make payable to IDG Books Worldwide, Inc.

Send orders to:
IDG Books Worldwide, Inc.
10475 Crosspoint Blvd.
Attn: Order Services
Indianapolis, IN 46256